# ONE CIRCLE

## How to Grow a Complete Diet in Less Than 1,000 Square Feet!

by David Duhon

AN ECOLOGY ACTION PUBLICATION

# ILLUSTRATIONS

Chapter and section symbols by Sahnta
Pannutti.

p. 131 Cultivo de Hortalizas en la Huerta
Familiar, Hans Carlier, 1978, Instituto
de Estudios Andinos, Apartado 289, Huancayo, Peru.

p.135 Demystifying Evaluation, Noreen
Clark and James McCaffery, 1979, $5.00
from World Education, 1414 Sixth Avenue,
New York, New York, 10019.

The two illustrations listed above
appeared in Appropriate Technology
Sourcebook, Volume II, Ken Darrow,
Kent Keller, Rick Pam, A Volunteers in
Asia Publication, 1981, available for
$6.50 + $1.38 postage per single copy
from: Appropriate Technology Project,
Volunteers in Asia, Bos 4543, Stanford,
CA 94305.

# Acknowledgements

*One Circle* was made possible in large part due to the financial support of the
following organizations and individuals:
        The Zaffaroni Foundation
        Syntex Corporation
        The CS Fund
        Pendred Noyce
        Bob Noyce
        Paul Hwoschinsky
        *and, especially,* Dr. Alejandro Zaffaroni, whose farsighted and continued efforts
                have been so important to Ecology Action since the very beginning.
To these organizations and individuals I extend my warmest thanks for their
assistance in this effort.

This work is another step within the longterm efforts of Ecology Action.  All those
who have supported Ecology Action over the years deserve thanks: financial contri-
buters, staff, apprentices--all those whose good efforts have sustained this
organization in its important work.  Earlier unpublished works by John Jeavons and
Robin Leler, and by Dan Cook helped point the direction as to what was possible--
a complete balanced diet produced from a truly minimal area.  I am thankful for all
the help and support of my co-authors:  my wife, Cindy, who helped in so many ways;
John, whose unending efforts were so important; and Gary, who also contributed a
great effort to the creation of the overall text.

Other individuals to whom I wish to extend my personal thanks include Michele and
Jay Cortright, Sam Rubuttom, Dick Graham, Bob Bragdon, Virginia Jeavons, Carol
Ankrom, and Paka.

# CONTENTS

## NUTRITION RECONSIDERED - 1

## THE NUTRIENTS - 17

## THE CROPS - 73
*by Cindy Gebhard*

# THE FUTURE - 129

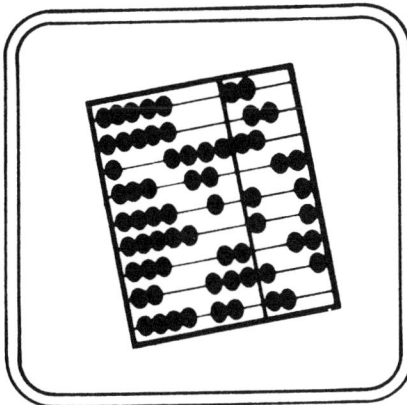

# SOLVING THE DIET - 150

# SAMPLE DIETS - 181

For an easier first reading, or for those wishing to skip some of the more technical and mathematical sections, you may wish to skip all the "Solving the Diet" sections, which appear throughout the book. These are indicated by the abacus symbol and/or by being boxed in. These sections will, however, be needed by anyone wishing to create a more precisely designed plan.

# FOREWORD

One Circle is meant as a tool and not a final answer.  I hope that it can be another lamp along the path.  This book can be read on a theoretical level, but it is intended primarily as a practical tool for those seeking to improve the world food system.  One Circle enables you to design your own minimal area diet, and from there to be able to help others.  For gardening methods covering vegetables, fruits, grains, and even crops for fuel, fiber, and other uses, study the biointensive techniques which are well explained in How to Grow more Vegetables... by John Jeavons.  The Backyard Homestead... by John Jeavons, J. Mogador Griffin, and Robin Leler is another important and useful resource.

One Circle presents a spectrum of possibilities and alternatives, with the assumption that one's diet is both a very personal and also a very important decision.  Deciding what your nutritional needs really are involves many choices.  Differing amounts of land and other resources will be needed according to which crops and methods you choose.  You may decide to act by changing the mix of foods that you buy, by making small changes in your garden plan, or by redesigning your entire approach to food.  We must each choose our own roles in the restoration and maintenance of the world food system.  While defining some of the choices available, One Circle does not advocate a particular set of choices for such important and personal matters.

While the problems addressed affect all of us, and particularly the poorer peoples of the world, the audience addressed, those who will actually read and use the book, will initially often be limited to those who are not poor or hungry.  The design techniques in One Circle no doubt have built-in biases that make them more easily understood and used by people familiar with the affluent culture from which the book comes.

The sort of special people who are needed to transfer this information are "cultural amphibians", world citizens who can empathize with and learn from the world as a whole, whether they travel the world or never leave their home village.  This might be the development volunteer who goes overseas to teach and finds herself the one who is enriched.  It might be the student from Botswana who has come to the States to learn, but teaches lessons of thoughtfulness, compassion and insight to all who cross his path.  It might be the person who succeeds within an American-based multinational corporation, and then later uses the skills he has developed to head a major development effort in his own country.

The socio-ecosystem cannot be divided along the boundaries of nature's eco-systems, nor those of humankind's political systems. From the clutter in space, to the whales in the ocean depths, to the pollution in the arctic, to our shrinking forests and expanding deserts, we are a worldwide socio-ecosystem. We are of one circle even though we are of many cultures.

Cultural amphibians can move from one culture to another and can bring with them the best (or the worst) of each culture. They can help correct problems from one place with solutions from another (or they can simply redistribute the problems). They can transfer values, technology, and even culture. These are the kind of people--from all over the world--who are needed to help *develop* a better world. Such *development work* is needed everywhere. While acute symptoms of the world's problems are focused in the poorer countries, the problems themselves exist worldwide.

The citizens of affluent nations cannot "lead" other people out of the problems which we are in great part responsible for. We can help decrease the damage that we are all doing. We must also help repair the damage which has occurred in the past. Most importantly, though, we must search for answers within our own lives. We should remember, however, that some of the best models of resource-conserving systems will be found among cultures that are poorest in resources, but rich in tradition, wisdom, and an understanding of natural systems. New cross-cultural syntheses are needed. If we can make these new approaches work in our own lives, then elements in our work or in our example may become truly helpful to others.

Within each culture we need another kind of amphibian, people who can transmit values, technology, and culture from one generation to another--people who can teach the children. If we are to see that what we should be trying to do is not to produce food, but to maintain and use the living, food-producing organism that is our planet, then we must see the connection between our children, our gardens, and the living soil. We produce food for today. We maintain a living soil for tomorrow. We must let the children share in both.

Work in many distant parts of the world needs to be done, and there are special individuals capable of helping from within other cultures, but cures for the long-term problems must come primarily from within each culture, each community, each individual. We can share the results of our progress toward answers--but only if we share common goals. If we wish to help others produce their food using minimal resources, then we must first take this on as our own, personal, long-term goal. I hope One Circle can help people in this process.

David Duhon
Willits, California
March, 1985

# INTRODUCTION

For most of us, our primary link to the soil is the supermarket where we buy the food we eat. This is the place where we cast our "dollar-votes" for the kind of world food system that we want. Our choices always seem more limited than our rationalizations:

> Best not to read the ingredient labels; worrying about all those chemicals might raise one's blood pressure. Nutritious foods won't do the family any good anyway if they won't eat them, so no use buying them. Why aren't there ever any coupons for healthy foods? What was that new cereal that the youngest wanted?
>
> Too bad about the conditions of the farm workers--maybe the grape and lettuce boycotts helped. So many of them are illegal aliens; but who'd want to work out in the sun all day for less than minimum wage, with your back bent and all those pesticides. Of course, if we had to pay minimum wage to the people who produce our food our grocery bills would be a lot higher.
>
> Which cheese company was being investigated for criminal activities, or was that the meat packing company, or the company that produces the waxed boxes for the produce? Oh well, let's hope the government straightens all of that out soon. And bananas--which come from countries I shouldn't be supporting? Where does all the out of season produce come from? South Africa, Chile, New Zealand? Some comes from Mexico at least.
>
> Of course the worst problem is the farmers--spraying all those chemicals, depleting our soil and water, causing all that erosion--how can the government let them do that? And why are so many farmers still going broke? Organic farming can't be much of an alternative. Organic products aren't even in this store, and where you can get them they're usually so expensive. Anyway, everyone knows that some farmers cheat. At least there are name brands to choose from.
>
> Don't let the children put their mouths on anything--they must spray the store a lot to keep the board of health happy. Why do people move expressionlessly up and down the aisles like well-programmed machines? Well, supermarkets may not be perfect, but they're better than eating out all the time. People don't starve here like in some countries--or at least not many of them. Things could be worse.

And at the rate we are going things may get a whole lot worse, both here and around the planet. While political and economic constraints within society appear to deny us most real choices, we do in fact have the power to help make a better world.

By acting first as individuals, and letting a community of effort grow around our good work, we can sidestep the usual political and economic constraints which seem to hold us to our present course. Our food system was created in great part by individuals who worked hard and took risks to create something for their own benefit. If we are to take care of ourselves and our planet, then we will also have to work hard and take risks. By starting as individuals it is possible to create a new food system one person at a time and to begin today! We must act with both urgency and patience.

Most people believe that the area, time, and complexity involved in growing one's own food is more than they are capable of. This need not be the case. Biointensive techniques, which are explained in How to Grow More Vegetables, can allow people to grow food in a simple, sustainable, and ecologically sound way, while using a minimal amount of time, land, water, and other resources. This book, One Circle, will help you use these biointensive techniques to create your own diet that can be grown in an area smaller than you probably had ever before imagined was possible.

The area required, which can be less than a thousand square feet per person, is available to most, whether in their own yard, the yard of a friend or neighbor, or in a community garden. If less area is presently available to you, then choose a scaled-down version and still make a first step. Begin with parsley in a windowsill if need be. If you want to produce your own food, and are willing to keep your area needs minimal, you will almost certainly be able to find the land that you need.

The time required to grow your own food can be kept to as little as one or two hours a day, and much of the work can be saved for weekends. This is less time than most people spend watching television. It will be pleasant and rewarding time that will provide many of the things people expect from leisure activity, such as exercise, sunshine, and an escape from the normal turmoil of day-to-day life.

There are skills that will be needed, but these can be learned over time. The biointensive methods have been practiced, researched, and refined by Ecology Action over a period of fourteen years. A principle that has been observed constantly throughout this process has been the need to keep the method as simple, replicable, and easy to learn as possible without sacrificing yields or sustainability. The result is a system that with only minor alterations can be applied to nearly any crop in nearly any area of the world where agricultrure is practiced. These techniques have been learned and practiced by men and women, old and young, of large and small builds, in nearly every combination of soil and climate, and in nearly every area of the globe.

The biointensive method is neither new, nor some passing fad. There are indications that the method traces its history back, before the time of Christ to ancient kingdoms in both the Far East and the Middle East, possibly having been transferred from China to ancient Egypt and Persia. The earliest Christian monasteries, which began in Egypt around the second century A.D., adopted these methods and later moved these gardening techniques with them when they shifted their center of activity into Northern and Central Europe. These techniques were an important part of the self-reliant food system that helped preserve both the monks and the knowledge that they carried in their copied manuscripts through the troubled times of the Middle Ages.

During the Renaissance, these techniques moved into the gardens of the nobility, and from there into the market gardens springing up around the cities of Europe. Near Paris, in the nineteenth century, the methods were refined into the most economically successful form of agriculture of the time.

While these techniques represent a clear-cut, historical tradition, they have still been modified to meet the needs and resources of the times by everone who has used them. The monks had a sewage system that emptied into their compost piles. The food they produced was mostly for their own use. The French market gardeners relied on large amounts of horse manure, supplied by the sizable urban horse population of the time, to produce fine produce for market, much of which was grown out of season.

John Jeavons and the staff of Ecology Action have worked to adapt the methods to meet the needs and resources of our current times. Today, we must deal with increasing population, decreasing amounts of available farm land, diminishing water resources, disappearing forests, and depleted agricultural soils. What is needed is an agriculture that can be self-sustaining with a minimum amount of start-up resources. Other agricultural technologies being developed to feed the world's hungry do not generally share this goal. Green Revolution, hydroponics, and other new technologies seeking to intensify production usually have built into their design a continuing, permanent need for the import of sizable amounts of costly fertilizers, pesticides, energy, and industrial products. The constraints we face today demand both the adoption of responsible goals, and also the careful planning and design that will be needed to meet these goals. One Circle deals with the process of designing diets that can sustain us within the constraints of the world's resources.

A typical vegetarian diet can provide better, more balanced nutrition than the standard American diet, and can do so using about ten percent of the area and other resources. By producing a vegetarian diet yourself using biointensive techniques, it is possible to use even less land and other resources. By shifting to a more efficient mix of vegetarian staples and growing your own food using biointensive techniques, the area required can be reduced to as little as 700 square feet for the average adult.

This book argues that calories rather than proteins should be considered the limiting factor in designing a minimal area diet. Protein-concentrating crops such as grains, beans, and seeds can provide large amounts of both protein and calories per pound of food, but when compared with many other crops, produce relatively little of either nutrient per unit of area. Nutritionists view our protein needs differently now than they did ten years ago. We need not rely heavily on these less-efficient, high-protein foods in order to have a nutritionally sound diet. Foods that are more efficient at producing calories and protein from a limited area, such as roots and tubers, may serve as staples in a mix of foods forming a complete, wholesome diet.

There is a wide spectrum of choices between a typical vegetarian diet and a diet requiring the very least possible area. There are also staples other than those in this edition of One Circle that can form the basis of efficient diets. The use of animal products will generally significantly increase the area required for a diet. It is possible though, to design minimal area diets for animals. What is being advocated is not a certain kind of diet, but a process of diet design which among other things also attempts to minimize the area required.

This design process is intended to allow individuals, families, and other groups to free themselves by reclaiming responsibility for their own food production. It can help people in developing countries to rebuild the self-reliant food production they once had. While many of the principles that governed traditional food systems will again be needed, a shift to more efficient food mixes will be required due to the decreasing area of arable land available per person in the Third World. Livestock, which plays an important role in many traditional food systems, will generally need to give way to more area efficient food choices, unless ways can be found to drastically reduce the area required to produce the food for the livestock.

Whether we live in the cities, suburbs, or rural areas of an industrialized country, or whether we work in mines or on plantations, or live in urban slums or in a famine relief camp in a country whose food self-reliance has been mostly destroyed by the process of "development", we have nearly all become disconnected from our resource base. The circle that connects us to our crops and the soil has been broken. The circle that connects us to each other has also been broken. Governments, industry, and other institutions rely on this disconnection. Think of the worker in an arms plant or the shopper in a supermarket. If a solution is to be found, it will not come from these institutions. It must begin with individuals, and build to families, neighborhoods, and communities. If a solution is successful, and can be initiated by individuals, then it has the potential to spread by itself. This may be critical.

Blaming the world's problems on leaders, governments, and corporations will not produce any solutions. Modern society for the most part reflects accurately the values held by its members. We can be fooled into some things, and forced into other things, but even this is generally done by people who are products of society. The food system is this way. We are offered the foods and conveniences we desire. Advertising may sway our tastes this way or that, but even it largely reflects the trends of society.

A change in technology by itself, then, cannot make the necessary evolution in society unless it is able to change and influence values. Technologies are not simply

*vi*

tools--innocuous things whose use is determined by an external value system. They are born of certain values and encourage certain values and ways of thinking. Medical technology reduces health to matching the right treatment or mix of chemicals to a disease. Computers reduce people and nature to numbers used to form models, when we should be observing more and making better use of the analogue computer of our mind and senses. While these technologies do have their advantages, it is the negative effects that we are too often unaware of that cause the greatest problems. Our modern technologies have repeatedly led us to believe that we understand and can control matters that we do not understand and often lose control of.

Gardening has its own biases. It stimulates a slow approach to declaring what is true, for the awe that comes from working with nature, the soil, and plants will not let us easily declare truths from an organized collection of data that is only a faint shadow of reality. We learn to seek the whole with all our senses. We learn to value steady, skilled maintenance over flashy, broad strokes toward sudden progress. We learn to take care in all our work, for any link can become the weak one. Our crop yields more often define subtle mistakes than any clever improvements in technique. Perhaps we find lower yields with a three crop interplanting only because our transplanting technique suffered while trying to sort out the complexities of the pattern. Generally it is better to do things simply and well.

A technology is a tool, but it is also an important link to how we view the world and the values that we hold. Values reflect themselves in the kinds of individuals, families, communities, and societies that are created. Different kinds of agriculture encourage different kinds of values. Eating food from a supermarket will encourage different values and patterns of creativity than those we might have if we produce our own food. Producing food from a small garden--a small plot of land that we work by hand and attend to with care--can help change our values, and improve the way that we look at and think about the world. Self-reliant food production can help us fine-tune our body, mind and senses. It can help us pass on to our children the values that a better tomorrow will require. Just as we put life into the soil, so can the soil add to our life. The choice for producing our own food is a choice for improving our own lives and the lives of our children.

If we accept--as given--the options offered to us by the institutions of society, then, as the person in the supermarket found, our choices are very limited. But if we create our own choices--as we can do by growing our own food--then we have more complete choices and can begin to create a better future. The paradise we seek, we must create for ourselves, and there is no better place to start than in our gardens.

# A CHALLENGE

## by John Jeavons

### LIVING CIRCLES

Our world is One Circle -- a living circle of life with many forms each interdependent upon one another. The fresh smell and the sound of silence we encounter as we walk through a forest are part of this circle -- so are the diversity and amazingly fragile balance of the soil and its microscopic microbial life, the touch of a gentle breeze upon our faces, the exhilarating force of a strong gust of wind, the sight of the delicate colors of an unfolding flower, the laughter in a child's eyes, and the character in the lined face of an older person wise in the ways of this planet.

A seed is One Circle of life, as is each person, this planet, and a garden. Another kind of circle is the first section we planted at our new garden/mini-farm in 1982. This circle is 1,000 square feet of planted area. The shape was chosen because it fit naturally into a bowl-shaped area at the bottom of a moderate to steeply sloping, one and one-quarter acre area we had fenced off for growing food.

### THE GARDEN/MINI-FARM CIRCLE

As people came to visit our new Ecology Action biointensive demonstration and research site on the first Saturdays of June, July, August, and September, the thousand square foot circular area began to be used as a point of reference because of its unusual shape among many rectangular growing beds, and because it was a natural focal point, some one hundred feet below one's first view of the garden. It was also a good unit of area for comparison. Four circles would be the size of our economic mini-farm model, and three-quarters of a circle to three circles would be the size of the area we believed a complete balanced vegetarian diet could be grown on. In contrast, a vegetarian diet grown by standard commercial United States agricultural practices would take about ten circles, and a meat diet from forty-five to eighty-five circles.

### TREES DISAPPEAR

On the tours, as people looked down to the circle in the garden below, it was a good time to reflect on how the Earth's circle of life was rapidly deteriorating. In about 1800 the Earth had a heavy cover of trees -- perhaps close to as much as had ever existed -- though many had already been logged in China and Europe. In 1950, only about twenty percent of these trees remained, and by 1975 only about ten percent were left. Today, there are even less. One-third of the world's countries depend on wood for fuel and many no longer have enough. At the same time, the remaining trees, the "skin of the Earth", as Alan Chadwick often said, are still being cut down. In vast areas of this planet, they are no longer there to retain water in the soil, protect the soil's microbial life and breathe out oxygen after taking in excess atmospheric carbon dioxide. This disappearance of trees is also creating many environmental and climatic problems which are dramatically reducing the number of plant and animal forms left on this planet.

DESERTS INCREASE DRAMATICALLY

By 1975, about forty-nine percent of the Earth's land surface had become desert. By the year 2000, the U.N. estimated that sixty-three percent or more of the Earth's land surface will have become desert or will have become otherwise unusable for food-raising due to the combined effects of deforestation, salinization and suburbanization. This problem is not limited to the Third World, as one-third of all the desertification expected to occur in the world between 1977 and the year 2000 may come from the United States.

POPULATIONS

In the year 2000, many estimate that the Earth will be the home for about five and one-half billion people -- up from four billion in 1975. About seventy-five to eighty percent of the people are expected to live in the Third World.

AGRICULTURAL LAND USAGE

A study by the Environmental Fund in Washington, D.C. indicates that up to ninety percent of the agricultural land available to the Third World in 1975 may no longer be farmable by the year 2000 due to the processes described above. Should this occur, only a little over two circles of farmable land, a mere 2,100 square feet, might be available to each man, woman, and child for food, fuel, building materials, fiber for clothes, and income crops. Yet, if we take the most productive form of mainstream agriculture today -- Japanese mechanized, chemical, commercial techniques -- about five circles would be required to grow a vegetarian diet for one person. If everyone practiced this kind of agriculture, by the end of the century for the Third World, there might only be enough land to feed forty percent of the people . The point in time when five circles per person might be left for the agriculture of these countries is possibly about 1997. But these Japanese techniques are expensive and use very high inputs of chemical fertilizers, pesticides, and water. Few can afford them.

So let's choose a less capital-, fertilizer-, and pesticide-intensive form of agriculture -- United States mechanized, chemical, commercial techniques. These techniques produce one vegetarian diet on <u>ten</u> circles. Ten circles of farming land per person of good agricultural soil might remain in the Third World in, say, 1992, extrapolating from the Environmental Fund report, but most people could not afford the equipment and materials involved for even these techniques.

Other evaluations of how much agricultural land will be available to each person in the Third World vary. United Nations' Food and Agricultural Organization data indicated that in 1975 there were 41 circles of agricultural land avaiable to each person in the world, and 37 circles, or 37,000 square feet, for each person in the Third World. A separate U.N. projection notes that these figures are expected to change to 18 circles for each person in the world and about 16 circles for each person in the Third World in the year 2000.

Why is there a difference in the estimates of agricultural area availability by the year 2000 -- between 16 circles and 2 circles? Both evaluations are derived from close studies of detailed U.N. data. One possibility is that each reflects a different estimate as to the quality of the land expected to be under cultivation in the year 2000 with the Environmental Fund report expecting a more significant level of depletion in the world's agricultural soils. Sixteen circles of farmable land might be available to each Third World person in the year 2000, but the productivity level of each circle might be poor. More research needs to be performed in this area so that a good qualitative as well as quantitative understanding results.

An analysis of recent finding of the United Nations' Food and Agriculture Organization's "Land Resources for Populations of the Future Project" indicates that in about 1982 the Third World as a whole (assuming actual diets being eaten and assuming actual agricultural practices being used) had just enough agricultural land to feed its people. Actually, Latin America had almost twice the land needed to feed its people at this point and the rest of the Third World had less than enough. The need for food raising approaches that are personal, use the smallest possible area, produce complete diets, and are resource-conserving becomes apparent in light of this overall world picture.

With efforts directed into this kind of local food-raising a personal "Marshall Plan" based on local resources could rapidly reverse the deteriorating world situation. The real world energy crisis is one of human energy, and we can make the difference by using our resources more effectively. We each need to cultivate our own One Circle. Some ways in which we can do this will be described in this book.

## STARVATION

Even in periods of adequate agricultural land, millions of people have died from starvation, and this number has increased as agricultural land has became more scarce. According to certain estimates, in 1978, fourteen million people died from starvation, in 1981, twenty-one million, and in 1984 people were starving to death at the rate of forty-five million or more. In 1982, Orville Freeman, former Secretary of Agriculture, said that he expected 500 million people to starve to death by the end of the decade. In addition, the United Nations recently indicated that 485 million individuals are in the process of starving to death and that another one billion are significantly malnourished.

## CHILDREN

Generally, two-thirds of those who starve each year are children. Yet, there is another more hidden side to the effects of malnourishment. UNICEF estimated for 1983 that "for every child under age five who has died, another has been left blind or deaf or crippled or retarded." In India, 85% of the children (perhaps about 200 million) will never be physically and/or mentally normal due to the malnutrition which has already occurred -- even if they are fed perfect diets the rest of their lives.

## THREE CRISES: ENERGY, FOOD, AND HEALTH AND NUTRITION

Dr. E. F. Schumacher, noted English economist and author of Small Is Beautiful, noted that the world would be experiencing three major crises: Energy, Food, and Health and Nutrition. The industrialized world is very aware of the first crisis. The next two crises have arrived for many people. Many point to the fact that there is enough food currently grown in the world; that growing enough food is not the problem. They point to the physical distritution difficulties, inadequate storage facilities, and political problems. These points are well taken and are true, but soon, due to deforestation, desertification, population increase, and losses of agricultural land, there will not be enough land, using current agricultural practices, for most of the world's people to grow all their food -- even with good distribution, adequate storage facilities and supportive political institutions.

U.S. AGRICULTURE?

What about U.S. agricultural practices? Cannot they feed the world? The United States has depleted almost one-half of its soil base, over one-third of its topsoil and one-half of its organic matter in the last 200 years. This level of depletion probably took 3000 years to occur in China using different agricultural practices.

It takes the United States somewhere between six and twenty calories of energy input to produce one calorie of food. In fact, today, if all the world were to use U.S. agricultural, processing, and distribution techniques for its food needs, about 2 1/2 times all the energy used in the world for all purposes would be required just for agricultural processes!

In addition, it is this same mechanized, chemical form of agriculture which, on the average, has depleted about 1 million acres of farmland per year over the last 14 years. Combined with the loss of agricultural land due to urbanization and suburbanization, this rate of depletion, if it continues, will mean that the United States may have no food to export by the year 2000, assuming diets similar to those eaten today and no significant increase in population. This situation could produce significant difficulties, as much of our trade deficit from fuel imports has been balanced by our trade earnings from agricultural exports.

A RESOURCE-CONSERVING ALTERNATIVE IS NEEDED

In light of such a perspective it seems appropriate to be looking for a more resource-efficient food-raising system which is capable of building and maintaining soil fertility. Since the situation is so widespread, it seems appropriate to involve as many people as possible, including children, in its solution. With positive energy it should be possible for all of us, working together, to revitalize the world's soils and to develop resource-conserving food-raising systems locally.

DESIGNING A NEW DIET

Even in many vegetarian diets large amounts of farmland are used to produce the oils and sweeteners needed for the recipies involved. Other alternatives can provide the needed calories. One approach utilizes grains and/or beans as a base. This practice also requires a large area for cultivation. Other practices emphasize root and tuber crops for the por-vision of calories. These crops require less space to be grown, but are often unable to provide all the nutrients needed for a complete, balanced diet. Also, a large amount of roots and tubers need to be eaten if enough nutrition is to be obtained. A more complete study of crop nutrients and crop yield levels provides a number of different ways in which a person can grow a balanced diet in a small area. It is the purpose of One Circle: How To Grow A Complete Balanced Diet In 1,000 Square Feet Or Less to enable the reader to design his or her own diet according to personal preferences, dietary needs, space limitations and the amount of time available for food growing. The design goal of One Circle is to determine how one adult woman can grow all her food on as little as 550 square feet, and how one man can do the same on as little as 850 square feet -- an average of 700 square feet per person (less than one circle). Many detailed charts are provided along with easy-to-use slide rules that make this process easier. The diets developed by a person may require as little as one circle (or less) for cultivation in an eight-month growing season, and as much as two, three, or more circles depending on how efficient the crops grown are in producing adequate nutrition within a limited area of land and within the limit of the weight of food that can easily be consumed each day. The tables provided indicate the levels of efficiency for key crops and provide the information necessary for the reader to develop this efficiency information for other crops. Fourteen especially efficient crops are emphasized in One Circle, but any crop may be used in the diet-designing process. This process is an exciting way to understand nutrition and to evaluate the effectiveness of your food-raising practices!

*Also available, by David Duhon:*

A History of Intensive Food Gardening

    Part 1: Europe

*Available from the author:*

    *David Duhon*
    *5798 Ridgewood Road*
    *Willits, CA, 95490*

*$6.00 postpaid*

# NUTRITION RECONSIDERED

## INTRODUCTION

Nutritional science has produced a growing list of
essential nutrients. It is quite likely that more will be
added to this list as time goes on. These nutrients include: 1) calories, sources of energy in the form of fats,
carbohydrates, and proteins; 2) vitamins, catalysts which
are essential to the body's chemical transformations; and 3)
minerals, such as iron, iodine, calcium, and zinc, which
the body uses for a variety of purposes.

For most of these essential nutrients, various groups
have made estimates of the minimum requirements for maintaining the health of a person of given characteristics.
An example might be a person who was female, age 23,
pregnant, weighed 123 pounds, and had a light level of
activity. These minimum needs have a safety factor added
to them to allow for variation between individuals.

The nutrient requirements set by the National Academy
of Science, the RDA's, have been used in most of the analysis in this book. In the section discussing individual
nutrients, both the requirements from the National Academy
of Science, and some alternative suggestions from other
sources have been presented and discussed. The annotated

The Recommended Dietary
Allowances are set by
the Food and Nutrition
Board of the National
Academy of Sciences.

bibliography at the end of the nutrients section can help you investigate nutrition and form your own understanding of what constitutes a healthy diet.

The RDA's for some nutrients are determined not only by the body's needs, but also by other factors more accurately related to the composition of the average U.S. diet. In stating protein requirements, a certain protein quality, based on amino acid content and digestability, is assumed, even though this is a factor of diet rather than of protein needs. For iron, it is assumed that only 10 percent of the iron we take in will be absorbed. Depending on the mix of foods in our diet and other factors, our actual absorption might be better or worse than this. For calcium, a high protein intake and high customary calcium intake are assumed and these assumptions result in a very high recommendation for calcium.

The RDA's make many assumptions as to diet, and are not a simple statement of our body's needs. While the diet that is assumed may be accurate for many Americans, it is a diet of excess and not one that should be recommended. Its assumptions may not always be applicable in the design of a diet seeking to make efficient use of our planet's resources.

The instructions and tools in this book will allow you to use whatever nutrition standards you select. You will then be able to design a minimal area diet based on your own best sense of your personal dietary needs.

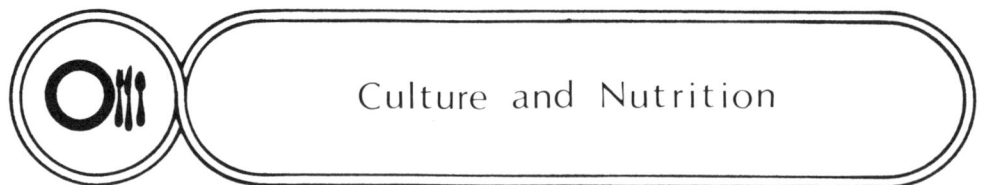

## Culture and Nutrition

Health is a culturally defined term. What one culture might consider healthy might be considered unhealthy by another. A culture that tends to define health only in terms of nutrition and exercise will have different definitions of health and what a healthy diet is than a culture that considers nutrition together with other factors such as lifestyle, soil health, and food system vulnerability.

Much of what Americans know about health is strongly influenced by a food industry that sells nutritional information along with its products. Healthful eating is often reduced to a matter of meeting minimal requirements of all the nutrients, while other aspects of nutrition are ignored by many. We should also be concerned with not getting too much of certain nutrients and getting our nutrients in a balanced, healthful mix.

Nutritional science increasingly recognizes the importance of eating a mix of foods that provides nutrients in the proper proportions without taking in excess amounts of certain nutrients which might be harmful to our health. The most widespread nutritional ills of American society are not affected by whether or not our morning breakfast cereal contains 25% or 100% of the requirements for all the vitamins and minerals. The amount of sugar in the cereal is much more likely to affect our health. The nutritional ills of an affluent society are more likely to be due to nutrient excess than nutrient deficiency.

A Nutritious Breakfast?

The food industry is quick to list the "healthy" amounts of protein, vitamins, or minerals in a product, but is less likely to give information relating to the problems of excess fat or cholesterol or of the excess empty calories of sugar. Whether a product lists it as dextrose, brown sugar, or honey, it is still sugar and supplies relatively empty calories lacking the nutrients needed to properly metabolize these calories. In the quantities consumed by most Americans, sugar is not healthy--no matter what form it comes in.

Getting enough protein is emphasized by many as an important and difficult choice. In reality, *if we avoid foods such as sugars and oils, it is difficult to get enough calories without also getting enough protein*. The problem lies not in our protein needs, or in the protein content of nutritious, whole foods, but in a national diet reliant

3

on foods which have had the protein and other nutrients removed from them.

Our nutritionists tend to focus on problems generated by such a culturally determined diet, and to set requirements based on this same diet. The nutrients they select often reflect problems in our diet and not our true needs. The requirements that are set also assume an unhealthy diet, the typical American diet, and are not necessarily a reflection of our true needs either. An effort to produce a complete human diet from a minimal area will have to focus on different problems, and to a degree, on different nutrients. Individuals truly committed to this effort may have to make difficult choices as to what their true needs are.

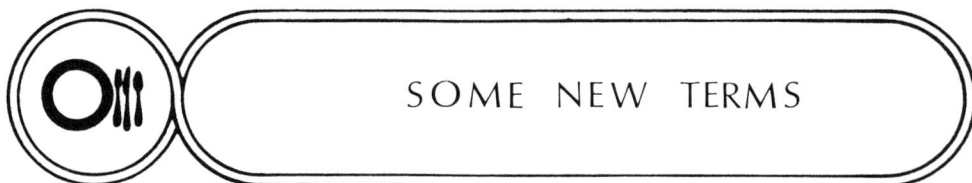

## SOME NEW TERMS

Which are the nutrients that are the most difficult to design into a complete, minimal area human diet? The _essential nutrients_ are those the body needs for proper functioning. Any of these may be problematic. In trying to correct the typical American diet, fat is a problem, since most Americans consume too much of it. _In trying to design a minimal area diet, calories are a good example of a problem nutrient, because there are few crops that both concentrate calories and also produce a sizable yield per unit of area._ A nutrient that is difficult to supply either because of low concentrations of the nutrient in food, or because of low yields of the nutrient per unit area for the various crops will be called a _Critical Nutrient_.

Nutrient concentration per pound of food, and the yield of the nutrient per 100 square feet of growing area are the primary design criteria in a complete, minimal area diet.

For information on the nutritional patterns of nine healthier societies, see The Appetites of Man, by Sally Devore and Thelma White.

4

While you may like a food such as asparagus--it may taste good to you--you would have great difficulty eating the amount that would be required to meet your daily nutritional requirements for most nutrients. The nutrients contained it it are not concentrated enough. To get 2,000 calories eating asparagus would take nearly 20 pounds-- more than could be eaten by the most ardent asparagus lover. A factor not generally considered in nutrition books is that the bulk or weight of the food consumed is an important element in diet design, just as are the requirements for specific nutrients. A weight of between four and six pounds per day of food as served is probably a reasonable solid food consumption level for most people.

A good approach to determine your own personal consumption level is to spend a week weighing everything you eat and see what your average daily consumption is. Since most Americans are accustomed to eating a fairly concentrated and therefore low bulk diet, the weight you are used to eating is probably less than what you could get used to eating if you ate a less concentrated diet. *If you can increase the weight that you can comfortably consume each day, while keeping your calorie level the same (by switching to less concentrated foods), you will be able to greatly decrease the area required to grow a complete diet.* This will be explained in a later section.

For this analysis, if a food can provide all of a particular nutrient in six pounds or less for men, or in five and a half pounds or less for women, then it will be defined as being *Weight Efficient* for that nutrient. In designing your own diet you may wish to choose a different food weight to define *Weight Efficient*, and may even wish to change this value again later, as you are able to eat more weight from a less concentrated diet. If a nutrient has few crops that are *Weight Efficient* for it, then it is defined as being a *Weight Critical Nutrient*.

The production level for a crop is determined by the yield per unit area and the total area. To achieve high

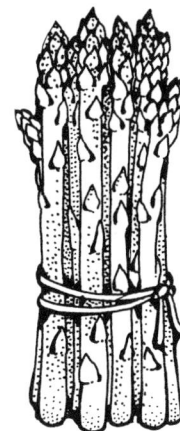

The nutrients in asparagus are not concentrated enough.

A crop that can provide all of a nutrient is six pounds or less is *Weight Efficient* for that nutrient.

5

yields in a sustainable way requires skill and experience in order to improve soil and provide good crop care. The area each of us can maintain is limited by the time and effort we have available. Skill and experience make the most of these factors.

In many parts of the world available cropland area is especially limited. While political and economic factors can be the prime cause of this scarcity, it is easier to improve agricultural production than it is to change the political and economic structure of a country. Even if land reform is not easily achieved, it is still possible to gain increases in production. Such yield increases can bring benefits to the small farmers who were passed over by the insustainable, high-input agriculture of the Green Revolution.

When we are provided with a means of increasing our productivity in a sound, sustainable way, we are enpowered in a way in which we can sustain ourselves. This will help make more difficult changes easier. An agronomic solution can help provide a stable base from which to build. If we must wait for massive global starvation and chaos to trigger changes in governments and the world food system, we have waited too long.

Few people growing food in small areas take yield data. Without actually weighing your harvest, crop yields are difficult to estimate. Yield estimates from How To Grow More Vegetables..., by John Jeavons, have been used in this analysis. Some of the yield levels have been lowered in consultation with him after further analysis, so that the yield estimates here will be more immediately applicable to a broad range of situations.

In How To Grow More Vegetables..., three yield figures are given for each crop, Beginning, Good, and Excellent. One way to interpret these is that an average person with average soil and climate can get Beginning yields for most crops in the first year or two if the directions in the book are carefully followed. Rather than worry about the

Taking yield data is an important first step.

6

ambiguity of such a statement, one should simply try it, take yield data, and use the results for the next year's planning.

By the third year, with continued building of soil and skill, and the completion of a "complete texturizing dig"* for all the beds, <u>Good</u> yields can be achieved. (<u>Good</u> yields may even be achieved the first year.)

<u>Excellent</u> yields include figures that have been achieved and even surpassed for some crops. For other crops that have been less well studied, the projections have been based either on yields from other sites or sample testing in Ecology Action research beds. While more tentative, <u>Excellent</u> yields can be used to estimate a plateau of optimal yields which may be reached in the seventh year of a well focused effort on a single site. These assume careful studies that could even be undertaken by someone with a full-time job, given the small area and limited number of crops being considered in this book.

Networking with others and sharing results will also be helpful. In fact, if the research is kept within narrow design limits, this process could facilitate revolutionary increases in food production worldwide. Cooperation within a common framework makes it possible for individuals anywhere to make significant contributions toward solving the world food crisis. Once a key technique for growing a crop well is discovered by one person or group, everyone can benefit from the result.

For this book's analysis, <u>Good</u> yield figures have been assumed and the area 550 square feet for women and 850 square feet for men set as the area objectives. If a crop can meet the needs for a nutrient within the area objectives, then it will be defined as *Area Efficient* for that nutrient. If there are few crops that are *Area Efficient* for a particular nutrient, then it is defined as an *Area*

A crop that can provide all of a nutrient in 700 square feet or less is *Area Efficient* for that nutrient.

* For complete instructions, see John Jeavons, <u>How to Grow More Vegetables</u>, 3rd edition, 10 Speed Press, Berkeley, CA, pp. 16-17.

*Critical Nutrient.*

Using these criteria, the following chart indicates which nutrients are *Critical Nutrients* for men or women, and whether they are critical relative to weight or area:

| | WEIGHT CRITICAL | | AREA CRITICAL | |
|---|---|---|---|---|
| | MEN | WOMEN | MEN | WOMEN |
| Calories | | | x | x |
| Protein | | | | x |
| Isoleucine | | | | x |
| Leucine | | | | x |
| Cystine + Methionine | | | x | x |
| Tryptophan | | | | x |
| Carbohydrates | | | x | x |
| Fat | x | x | x | x |
| Linoleic Acid | x | x | x | x |
| Vitamin A | x | x | x | x |
| Riboflavin | | | x | x |
| Niacin | | | x | x |
| Vitamin $B_6$ | | | x | x |
| Pantothenic Acid | | | x | x |
| Iodine | x | x | x | x |
| Zinc | | | x | x |
| Calcium | | | x | x |
| Iron | | | | x |

These are the nutrients that will be the most difficult to provide the recommended allowances for in a daily diet of five and a half or six pounds produced on an area of 700 square feet.

The following fourteen crops have been selected due to their efficiency in meeting the requirements for the *Critical Nutrients*

| | |
|---|---|
| collards--leaf and stem | potatoes--tuber |
| filberts--seed | peanuts--seed |
| garlic--bulb | soybeans--seed |
| leeks--bulb | sunflower--seed |
| onions--bulb | sweet potatoes--tuber |
| parsley--stem and leaf | turnips--root and leaf |
| parsnips--root | wheat--seed |

Using this list of efficient crops, all nutrients for

which requirements have been set* have at least three
sources that are *Weight Efficient,* and at least three
sources, not necessarily the same, that are *Area Efficient.*
In this analysis, the *Critical Nutrients* that were listed
have six or less efficient crops relative to weight or to
area. *By using these fourteen crops in the right propor-*
*tions it will be possible to design a balanced, healthy*
*diet that requires only a minimal amount of growing area.*

It is possible (and will probably be desirable) to add
other crops to this list and still design a minimal area
diet. If either different yield figures are used, or if a
different set of nutrient requirements are used, a different list of *Critical Nutrients* and *Efficient Crops* might
be generated. The instructions for completing such a
process are given in the boxed section at the end of this
chapter.

The following lists give the *Weight Efficiency Values*
and the *Area Efficiency Values* for the fourteen efficient
crops. The methods for calculating these are given in the
boxed section that follows. The *Weight Efficiency Values*
express the number of pounds that it would take of a certain
crop to meet the needs for a certain nutrient. The *Area*
*Efficiency Values express the number of 100 square foot beds*
*that it would take to produce all of a given nutrient from*
*a particular crop.*

* The one partial exception is vitamin $B_{12}$. For this
nutrient, it is important to see the special treatment
given to it in the individual nutrients section on
page 63.

| WEIGHT EFFICIENCY VALUES / Nutrient | | Collards | Filberts | Garlic | Leeks | Onions | Parsley | Parsnips | Peanuts | Potatoes | Soybeans | Sunflower Seeds | Sweet Potatoes | Turnips | Wheat |
|---|---|---|---|---|---|---|---|---|---|---|---|---|---|---|---|
| Calories | M | 14.8 | .94 | 4.34 | 11.4 | 15.6 | 13.6 | 7.92 | 1.05 | 6.40 | 5.04 | 1.06 | 4.22 | 20.9 | 2.47 |
| | F | 11.0 | .69 | 3.22 | 8.47 | 11.6 | 10.1 | 5.87 | .78 | 4.74 | 3.73 | .79 | 3.13 | 15.5 | 1.83 |
| Protein | M | 3.44 | .98 | 1.99 | 5.60 | 8.24 | 3.44 | 7.27 | .47 | 4.75 | 1.26 | .51 | 5.89 | 4.98 | 1.28 |
| | F | 2.82 | .80 | 1.64 | 4.60 | 6.76 | 2.82 | 5.97 | .39 | 3.90 | 1.03 | .42 | 4.84 | 4.09 | 1.06 |
| Isoleucine | M | 2.48 | .19 | -- | 1.58 | 13.9 | -- | -- | .28 | 3.65 | .44 | .44 | 5.78 | 3.30 | .90 |
| | F | 2.06 | .16 | -- | 1.31 | 11.5 | -- | -- | .23 | 3.03 | .37 | .36 | 4.79 | 2.73 | .75 |
| Leucine | M | 1.83 | .25 | -- | 1.23 | 10.0 | -- | -- | .20 | 3.06 | .34 | .39 | 5.22 | 2.25 | .59 |
| | F | 1.52 | .21 | -- | 1.02 | 8.29 | -- | -- | .16 | 2.54 | .28 | .32 | 4.32 | 1.86 | .49 |
| Cystine + Methionine | M | 2.20 | .80 | -- | 1.16 | 14.4 | 12.8 | -- | .33 | 6.07 | .64 | .46 | 6.44 | 5.13 | .61 |
| | F | 1.84 | .67 | -- | .96 | 12.0 | 10.7 | -- | .27 | 5.06 | .54 | .38 | 5.37 | 4.28 | .51 |
| Tryptophan | M | 1.39 | .26 | -- | -- | 3.46 | .94 | -- | .23 | 2.10 | .39 | .34 | 3.15 | 1.96 | .69 |
| | F | 1.15 | .22 | -- | -- | 2.87 | .78 | -- | .19 | 1.74 | .32 | .28 | 2.61 | 1.62 | .57 |
| Carbohydrate | M | 12.4 | 5.34 | 2.90 | 7.97 | 10.3 | 10.5 | 5.09 | 5.07 | 4.23 | 8.82 | 4.49 | 2.73 | 16.5 | 1.74 |
| | F | 9.17 | 3.96 | 2.15 | 5.91 | 7.6 | 7.77 | 3.77 | 3.75 | 3.13 | 6.54 | 3.32 | 2.02 | 12.2 | 1.29 |
| Fat | M | 9.38 | .11 | 33.3 | 21.4 | 60 | 11.1 | 13.0 | .14 | 60 | 1.29 | .14 | 13.0 | 24.2 | 4.57 |
| | F | 6.88 | .08 | 24.4 | 15.7 | 44 | 8.15 | 9.57 | .10 | 44 | .95 | .10 | 9.57 | 17.7 | 3.35 |
| Linoleic Acid | M | -- | .10 | -- | -- | -- | -- | -- | .07 | 17.3 | .33 | .03 | 5.84 | 26.5 | 2.05 |
| | F | -- | .07 | -- | -- | -- | -- | -- | .05 | 12.7 | .24 | .02 | 4.29 | 19.4 | 1.51 |
| Vitamin A | M | .20 | 12.4 | -- | 33.3 | 33.3 | .16 | 43.5 | -- | -- | 44.1 | 26.3 | .16 | .23 | -- |
| | F | .16 | 9.88 | -- | 26.7 | 26.7 | .12 | 34.8 | -- | -- | 35.2 | 21.1 | .13 | .19 | -- |
| Riboflavin | M | 1.13 | .66 | 4.44 | 5.93 | 8.89 | 1.36 | 3.90 | 2.71 | 8.89 | 3.90 | 1.54 | 5.00 | 1.15 | 4.10 |
| | F | .85 | .50 | 3.33 | 4.44 | 6.67 | 1.02 | 2.93 | 2.03 | 6.67 | 2.93 | 1.15 | 3.75 | .86 | 3.08 |
| Niacin | M | 2.34 | 4.39 | 7.93 | 7.83 | 20.0 | 3.30 | 20.0 | .25 | 2.34 | 6.67 | .73 | 5.63 | 5.31 | 1.28 |
| | F | 1.69 | 3.17 | 5.73 | 5.65 | 14.4 | 2.39 | 14.4 | .18 | 1.69 | 4.81 | .53 | 4.06 | 3.83 | .92 |
| Vitamin $B_6$ | M | 2.25 | .77 | -- | 2.20 | 6.89 | 2.74 | 4.88 | 1.52 | 1.89 | .69 | .35 | 2.02 | 4.65 | .65 |
| | F | 2.25 | .77 | -- | 2.20 | 6.89 | 2.74 | 4.88 | 1.52 | 1.89 | .69 | .35 | 2.02 | 4.65 | .65 |
| Pantothenic Acid | M | 2.50 | .97 | -- | -- | 62.5 | 3.62 | 1.84 | .46 | 3.03 | .66 | -- | 1.34 | 10.6 | 1.41 |
| | F | 2.50 | .97 | -- | -- | 62.5 | 3.62 | 1.84 | .46 | 3.03 | .66 | -- | 1.34 | 10.6 | 1.41 |
| Iodine | M | 1.69 | 14.4 | 10.6 | -- | 2.03 | -- | 7.96 | 1.43 | 1.91 | -- | -- | 2.60 | .50 | 39.7 |
| | F | 1.30 | 11.1 | 8.13 | -- | 1.56 | -- | 6.73 | 1.10 | 1.47 | -- | -- | 2.00 | .39 | 30.5 |
| Zinc | M | -- | .72 | 1.65 | 7.09 | 6.25 | 2.44 | -- | .66 | 3.67 | 3.30 | -- | 28.6 | .85 | 1.26 |
| | F | -- | .72 | 1.65 | 7.09 | 6.25 | 2.44 | -- | .66 | 3.67 | 3.30 | -- | 28.6 | .85 | 1.26 |
| Calcium | M | .54 | .53 | 3.80 | 2.12 | 4.07 | .54 | 2.20 | 1.87 | 12.2 | 1.51 | .92 | 2.75 | .57 | 3.72 |
| | F | .54 | .53 | 3.80 | 2.12 | 4.07 | .54 | 2.20 | 1.87 | 12.2 | 1.51 | .92 | 2.75 | .57 | 3.72 |
| Iron | M | 2.22 | .65 | 1.47 | 2.08 | 4.35 | .36 | 3.13 | 1.10 | 3.13 | .81 | .31 | 2.44 | 1.50 | .92 |
| | F | 4.00 | 1.17 | 2.65 | 3.60 | 7.83 | .64 | 5.63 | 1.98 | 5.63 | 1.46 | .56 | 4.39 | 2.70 | 1.66 |

| AREA EFFICIENCY VALUES / Nutrient | | Collards | Filberts | Garlic | Leeks | Onions | Parsley | Parsnips | Peanuts | Potatoes | Soybeans | Sunflower Seeds | Sweet Potatoes | Turnips | Wheat |
|---|---|---|---|---|---|---|---|---|---|---|---|---|---|---|---|
| Calories | M | 18.1 | 27.6 | 13.2 | 17.4 | 7.12 | 70.9 | 6.07 | 38.3 | 6.21 | 76.7 | 38.7 | 22.7 | 14.1 | 32.6 |
|  | F | 13.4 | 20.3 | 9.79 | 12.9 | 5.29 | 52.7 | 4.50 | 28.5 | 4.60 | 56.7 | 28.8 | 16.8 | 10.5 | 24.1 |
| Protein | M | 4.19 | 28.8 | 6.05 | 8.52 | 3.76 | 17.9 | 5.57 | 17.2 | 4.61 | 19.2 | 18.6 | 31.6 | 3.37 | 16.9 |
|  | F | 3.43 | 23.5 | 4.99 | 7.00 | 3.08 | 14.7 | 4.58 | 14.2 | 3.78 | 15.7 | 15.3 | 26.0 | 2.76 | 14.0 |
| Isoleucine | M | 3.02 | 5.58 | -- | 2.40 | 6.32 | -- | -- | 10.2 | 3.54 | 6.69 | 16.1 | 31.0 | 2.23 | 11.9 |
|  | F | 2.51 | 4.70 | -- | 1.99 | 5.23 | -- | -- | 8.40 | 2.94 | 5.63 | 13.1 | 25.7 | 1.85 | 9.89 |
| Leucine | M | 2.23 | 7.35 | -- | 1.87 | 4.56 | -- | -- | 7.30 | 2.97 | 5.17 | 14.2 | 28.0 | 1.52 | 7.78 |
|  | F | 1.85 | 6.17 | -- | 1.55 | 3.87 | -- | -- | 5.84 | 2.46 | 4.26 | 11.7 | 23.2 | 1.26 | 6.46 |
| Cystine + Methionine | M | 2.68 | 23.5 | -- | 1.76 | 6.58 | 66.7 | -- | 12.1 | 5.89 | 9.73 | 16.8 | 34.6 | 3.47 | 8.05 |
|  | F | 2.24 | 19.7 | -- | 1.46 | 5.48 | 55.8 | -- | 9.86 | 4.91 | 8.21 | 13.9 | 28.8 | 2.89 | 6.73 |
| Tryptophan | M | 1.69 | 7.64 | -- | -- | 1.58 | 4.90 | -- | 8.40 | 2.04 | 5.93 | 12.4 | 16.9 | 1.32 | 9.10 |
|  | F | 1.40 | 6.47 | -- | -- | 1.31 | 4.07 | -- | 6.94 | 1.69 | 4.87 | 10.2 | 14.0 | 1.09 | 7.52 |
| Carbohydrates | M | 15.1 | 157 | 8.82 | 12.1 | 4.68 | 54.7 | 3.90 | 185 | 4.10 | 134 | 164 | 14.7 | 11.2 | 23.0 |
|  | F | 11.2 | 116 | 6.54 | 8.99 | 3.47 | 40.5 | 2.89 | 137 | 3.03 | 99.5 | 121 | 10.8 | 8.25 | 17.0 |
| Fat | M | 11.4 | 3.23 | 101 | 32.6 | 27.4 | 57.9 | 10.0 | 5.11 | 58.2 | 19.6 | 5.1 | 69.8 | 16.4 | 60.3 |
|  | F | 8.37 | 2.35 | 74.2 | 23.9 | 20.1 | 42.5 | 7.34 | 3.65 | 42.7 | 14.4 | 3.65 | 51.4 | 11.9 | 44.2 |
| Linoleic Acid | M | -- | 2.94 | -- | -- | -- | -- | -- | 2.56 | 16.8 | 5.02 | 1.10 | 31.3 | 17.9 | 27.0 |
|  | F | -- | 2.06 | -- | -- | -- | -- | -- | 1.83 | 12.3 | 3.65 | .89 | 23.0 | 13.1 | 19.9 |
| Vitamin A | M | .24 | 363 | -- | 50.6 | 15.2 | .83 | 33.4 | -- | -- | 670 | 960 | .87 | .16 | -- |
|  | F | .19 | 290 | -- | 40.6 | 12.2 | .63 | 26.7 | -- | -- | 536 | 770 | .70 | .13 | -- |
| Riboflavin | M | 1.37 | 19.4 | 13.5 | 9.02 | 4.06 | 7.09 | 2.99 | 98.9 | 8.62 | 59.3 | 56.2 | 26.8 | .78 | 54.1 |
|  | F | 1.03 | 14.7 | 10.1 | 6.75 | 3.04 | 5.32 | 2.25 | 74.1 | 6.47 | 44.6 | 42.0 | 20.1 | .58 | 40.6 |
| Niacin | M | 2.85 | 129 | 24.1 | 11.9 | 9.13 | 17.2 | 15.3 | 9.13 | 2.27 | 101 | 26.6 | 30.2 | 3.59 | 16.9 |
|  | F | 2.06 | 93.2 | 17.4 | 8.59 | 6.59 | 12.5 | 11.0 | 6.57 | 1.64 | 73.2 | 19.3 | 21.8 | 2.59 | 12.1 |
| Vitamin B$_6$ | M | 2.74 | 22.6 | -- | 3.35 | 3.15 | 14.3 | 3.74 | 55.5 | 1.83 | 10.5 | 12.8 | 10.8 | 3.15 | 8.57 |
|  | F | 2.74 | 22.6 | -- | 3.35 | 3.15 | 14.3 | 3.74 | 55.5 | 1.83 | 10.5 | 12.8 | 10.8 | 3.15 | 8.57 |
| Pantothenic Acid | M | 3.04 | 28.5 | -- | -- | 28.5 | 18.9 | 1.41 | 16.8 | 2.94 | 9.97 | -- | 7.19 | 7.19 | 18.6 |
|  | F | 3.04 | 28.5 | -- | -- | 28.5 | 18.9 | 1.41 | 16.8 | 2.94 | 9.97 | -- | 7.19 | 7.19 | 18.6 |
| Iodine | M | 2.06 | 423 | 32.2 | -- | .93 | -- | 6.10 | 52.2 | 1.85 | -- | -- | 14.0 | .34 | 522 |
|  | F | 1.58 | 327 | 24.7 | -- | .71 | -- | 5.16 | 40.2 | 1.43 | -- | -- | 10.7 | .26 | 402 |
| Zinc | M | -- | 21.2 | 5.02 | 10.8 | 2.85 | 12.7 | -- | 24.1 | 3.56 | 50.2 | -- | 154 | .57 | 16.6 |
|  | F | -- | 21.2 | 5.02 | 10.8 | 2.85 | 12.7 | -- | 24.1 | 3.56 | 50.2 | -- | 154 | .57 | 16.6 |
| Calcium | M | .66 | 15.6 | 11.6 | 3.22 | 1.86 | 2.82 | 1.69 | 68.3 | 11.8 | 23.0 | 33.6 | 14.8 | .39 | 49.1 |
|  | F | .66 | 15.6 | 11.6 | 3.22 | 1.86 | 2.82 | 1.69 | 68.3 | 11.8 | 23.0 | 33.6 | 14.8 | .39 | 49.1 |
| Iron | M | 2.70 | 19.5 | 4.47 | 3.04 | 1.98 | 1.86 | 2.40 | 40.2 | 3.03 | 12.3 | 11.3 | 13.1 | 1.02 | 12.1 |
|  | F | 4.87 | 34.4 | 8.06 | 5.47 | 3.57 | 3.34 | 4.31 | 72.3 | 5.46 | 22.2 | 20.4 | 23.6 | 1.82 | 21.9 |

## SOLVING THE DIET

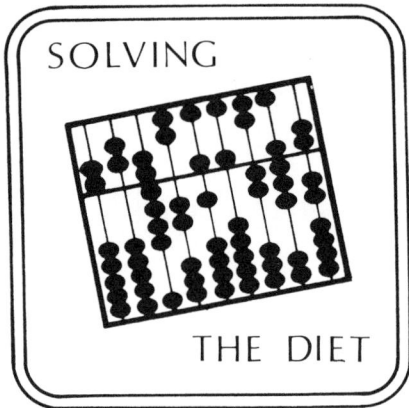

Determining *Critical Nutrients* and *Efficient Crops* can be a tedious task. The first step, gathering the data, is the most difficult. There is no single source that will give the amounts for all nutrients. The table on the following page will greatly simplify this process by giving some of the more common and useful sources for this information and indicating which nutrients are included in each source. They are listed in priority order, so that when more than one figure is given for a nutrient in a particular food, the source higher up has been given preference. An attempt has been made to give priority to sources that are more respected, commonly used, and commonly available.

Another important reference is Nutrient Content of Foods, Selected References and Tables.* This lists important books and journal articles that give the nutrient content of various foods. Good resource librarians can open doors to information that you did not know existed. Many universities also have computer search systems. Abstracts of books and articles can help locate some of the more obscure pieces of information.

The amounts given for the nutrient content of a food may vary considerably between sources. Testing errors are part of the cause, but there is also variation between samples of the same type of food. Nutrient content may vary because of crop location, time of harvest, soil type, crop variety, agricultural practice, or a number of other factors.

Many of the figures for the nutrient content of a food, such as those contained in the U.S.D.A.'s Composition of Foods by Watt and Merrill (last revised in 1963) are by now quite old. A quick sampling of more current sources reveals that most rely heavily on the figures used in Composition of Foods. It is argued by some that as our soils have decreased in quality and nutrients and as hybrid seeds have become the norm for many crops, that the nutritional content of our foods may have decreased from these earlier figures.

Some sources give the nutrient content per pound, some per 100 grams, and some per serving portion. There are about 454 grams (g) in a pound (lb.), 1,000 milligrams (mg) per gram, and 1,000 micrograms (mcg) in a milligram. If you are

* Boston Area Research Dieticians Special Practice Group, Massachusetts Dieticians Association, 1978.

## RESOURCES GIVING NUTRITIONAL CONTENT OF FOODS

*(sources are listed in order of priority as used in the researching of foods for this book.)*

| Nutrient | Composition of Foods, Merrill, Annabel L. and Watt, Bernice K. Agriculture Handbook #8, USDA Gov't Printing Office, 1964. (Extensive foods list. Last time revised was 1963.) | Amino Acid Content of Foods, FAO Nutritional Study #24, FAO Food Policy and Food Service, Rome, 1970. (Covers protein digestibility. Expensive; try your library.) | Food Values of Portions Commonly Used, 13th ed. Church, Helen Nichols, and Pennington, Jean A.T. Harper and Row, N.Y. 1971. (Good reference list.) | Nutrition Almanac, Nutrition Search, Inc., John D. Kirschmann, dir. McGraw-Hill Book Company, N.Y. 1975 (Also covers nutrient deficiency symptoms.) | Laurel's Kitchen, Laurel Robertson, Carol Flinders, Bronwen Godfrey, Bantam Books/Nilgiri Press, Petaluma, CA, 1976. (Good reference list. Not all listings have weights reported.) | Composition and Facts about Food, Ford Heritage, republished by Health Research, Mokelumne, CA, 1971. (Ordered Nutrient concentration lists, and food digestion times.) |
|---|---|---|---|---|---|---|
| Linoleic acid | ● | | | | ● | ● |
| Valine | | ● | | ● | | |
| Tryptophan | | ● | | ● | | |
| Threonine | | ● | | ● | | |
| Tyrosine + phenylalanine | | ● | | ● | | |
| Cystine + methionine | | ● | | ● | | |
| Lysine | | ● | | ● | | |
| Leucine | | ● | | ● | | |
| Isoleucine | | ● | | ● | | |
| Vitamin E | | | | | ● | |
| Vitamin C | ● | | ● | ● | | ● |
| Pantothenic acid | | | | ● | | |
| Niacin | ● | | ● | ● | ● | ● |
| Inositol | | | | ● | | |
| Folic acid | | | | ● | ● | |
| Choline | | | ● | ● | | |
| Biotin | | | | ● | | |
| Vitamin B6 | | | | ● | | |
| Riboflavin | ● | | ● | ● | | ● |
| Thiamin | ● | | ● | ● | | ● |
| Vitamin A | ● | | ● | ● | | ● |
| Zinc | | | ● | ● | | |
| Sodium | ● | | ● | ● | | |
| Potassium | ● | | ● | ● | | |
| Phosphorous | ● | | | ● | | |
| Magnesium | ● | | ● | ● | | ● |
| Iron | ● | | ● | ● | ● | ● |
| Iodine | ● | | | ● | | ● |
| Calcium | ● | | ● | ● | ● | ● |
| Protein | ● | ● | ● | ● | ● | ● |
| Fats | ● | | ● | ● | ● | ● |
| Carbohydrates | ● | | ● | ● | ● | ● |
| Calories | ● | | ● | ● | ● | ● |

given a nutrient content in a form such as 32 mg of the nutrient per 100 g of food, this may be converted into mg per pound as follows.

$$\frac{32 \text{ mg nutrient}}{100 \text{ g food}} \times \frac{454 \text{ g food}}{1 \text{ lb. food}} = \frac{145 \text{ mg nutrient}}{1 \text{ lb. food}}$$

See the section on vitamin A in the nutrients chapter for a discussion of the two different measurement units used and the method for converting into the unit currently in use.

All the figures have been converted, both for nutrient content and for yields, to the amounts as consumed--e.g. the yield for soybeans expresses the number of pounds of cooked beans that can be provided from a single 100 square foot bed, and the *Weight Efficiency* figures for wheat convert the nutrient amounts for whole wheat flour to figures that would be of an appropriate concentration level for a simple bread. Changes in nutrient concentration due to preparation have not been accounted for in all of the foods, but this refinement should be made once optimum preparation techniques have been defined. The methods of preparation and other assumptions and a nutrient chart are given as appendices to the crops chapter. Steaming generally increases water weight while baking generally decreases it, explaining why the nutrient concentration of a baked potato or sweet potato may be higher than that of a steamed or raw one.

Once a nutrient list is complete, *Weight Efficiency* values may be calculated from this information and a corresponding set of values for nutrient requirements. A chart giving the Recommended Dietary Allowances (RDA's)* from the National Academy of Sciences is given at the end of the nutrients section. Where possible, the information and methods used in calculating the RDA's have been given to allow you to custom fit the RDA's--which have been calculated for people of average characteristics--to fit your own personal set of characteristics. If nutrient requirements other than the RDA's have been selected, then these should be used in the calculation of the *Weight Efficiency* values.

To calculate *Weight Efficiency* for a given food and nutrient, simply divide your needs for the nutrient by the amount of the nutrient in the food as consumed. For example, if you calculate your calorie needs to be 2,000 per day, and a food can provide 500 calories per pound, then you would need to consume four pounds of that food to get your 2,000 calories. This does not assume that all the calories will come from a single food. This figure is simply to help in comparing the

* Recommended Dietary Allowances, Eighth Revised Edition, Food and Nutrition Board, National Research Council, National Academy of Sciences, Washington, D.C. 1974.

14

various crops.

Once *Weight Efficiency* has been calculated, you can calculate the food's *Area Efficiency* from this figure, an estimate of yield per 100 square feet, and information as to whether the crop requires half a growing season or a whole growing season. To estimate if a crop requires a half season or a whole season, first estimate the number of weeks in your overall growing season, from the last frost in the spring to the first frost in the fall.* Next, use How to Grow More Vegetables' master charts to estimate In Ground Time by adding Time to Maturity (column 0) to the Harvesting Period (Column P) plus a two week safety factor. If the total of these factors for In Ground Time is more than half your growing season, it is best to count the crop as a full season one. If the In Ground Time is half your growing season or less, count the crop as a half season one.

Realize that these are over-simplifications to aid in the design process, and that you will later have to fit the proposed crops within the growing season and that their climatic and seasonal needs will have to be considered as well. Adjustments in the plan may then be needed. Extensions of growing seasons may sometimes be necessary for certain crops. This can be facilitated through the use of mini-greenhouses in cooler weather (see The Backyard Homestead, pp. 135-141) and by shade netting or the appropriate shading of one crop by another to help plants grow in the summer heat.

For crops that require a whole season, simply use or adjust the appropriate figures from How to Grow More Vegetables, the adjusted ones used in this book, or use your own figures, adjusted to express the amount "as consumed". For half season crops that can be "double-cropped" back-to-back with another crop, two crops per year--not necessarily the same crop--can be grown, so the yield figures for each half season crop may be doubled. Until crop combinations are fine-tuned, a process already underway by Ecology Action and one that you can help in, full yield potentials may not be realizable for both crops. The problem is how to work out the timing so as to mesh the two crops into a growing season without a reduction of yields for either one.

To calculate the *Area Efficiency* for a crop and nutrient, take the yield figure per 100 square feet for the entire growing season** and divide this figure into the weight of the food that you would need to get all of the nutrient in question for one year.

For example, if you know from the *Weight Efficiency* value that it would take

* For maps to help estimate growing season, see The Backyard Homestead, pp.148-150.
** Doubled for half season crops and corrected for "weight as consumed".

four pounds per day of a food to provide all of your calorie needs, then it would take 365 times that, or 1,460 pounds to provide your calorie needs for a year. Dividing the 1,460 pounds needed by an estimated 200 pounds per crop for two crops, or 400 pounds per year per 100 square feet, produces an _Area Efficiency_ of 3.65-- it would take 3.65 beds of 100 square feet (or 365 square feet) to produce all your annual calorie needs from this one crop.

The list of _Critical Nutrients_ has been obtained by examining a sample of crops suspected to be good choices for a minimal area diet. Most nutrients have many crops that are _Weight Efficient_. Many nutrients have only a few that are _Area_ Efficient. Additional crops have been added to the original group to fill-in for _Critical Nutrients_ that were short in _Efficient Crops_. Crops that made no significant contributions to either _Weight Critical_ or _Area Critical Nutrients_ have usually been eliminated. The list of fourteen crops used in this book is the result of this process.

The aim in limiting this book to only fourteen well-matched, highly efficient crops was to create a simple model that could be tested over a broad range of soil and climate conditions. What is intended, is not to define the answer, but to define a process for searching for answers. While a good answer can be created from these crops, they are only training wheels intended to lead to regionally specific mixes of crops that will be better matched to local conditions, more diverse, and more efficient.

When we study a traditional culture whose diet is diverse and well suited to to its environment, we are tempted to sit at our desks and try to design a similarly elegant solution. To follow the path of such cultures, we must begin as they did, with only a few crops, and let the richness of our experience over years and generations mold a food system that is bountiful, diverse, and efficient. By testing the same crops and using the same techniques across a diversity of soils and climates, we should be able to make quantum leaps down this path that would not be possible through scattered efforts, each attempting to find their own answer. The answer is as singular as it is diverse.

# The Nutrients

Ecology is what connects us to plants, either directly or through animals who consume plants, and from there to sun, air, and soil. This continuum of soil to plants and animals and humans and then back to soil is bridged by a flow of water, nutrients, and energy. The water and nutrients are continually recycled in a circle turned by the energy of the sun.

The soil is fed by weathering rock, plants and animals, and the atmosphere. Micro-organisms in the soil help in this process. Plants use the sun's energy together with water, soil minerals, and elements from the air to create carbohydrates, proteins, fats, vitamins, and other substances needed by the plants.

Powered by energy originally from the sun, we help as part of the circle of nutrient flow. Animals consume plants and each other, use up some of the sun's stored energy in their metabolism, and form new mixes of nutrients. Micro-organisms in the intestines of humans and other animals help in this process.

We excrete some amounts of all the nutrients we take in. Our body's nutrient stores could, if allowed, feed

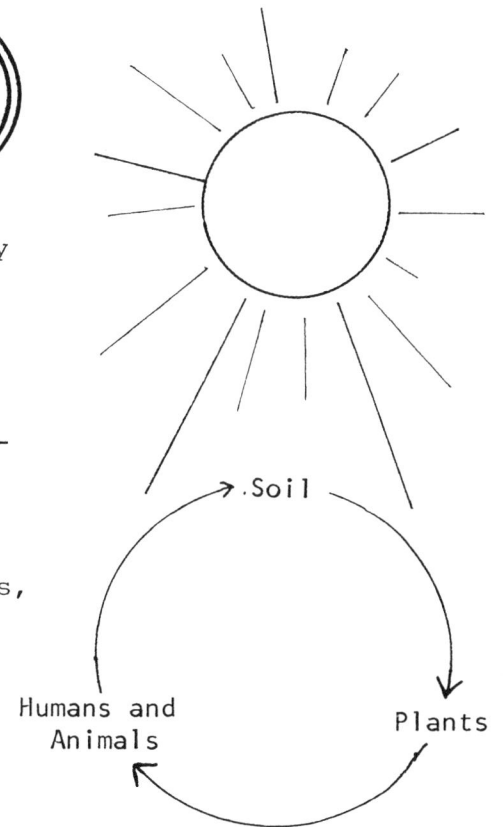

The Nutrient Cycle

Ecology - the pattern of relations between organisms and their environment.

17

the soil so that even in death we could continue the circle of life. Micro-organisms and other decomposers in the soil link us back to the soil to complete the circle.

Nutrition in its broadest sense traces our connection to the sun and earth--our role in the circle of life. Even the moon and the planets may have their influence on plants and on us.

Unless we can extend our concept of nutrition beyond what we find in our cupboards and refrigerator, and connect to our gardens, the soil, and the planet, we will not be able to fully achieve and sustain the health we seek in nutrition. To improve our health--to improve our life-- we must care for the entire circle of life of which we are a part.

Our connections to the physical cosmos are not the only ways that nutrition extends beyond the food in front of us. For humans, our analysis must expand beyond the ecosystem of earth, air, and sun. We affect this planet in ways vastly more extreme than an organism simply playing out its niche in an ecosystem. We must relate to the broader socio-ecosystem, and examine a part of it, the world food system.

The sun's energy together with soil nutrients, and elements from the air are stored as wheat and shipped from the United States to locations around the world. Petroleum, which is also a form of stored solar energy, soil, and air elements, is shipped from places around the world into this country to help produce wheat (and other products). Our world food system is dependent upon this movement of stored energy and nutrients across the boundaries of ecosystems and countries. We cannot draw boundaries to delineate a particular ecosystem or country as *the* source of our food. We must consider the earth as *one circle* of nutrient flow, turned by the energy of the sun. The paths of the nutrient flow are determined in part by the principles of ecology and in part by those of the world food system.

Today, the world food system determines the nutritional intake of individuals far more than do the local

Nutrition connects us to the sun, the moon, and in subtle ways to the entire cosmos.

Sociology - the patterns of relations between people in society.

18

influences of earth, air, and sun.  Our socio-ecosystem
has tied many peoples of the planet, people who were once
fed within their local ecosystem, to a world food system
not controlled by them--one which is often disrupted by
wars, famine, pestilence, and other malfunctions (and
sometimes functions) of our socio-ecosystem.  As has been
pointed out by many, the *current* causes of hunger and
starvation lie mostly outside the boundaries of natural
local flows of nutrients and energy, and within the
entangled web of local politics and economics.

For more information on the politics and economics of the world food problem, see Food First, by Francis Moore Lappé and Joseph Collins.

Changing the politics and economics of a socio-
ecosystem is very difficult.  Even if this could be
rapidly accomplished, it is possible that very shortly
a reality awaits us that would cripple even a "corrected"
or perfected socio-ecosystem.  Soon there may only be
as little as "one circle" of growing area for food, a mere
thousand square feet, for each person living in the Third
World.  This *growing* problem necessitates an approach to
nutrition that asks how to *sustain* a circle that is being
stretched to its limits.

Whether considered from the point of view of ecology,
economics, or politics, the earth is one circle, which from
any viewpoint is also being stretched to its limits.  This
globe we call earth is the multi-dimensional product of
the circle of nature and the circle of man.  A science of
nutrition is needed that can be applied to the entire
planet, and bring health to soil, plants, animals, and
people.

Socio-ecology - the complex of relations connecting individuals, society, and the eco-system.

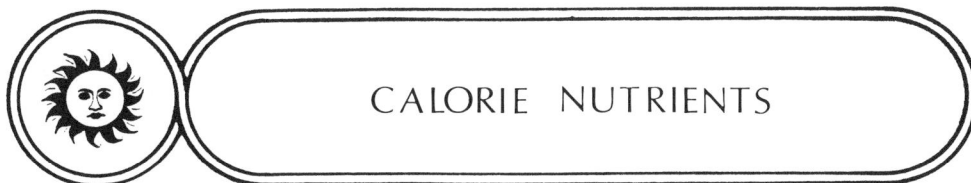

## CALORIE NUTRIENTS

Calories are energy, the sun's energy, taken in by
plants through photosynthesis, stored as carbon bonds which
eventually take the form of fats, proteins, carbohydrates,
and other substances needed by the plants.  Of these, the

fats, proteins, and carbohydrates can be utilized by our bodies to supply the energy needed for building and maintaining tissues and powering our activities. A gram of fat stores about nine calories, and a gram of protein or carbohydrates about four.

These three energy storing substances--fats, proteins, and carbohydrates--have other characteristics which determine the best mix of them for our nutritional needs. The actual mix, however, is best predicted today not by nutrition, nor by the capacity of the local ecosystem. The per capita gross domestic product of a country is a good predictor of the mix of fats, proteins, and carbohydrates consumed by the people of that country. (See graph at left.)

As can be seen by the graph, the major change that occurs as national per capita gross domestic product rises is that people consume a higher percentage of their calories as fats and a lower percentage of them as carbohydrates. The percentage of calories taken in as protein remains about the same. Changes also occur in the sources of these nutrients, with more calories coming from animal and processed foods as incomes rise.

The other change which occurs, which makes this graph somewhat deceptive, is that the total intake of calories rises with income. *While the percentage of protein remains the same, the amount of protein rises as national income rises.* For the poorest people of the world, calorie levels are generally inadequate, a condition which often manifests itself as kwashiorkor, the protein deficiency disease which we know from the pictures of starving children with swollen bellies. When calorie levels are low, protein is burned by the body for energy, robbing it from other uses such as the building and maintenance of body tissues.

According to this graph, however, even in the poorest countries, if people just had more to eat, even of the same mix of foods they are consuming presently,

Percentage of Calories from Proteins, Carbohydrates and Fats According to Income (1962, 85 Country Study)

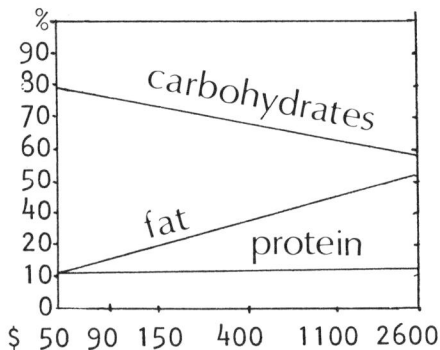

Gross Domestic Product Per Person Per Year in US$. (logarithmic scale)

*Adapted from: Perisse, et. al. (1969) FAO Nutrition Newsletter, 7, 3, p.1.*

they would then also have an adequate protein level.
There is in most cases no need for shifts to foods with
higher concentrations of protein, *rather there is simply
a need for more calories through the consumption of more
food.*

From a different perspective, that of the design of a
minimum area diet, calories again appear to be one of the
most limiting factors.  While there are many other nutrients that are either *Weight Critical* or *Area Critical*, all
the other *Critical Nutrients* generally have at least one
or two crops that can be used as a supplement--crops which
are both very *Weight Efficient* and also *Area Efficient*.
Such crops can supply a good proportion of the needs for
the nutrient from a small amount of food grown in a small
area.  This is not the case for calories.

As can be seen from the following table, there is no
such supplement for calories.  By the definitions given
in Chapter One, there is no food that is both *Area Efficient* and *Weight Efficient* for calories.  The only crop
that comes close is potatoes, which is efficient for both
for women, but not for men.

| WEIGHT EFFICIENCY | | | AREA EFFICIENCY | | |
| --- | --- | --- | --- | --- | --- |
| Crop | Men | Women | Crop | Men | Women |
| Filberts | .9 | .7 | Parsnips | 6.1 | 4.6 |
| Sunflower seeds | 1.1 | .8 | Potatoes | 6.2 | 4.6 |
| Peanuts | 1.1 | .8 | Onions | 7.1 | 5.3 |
| Wheat | 2.4 | 1.8 | Garlic | 13.2 | 9.8 |
| Sweet potatoes | 4.2 | 3.1 | Turnips | 14.1 | 10.5 |
| Garlic | 4.3 | 3.2 | Leeks | 17.4 | 12.9 |
| Soybeans | 5.0 | 3.7 | Collards | 18.1 | 13.4 |
| Potatoes | 6.4 | 4.7 | Sweet potatoes | 22.7 | 16.8 |
| Parsnips | 7.8 | 5.9 | Filberts | 27.5 | 20.3 |
| Leeks | 11.4 | 8.5 | Wheat | 32.6 | 24.1 |
| Parsley | 13.6 | 10.1 | Peanuts | 38.3 | 28.5 |
| Collards | 14.8 | 11.0 | Sunflower seeds | 38.7 | 28.9 |
| Onions | 15.6 | 11.6 | Parsley | 70.9 | 52.7 |
| Turnips | 20.9 | 15.5 | Soybeans | 76.7 | 56.7 |

Crops are listed in order for *Area Efficiency* and for *Weight
Efficiency*.

Bracketed numbers indi-
cate efficient crops.

Remember to interpret *Weight Efficiency* as the weight
of the food needed to produce a day's supply of calories,
and *Area Efficiency* as the number of 100 square foot beds
that would be required.

What can also be seen from this table is that crops that are good at concentrating calories tend to be less efficient in producing calories per area--there is a trade-off between *Weight Efficiency* and *Area Efficiency*. This means that if you increase the number of calories in a diet from 2,000 per day (the amount needed by the typical American woman) to 2,700 per day (the amount needed by the typical American man), the area needed to produce such a diet will increase both because of the increased caloric needs, and also because of the need for increased amounts of concentrated foods. Crops producing more concentrated foods, ones which are more *Weight Efficient* for calories, are also crops that are less *Area Efficient* and that will therefore require a greater area to produce the same amount of calories.

If we simply increase by 35% the area for all the crops of a woman's diet which supplied 2,000 calories in 5½ pounds, we would get the needed 2,700 calories for a man's diet, but the weight would go up to 7.43 pounds-- too much food to be comfortably consumed. Therefore it will be necessary to include in a man's diet crops which are more concentrated in calories--more *Weight Efficient*-- but which will take a greater area to produce a similar amount of calories because they are less *Area Efficient*. It will be necessary to make some shifts from foods such as potatoes, parsnips, and onions to more concentrated, lower yielding foods, such as sweet potatoes, peanuts, and wheat.

Taking this into consideration, a ten percent increase in calorie needs will probably result in between a twenty and thirty percent increase in the area required, so that the area needs of a man's diet may be as much as double that of a woman's. This is why as a working hypothesis, 550 square feet has been set as the area objective for women and 850 square feet for men. Further research may yield slightly different figures, but an average adult area objective of 700 square feet seems to be a reasonable

700 square feet is a reasonable target for a complete diet for an average adult.

and attainable target.

Even moderate improvements in the yields of certain crops such as sweet potatoes could both significantly decrease the area required, and also radically alter the mix of foods in a minimal area diet. Lower yields for other crops such as potatoes might also have significant but different effects.

Different nutritional needs, such as those of children or pregnant or lactating women may also generate remarkably different diets. The needs of these groups for especially high concentrations of certain nutrients-- calcium and protein for example--might possibly cause the area requirements to be as high or higher than the 850 square feet projected for men. More research is needed for the design of these diets.

It is important for anyone seriously interested in producing all their own food in a minimum area to have a good estimate of their own personal, minimum calorie needs, for a small amount of excess caloric intake will result in a considerable increase in area requirements. The boxed section that follows will enable you to estimate your calorie needs taking into consideration activity pattern, sex, climate, weight, and age. For a simpler approach, see the chart summarizing nutrient needs that is at the end of this chapter.

For most nutrients there is no good, simple way for monitoring whether or not you are getting enough for your actual needs. For calories, however, there is a simple method for monitoring yourself. If you know your ideal weight (see the chart next to Item 1 in the boxed section on calculating calories) and you monitor your calorie intake and weight, you can simply slowly lower your calorie intake until your weight begins to reach the lower half of your ideal range. If your weight is below your ideal range, you might consider the same process, only slowly increasing your calories. Find the point that is both comfortable and minimal, and you will then

Monitor calories and your weight to determine your minimum calorie needs.

have a good idea of your personal minimum calorie needs.

Continued monitoring will help you make adjustments related to seasonal or lifestyle changes, and may also reveal a long term downward shift in calorie needs. It is believed by some that as you improve your diet, your true calorie needs will decrease over time due to the more efficient use of nutrients by your body.

*Such a decrease in calorie needs would allow you to either keep the same diet and decrease the area required to produce it, or to shift to a diet higher in less efficient foods, but more attractive in its diversity.*

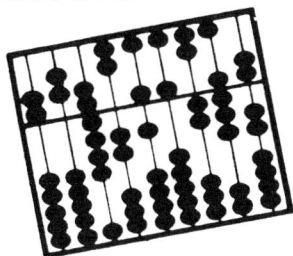

SOLVING

THE DIET

This method considers the factors of activity pattern, sex, climate, weight, and age. The needs of people under 23 and of pregnant or lactating women cannot be calculated using this worksheet, and will be dealt with in a later publication. The analysis assumes that a person is at their ideal weight. A person over or under weight will in most cases move toward their ideal weight if they consume an amount of calories appropriate for their height and size.

## CALORIES NEEDED PER HOUR OF SLEEP

| Height | | Men | | | | Women | | | |
| in  cm | lbs | +* | kg | +* | cal per hr | lbs | +* | kg | +* | cal per hr |
|---|---|---|---|---|---|---|---|---|---|---|
| 60 152 | -- | -- | -- | -- | -- | 109 | 9 | 50 | 4 | 52 |
| 62 158 | -- | -- | -- | -- | -- | 115 | 9 | 50 | 4 | 54 |
| 64 163 | 133 | 11 | 60 | 5 | 61 | 122 | 10 | 56 | 5 | 56 |
| 66 168 | 142 | 12 | 64 | 5 | 63 | 129 | 10 | 59 | 5 | 57 |
| 68 173 | 151 | 14 | 69 | 6 | 67 | 136 | 10 | 62 | 5 | 59 |
| 70 178 | 159 | 15 | 72 | 6 | 68 | 144 | 11 | 66 | 5 | 61 |
| 72 183 | 167 | 15 | 76 | 7 | 70 | 152 | 12 | 69 | 5 | 62 |
| 74 188 | 175 | 15 | 80 | 7 | 72 | -- | -- | -- | -- | -- |
| 76 193 | 182 | 16 | 83 | 7 | 74 | -- | -- | -- | -- | -- |

1. Use the table at the left and your height to estimate:

   a) your ideal weight _____
   b) cal/hr needed for sleep_____

2. Estimate calories needed per night's sleep by multiplying:

   _____ x _____ = _____
   cal/hr    hrs sleep   sleeping
                         calories

* This + or - range covers 50% of the population, from the 25th to 75th percentile. 109 pounds ± 9 pounds expresses a range from 100 pounds to 118 pounds.

3. Use the following list to estimate the number of hours spent daily per category:

Very Light - Seated and standing activities, painting trades, auto and truck driving, laboratory work, typing, playing musical instruments, sewing, ironing, planting flats*, planting beds*.

Light - Walking on level ground at 2.5-3 mph, tailoring, garage work, pressing, electrical trades, carpentry, restraunt trades, cannery workers, washing clothes, shopping with a light load, golf, sailing, table tennis, volleyball, watering*, harvesting*.

Moderate - Walking 3.5 - 4 mph, plastering, weeding, hoeing, loading and stacking bales, scrubbing floors, shopping with a heavy load, cycling, skiing, tennis, dancing, double-digging*, U-bar digging*, adding and mixing in compost and soil ammendments*.

Heavy - Walking with load uphill, tree felling, work with pick and shovel, basketball, swimming, football, difficult or rapid double-digging*, turning compost*.

* Categories for these activities estimated by experienced biointensive gardeners.

4. Use your estimates of time spent daily in each activity together with the information in the tables below to estimate your total activity factor.

| Activity Category | ACTIVITY FACTORS cal/lb/hr men | women | cal/kg/hr men | women |
|---|---|---|---|---|
| Very Light | .68 | .60 | 1.5 | 1.3 |
| Light | 1.32 | 1.17 | 2.9 | 2.6 |
| Moderate | 1.96 | 1.88 | 4.3 | 4.1 |
| Heavy | 3.81 | 3.52 | 8.4 | 8.0 |

| MEAN WORK TEMPERATURE | C° | F° | CLIMATE FACTOR |
|---|---|---|---|
| Below -- 14 | | 57 | 1.08 |
| | 14-30 | 57-86 | 1.00 |
| | 30 | 86 | 1.01 |
| | 32 | 90 | 1.02 |
| | 34 | 93 | 1.03 |
| | 36 | 97 | 1.04 |

| Activity | Hrs of Activity* | | Activity Factor | | Climate Factor | |
|---|---|---|---|---|---|---|
| Very light | _____ | x | _____ | x | _____ | = |
| Light | _____ | x | _____ | x | _____ | = |
| Moderate | _____ | x | _____ | x | _____ | = |
| Heavy | _____ | x | _____ | x | _____ | = _____ |

Total Activity Factor = _____

5. Multiply times your appropriate weight:  x _____

Total waking activity calories = _____

6. Add sleeping calories from Item 2:  + _____

Total daily calories for people 23-50 = _____

7. For people over 50, multiply by age factor from table below:  x _____

Total daily calories for people over 50 = _____

| Age: | 50 | 55 | 60 | 65 | 70 | 75 | 80 | 85 | 90 | 95 | 100 |
|---|---|---|---|---|---|---|---|---|---|---|---|
| Age Factor: | .90 | .89 | .88 | .87 | .86 | .85 | .84 | .83 | .82 | .81 | .80 |

* Total of column plus hours of sleep should equal 24.

This method is derived from information in: Recommended Dietary Allowances, 8th Revised Edition, Food and Nutrition Board, National Research Council, National Academy of Sciences, Washington, D.C. 1974.

Of the three sources of calories--proteins, fats, and carbohydrates--proteins have historically been emphasized as the most difficult to obtain in adequate amounts. To understand the causes of this emphasis, it is necessary to take a brief trip through history, and to see how our attitudes on protein have developed. When the best current thinking on protein and amino acids is applied to the design of a minimal area diet, calories rather than protein or amino acids seems to be the limiting factor.

Protein was given its name in 1838 by Garret Jan Mulder, a Dutch physician turned chemist, who first isolated and identified protein as a nutritionally required substance. Surveys of British diets taken in 1853 and 1865 showed protein intake to range between 57 grams for a "subsistance hospital diet" and 184 grams for the diet of a hard working laborer. This was assumed to show that hard work requires more protein, a belief which still persists among many today. Harder work actually requires *extra calories*, and extra protein consumption is simply a by-product of the additional calories.

By the turn of the century it was known that proteins were made of chains of amino acids. This explained the many and varied kinds of proteins that had been identified by earlier researchers. Each protein represents a different mix or pattern of amino acids. From about 1900 on, researchers concentrated on the relationship between amino acid patterns and the nutritional value of proteins. In the 1930's Rose and his assistants identified the eight essential amino acids and correlated their presence to protein quality. By 1935, the need for the eight amino acids in the proper proportions had been clearly established.

The concept of a limiting amino acid goes back to a paper by Block and Mitchell in 1946. The idea, still accepted in a modified form today, is that the body needs a certain amount of each of the essential amino acids, and that if one of them falls short of the needed amount,

## CHRONOLOGY OF PROTEIN RESEARCH

1838 - Protein named and researched by Mulder.

1853 and 1865 - Protein surveys taken of British diets.

Early 1900's - Amino acids become the focus of protein research.

1930's - The need for eight essential amino acids is recognized.

1935 - Need for amino acids in proper proportions is understood.

1946 - Concept of a limiting amino acid.

then it becomes the limiting factor to the quality of the protein and the body's ability to use the protein for certain functions. Milk, meat, and eggs suffered little from the problem of a limiting amino acid and therefore qualified as "complete" proteins. Plant proteins, however, were incomplete, and were therefore considered inferior. Anthropologists of the period even proposed that the "rice-eaters of the Orient" must be genetically different in order to explain how they could maintain their health with little or no animal proteins.* Part of the answer to the dilemma is that protein from different plant sources, such as grains and beans, can be combined to complement each other by supplying extra amounts of the amino acid that the other is lacking. We also know that our need for protein-foods is much less than we had thought then.

Food, the U.S.D.A. Yearbook of Agriculture for 1959, included a chapter on amino acids. This book made information on the somewhat complicated subject available in understandable terms to mainstream America. Food presented

Post World War II -
Protein needs of
Asians are questioned。

1959 - U。S。D。A yearbook
suggests food combining
to help poorer countries。

* Diet and Nutrition, Rudolf Ballentine, M.D., The Himalayan International Institute, Honesdale, Pennsylvania, 1978.

28

to Americans the concept of combining foods such as grains and beans to improve protein quality. The context, however, was not to change the eating habits of people in the U.S. where "...the supply of protein is generous and comes from a mixture of ordinary foods..." but to help "in countries where the protein supply is small and perhaps inadequate..."

In the 1960's the people of America learned of starvation. People starved in magazines and on television right before our eyes. We saw them in Biafra, in Bangladesh, in Southeast Asia, and in other places far away. We saw the children with distended bellies and were told the problem was protein. Some people may even have thought that if the starving had only been more aware of nutrition and protein combining, that they might have grown soybeans and not starved. No one told us that for most of these people the problem was insufficient food--not getting enough calories. It has more often been political and economic problems that have caused starvation, rather than ignorance.

1960's - Americans learn of the world food problem.

We were also warned of protein deficiency in our own country. The "rice-eaters" had invaded and people feared for their children's diets. The American Dietetic Association spoke of members of "philosophical, quasi-religious groups heavily influenced by Eastern thought..." as being a major component of the "new vegetarians". Vegetarianism was associated with yoga, drugs, and other strange and frightening aspects of youth. Few people noted the large numbers of healthy vegetarians already existent in our country. A pale, skinny-looking person in robes with a shaved head made more interesting news than a healthy-looking Seventh Day Adventist.

1971 - Ram Dass, formerly Harvard professor Dr. Richard Alpert, publishes Be Here Now.

No wonder people writing on vegetarianism in the 1970's were so careful in dealing with protein. The '70's brought higher food prices, heightened political and social consciousness, and a series of books concentrating on protein. It was important to separate this new movement of alternative eating from the "quasi-religious" groups of the 1960's. It was important to show people how to eat in a simple, cheap, healthy way, that was consistent with

1970's - World Food problem becomes politically defined.

29

1971 - <u>Diet for a Small
Planet</u> advocates protein
combining to help world
food problem.

OUR SMALL PLANET

See <u>The Home Grown Vege-
tarian</u> by Pat Labine,
George Burrill, and
James Nolfi for a
detailed analysis
of Amino Acids.

a set of social, political, and moral principles. Dealing
effectively and scientifically with protein gave a kind of
respectability, and protein combining soon came to be
perceived as the answer to the now politically defined
world food problem.

In 1971, Francis Moore Lappé's <u>Diet for a Small Planet</u>
came out. In the first sentence of the forward she states,
"This book is about PROTEIN--how we as a nation are caught
in a pattern that squanders it." A few pages later she
states, "What I will be suggesting in this book is a
guideline for eating from the earth that both maximizes
the earth's potential to meet man's nutritional needs and
at the same time, minimizes the disruption of the earth
necessary to sustain him."

Our "small planet's" ability to provide for its human
population was being examined, and this book performed
excellently the important task of focusing some of the
heightened consciousness of the 60's onto the world food
problem and the dietary habits of the U.S. Protein was
focused upon as the limiting factor in the earth's ability
to provide enough food, vegetarianism was given credibility
by being able to solve the"protein problem" in a scientifically sound way, and meal preparers were given recipes which
could hopefully please their families while "minimizing
the disruption of the earth...".

With hindsight, many of the problems of Lappé's book
can be pointed out, and many of them have been dealt with
in the 1982 edition. We know now that our requirements
can safely be met with much lower protein and amino acid
levels than were called for in the rules on combining
proteins. The two reasons for this are the shift from an
egg standard to a less demanding (and more accurate)
standard for the pattern of amino acids, plus a recognition
that only some of the body's protein needs, perhaps only
20 percent or less for adults, need to be met by a specific
pattern of amino acids. The full answer on protein is not
yet in, and our amino acid needs are even less well understood.

More important is that we should consider calories rather than protein as the limiting factor in the world's nutritional balance. In the 1853 and 1865 British surveys, protein was inaccurately focused upon rather than calories in comparing laborers and hospital invalids. Similarly, in an examination of grain and soybean fed beef, calories rather than protein should be emphasized. The waste of land is still outrageous when the conversion ratios for calories rather than protein are considered. *When calories are taken as the common denominator in examining diets, we then have a better tool with which to reduce the area needed for a complete human diet.*

People writing and using vegetarian cookbooks and recipes usually deal almost exclusively with protein combining as the means of living more lightly on the earth. A better way of asking this question is to examine the Area Efficiency for calories of the foods used in these recipes. *The oils and sweeteners in many vegetarian recipes may be as costly in the area required to produce a complete human diet as would the use of modest amounts of animal products.*

How can this be so? The explanation has two parts. First, the Area Efficiency for many of these oil and sweetener crops is very low for calories. The calorie production per area for olive, sesame, sunflower, and other oil plants are among the lowest for any food crop. Oils and sweeteners are both concentrated calorie sources which contain little protein or other nutrients. This means that when oils and sweeteners are included in the diet, the rest of the diet must include crops that are especially concentrated in all the other nutrients that were not provided for with these empty calories.

How much difference does this make? The average American consumes 16 to 17 percent of their calories as concentrated, separated fats, and a similar amount as sugars--fully one third of our calories comes from sources relatively empty of other nutrients. The fact that one

*Weight Efficient* for calories, but extremely inefficient for *Area Efficiency.*

*Weight Efficient* for calories, but inefficient for *Area Efficiency.*

Potatoes

Almost *Weight Efficient* for calories, one of the most *Area Efficient* crops for calories.

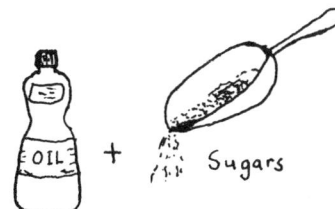

Very *Weight Efficient* for calories, but not *Area Efficient.*

THE SPECTRUM OF <u>AREA</u>
<u>EFFICIENCY</u> FOR
PROTEIN PRODUCTION。

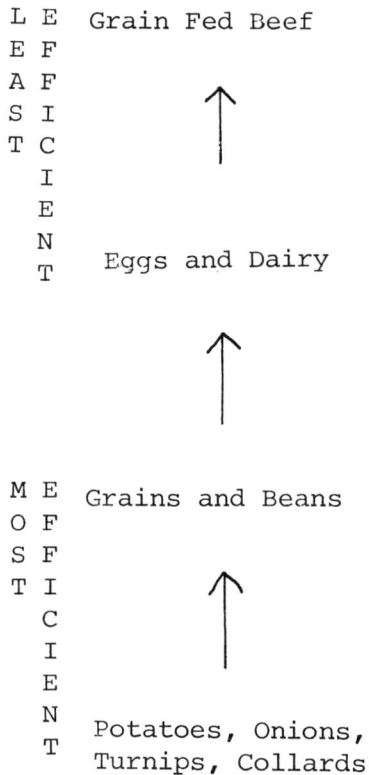

L E   Grain Fed Beef
E F
A F
S I
T C
  I
  E
  N
  T   Eggs and Dairy

M E   Grains and Beans
O F
S F
T I
  C
  I
  E
  N
  T   Potatoes, Onions,
          Turnips, Collards

type of oil may be less harmful to you than another or
that honey may not be quite as bad for you as white sugar
does not significantly reduce this problem.

One third of an average woman's daily energy needs
comes to 667 calories.  This could be surpassed with only
five tablespoons of oil and three tablespoons of honey.
One third of the energy needs for an average man would be
900 calories, which would be surpassed with seven tablespoons of oil and four tablespoons of honey.  For sunflower
oil, home pressing techniques can produce about three
tablespoons of oil from every pound of oil-type sunflower
seeds.  With <u>Good</u> biointensive yields of five pounds per
100 square feet, it would take 2,433 square feet of sunflowers for every tablespoon of oil that you add to your
daily menu.  This is two to three times the area in which
your entire diet can be grown just to get a tablespoon of
oil a day.

The second factor raising the area requirements in a
diet high in concentrated, empty calories, is that the rest
of the diet has to be more *Weight Efficient* for the other
nutrients without calories greatly exceeding the needed
amount.  For many nutrients this goal would require
the selection of crops which are either not *Weight Efficient*
or not *Area Efficient* for calories, or both.  Leafy greens
will need to be chosen to supply many of the vitamins and
minerals, yet, these are neither *Area Efficient* nor *Weight
Efficient* for calories.  Beans, grains, and seeds, which
are not *Area Efficient* for calories or for protein will be
needed to supply a concentrated protein source.  This will
further increase the area needed to supply calories (Remember that calories are the most difficult nutrient to provide
within the area constraint).  This second factor is somewhat
complex, and seemingly obscure, but can be easily understood
if you attempt to design a diet which assumes that one
third of your calories come from sugars and oils。

A vegetarian diet containing grains, beans, seeds, and
leafy greens that draws a third of its calories from oils

and sweeteners will probably take on the order of _twenty times_ the area to produce relative to what is minimally required. The factors that connect our diet to a conservant use of the earth's resources define a broad spectrum of choices that include both _what you consume_ and also _how it is produced_. These are personal choices, and this attempt to better define the spectrum of choices does not presume to answer what is best for any individual.

As the nutritional problems of this planet increase, we must continue to develop and apply better solutions. If we think we are already living the answer, then we may not be able to make the progress needed in time to circumvent these problems. There is a vegetarian answer to the question of a minimal area diet, and it may be the best answer; but the tools and recipes of most vegetarians, which focus on protein combining, and on encouraging vegetarian diets through recipes which use considerable amounts of oils and sweeteners, will not bring us to that vegetarian answer. Protein is an important aspect of diet design, but an undue emphasis on it or other isolated aspects of nutrition can be a barrier to determining the most efficient and environmentally sound path to a complete and balanced diet grown on the smallest scale.

## Nutrition Software

_Nutritionist I_ - nutrient calculator for IBM PC and Apple II family, from N-Squared Computing, 5318 Forest Ridge Rd. Silverton, OR 97381.

_Nutriplan_ - nutrient calculator for Apple II family and IBM PC/XT/jr, from Micromedx, 187 Gardiners Avenue, Levittown, NY 11756.

_Nutr-calc_ - nutrient calculator for Apple II family and IBM PC, from PCD Systems, Inc., 163 Main St, Penn Yann, NY 14527.

SOLVING THE DIET

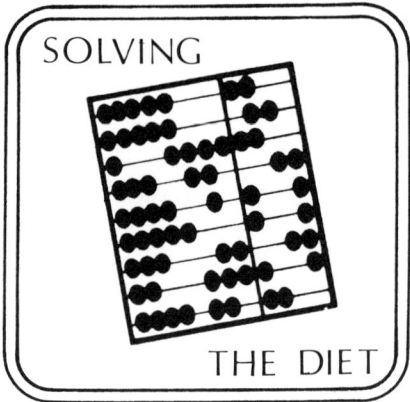

PROTEIN--How much protein do we need? We have what is called a dual requirement for protein. We need both the nitrogen which we get from all the amino acids, and also specific amounts of the eight essential amino acids. These essential amino acids cannot be synthesized by the body.

The amount of the total amino nitrogen that should be taken in as essential amino acids is estimated as about 20 percent for adults--pregnant and lactating women, however, need more. The following excerpt from Recommended Daily Allowances describes how protein is used in the body:

Food proteins provide amino acids for the synthesis of body proteins and nitrogen for the synthesis of many other tissue constituents. The body is in a dynamic state, with proteins and other nitrogenous compounds being degraded and resynthesized continuously. In fact, more protein is turned over daily within the body than is ordinarily consumed in the diet. Some of the amino acids released during the breakdown of tissue proteins are reutilized; but metabolic products of amino acids...are excreted in the urine. Nitrogen is also lost in the feces, sweat, and other body secretions and excretions, sloughed skin, hair, and nails. Therefore, amino acids and nitrogen are required continuously to replace these losses even after growth has ceased.

The amount of nitrogen required to replace these losses is considered a good estimate of adult requirements for protein (but pregnant and lactating women need more). Different proteins have different levels of efficiency. The common measure of this efficiency, net protein utilazation, or N.P.U., is the product of two factors, the coefficient of digestability and the biological value. The coefficient of digestability is an expression of the percentage of the nitrogen that is taken in by the body that is absorbed, and the biological value is the percent that is retained of that which is absorbed. The following list gives some values for the coefficient of digestability:

| Food | Coefficient of Digestability |
|---|---|
| fruits | .85 |
| brown rice | .75 |
| soy beans | .78 |
| wheat flour | .79 |
| potatoes and other root crops | .74 |
| other vegetables | .65 |

The biological value is determined by the amino acid mix of the total mix of foods in the diet. While the biological value is often given for lists of single foods, this is not really that useful, for it does not allow for the improvements that are possible through protein combining. The following list gives the mix of amino acids in milligrams per gram of protein that is needed to obtain a high quality protein:

| Amino Acid | Milligrams per Gram of Protein |
|---|---|
| isoleucine | 42 |
| leucine | 70 |
| lysine | 51 |
| sulfur containing amino acids | 26 |
| aromatic amino acids | 73 |
| threonine | 35 |
| tryptophan | 11 |
| valine | 48 |

If one or more of the amino acids falls short of this pattern for a high quality protein, then the one that is most short on a percentage basis is the limiting amino acid. This analysis is most accurately applied to the mix of foods that makes up the whole daily diet. The percentage that the limiting amino acid fulfills the requirement for a high quality protein determines the biological value.

The test proteins used in determining protein requirements had an N.P.U. of 70 percent. This could be achieved, for example, by a food with a digestability coefficient of about 90 and a biological value of about 78. Using this high quality protein in a diet that included enough calories to maintain body weight, 70 kilogram (154 pound) men were found to need an average of 5.2 grams of nitrogen to maintain an even nitrogen balance. Using the standard conversion factor of 6.25 grams of protein for each gram of nitrogen, this is the equivalent of about 33 grams of protein per day for a 70 kilogram man, or about .47 grams per kilogram of body weight. To this was added a correction factor of 30 percent to allow for the variation in needs between individuals. In the actual study, this adjusted value of about 0.6 grams per kilogram body weight was about equal to the amount needed by the man in the study requiring the most protein.

In addition to this, a correction was made to allow for a lower N.P.U. of 52.5 percent instead of the 70 percent that was tested for. This brings the protein requirements up to 0.8 grams per kilogram of body weight per day, or about 0.36 grams per pound of body weight.

If your protein needs are not in the highest end of the range for the population, or if your total daily protein mix has an N.P.U. greater than 52.5 percent, then this figure is probably an overstatement of your protein needs. In addition, the amino acid requirements for a high quality protein are based on the needs of infants, which are significantly higher per gram of protein than those of adults who have completed their growth. Since this will have the effect of underestestimating the N.P.U of food for adults, the protein requirements for adults may again be overestimated.

While a diet using whole foods will generally easily meet the full RDA for protein if enough calories are provided, it is interesting to reflect on the fact that there appears to be a consistent overstatement of average adult protein needs. There is evidence that excess protein consumption may cause a decline in endurance, have a role in obesity, and may cause an increase in the need for calcium. In a country with government policies influenced by special interest groups, such as the lobbies for milk, meat, and eggs, it is good to be cautious in considering these recommendations. Three separate components of the RDA for protein have been consistently weighted so as to overstate the needs of the average adult, while no mention is made of the possible adverse effects of excess protein. Yet, in the United States, the average protein intake has been running about 90 to 100 grams, double the needs of the average man, woman, and child. Protein is "sold" as a problem nutrient, using overstated requirements, not considering the excess levels that most Americans take in, or the problems that may result from excess consumption.

Still, protein requirements cause concern to someone choosing not to eat meat, eggs, or milk, and at the same time help other people to rationalize the excess amounts of fats and cholestorol they consume from animal products. A "science" generated by government groups and grants is inherently a politicized science, containing its own biases. The problem is worsened because these often reinforce our own biases and desires for certain foods.


Fats and Essential Fatty Acids--To understand fat, we must understand that our diets are determined by more than simply the factors of nutritional science, and that the non-nutritional factors come as often from within ourselves as from the outside. We consume as much fat as we do, not because we need it nutritionally, and not really because we are encouraged to (although animal products and rich deserts are certainly promoted as part of our diets). We consume as much fat as we do mostly because we like to.

Fats give food a consistency that we like. They act as a medium for many of the flavors that attract us to food such as the flavor of onions and garlic and many of the aromatic oils of herbs and spices. When we finish eating, that good, full feeling which we experience is in good part due to fats, and will linger longer with us after a high fat meal, because it takes fat longer to leave the stomach. It is understandable, then, that as people can afford to, they tend to derive a larger portion of their calories from fat.

People can easily synthesize the fat their bodies need from carbohydrates. With the exception of three essential fatty acids, which the body needs for specific functions, but cannot synthesize, we do not need fats for their nutritional value. They do, however, also serve as a carrier for the fat soluble vitamins which are essential to us. They are also a source of concentrated calories.

Many nutritional sources suggest an intake of fat of between 25 and 30 percent of our total calorie intake. Others point out that there is absolutely no evidence for an amount this high relative to the maintenance of health. The fact is that practically everyone in the United States gets more than 25 percent of their calories from fat, with 40 percent or more being the norm. Such excess levels of fat intake contribute to heart disease and other health risks. The lowest amount of fat ever reported in a survey of American diets was 26 percent from a survey of families in the south that was done about the turn of the century.

A diet of whole foods that is complete in all the other nutrients cannot help but have some fat in it. We can fulfill our needs for essential fatty acids by getting between one and two percent of our calories from linoleic acid. In Recommended Daily Allowances, it is stated that only 15 to 25 grams per day of appropriate food fats are needed to provide the needed linoleic acid and the delivery of the fat soluble vitamins. Twenty five grams would be about ten percent of the calories for the average man or woman. In the earlier graph relating income to the consumption of the three calorie sources, ten percent was about the percentage of fats used by the poorest peoples of the world. This is also the amount of fat typically found in many traditional Oriental diets. Ten percent, then, is perhaps a good guideline for the proportion of the calories in a diet which come from fat, with the linoleic acid needs being accounted for separately.

Carbohydrates--As with fats, there is no real requirement for carbohydrates. At the same time, if fats and proteins are kept close to their required amounts, without going too much over, you will obtain between 60 and 70 percent of your calories from carbohydrates.  Carbohydrates can generally be grown with more efficiency than either fats or protein.

Amino Acids--Our need for amino acids has been well established for a number of years.  Yet there is still considerable uncertainty as to exactly what the specific levels of those needs are.  We need to have a certain percentage of our protein intake supply the essential amino acids in a certain mix, within a certain period of time.  We do not yet know for sure what the percentage, the mix, or the period of time is.

The percentage of proteins that needs to come from a balanced mix of amino acids decrease with age at an unknown rate.  Twenty percent is generally used for adults.  This figure, however, assumes a <u>coefficient</u> <u>of</u> <u>digestability</u> higher than that of most vegetable proteins.  Some sources suggest doubling the amount of amino acids when using vegetable proteins.  This would be correct for a <u>coefficient</u> <u>of</u> <u>digestability</u> of 50 percent, but the fourteen crops in this book and many other foods of plant origin are more digestable than this.  Increasing the amino acid requirements by half is probably more accurate, or the actual <u>digestability</u> <u>coefficients</u> for each food can be worked in separately.  For example, if a food has an isoleucine content of 500mg/lb and a <u>digestability</u> <u>coeficient</u> of 60 percent, then 300 mg of isoleucine would actually be absorbed for each pound of the food eaten.

The essential amino acids include isoleucine, leucine, lysine, methionine, phenylalanine, threonine, tryptophan, and valine.  Histidine is needed by infants, and one source states that the need for adults has not been <u>disproven</u>.  Seventy-five percent of the need for methionine can be met by cystine, and the need for methionine is commonly stated as a joint need for the two, and often they are listed as the sulfur-containing amino acids or S-containing amino acids.  Similarly, sixty percent of the need for phenylalanine can be met by tyrosine.  These two are commonly listed together as the aromatic amino acids.

It was originally thought that the amino acids had to be balanced within a single meal.  Now it is thought that there is more leeway than this, and that amino acids can be balanced within the course of a day rather than within a single meal.  The answer to this question is not yet certain.

## PROTEIN

Primary uses in the body--people are 18-20% protein by weight.  It helps in the growth and maintenance of tissues, including muscles and internal organs, and also helps form hemoglobin, enzymes, anti-bodies, and most hormones.  It is burned for energy only if needed.

Intake and Metabolism--it supplies us with the nitrogen and amino acids which we need every day.  Amino acid content and digestability determine quality. Deficiency shows in hair, nails, skin, abnormal growth, poor muscle tone, and the slow healing of abrasions.

Tips for efficient use--grinding or cooking may aid digestion, as does dividing protein foods among all the meals and eating them first or perhaps after a little wine or cider vinegar.  Sprouting increases soy protein and depleted soils can decrease the protein in grains.

## FATS

Primary uses in the body--fats carry the fat soluble vitamins A, D, E, and K in the blood and supply essential fatty acids.  They are a concentrated energy source and also store energy.  Fats protect nerves and internal organs and also lubricate the intestinal tract.

Intake and metabolism--fatty foods slow the production of hydrochloric acid which slows the digestion of fats and particularly of protein.  Fats remain longer in the stomach.  Digestion breaks fat into fatty acids and glycerol.  The liver is important in fat utilization.

Tips for efficient use--Best is a low fat intake from whole, plant foods high in linoleic acid.  Fat utilization requires sufficient ammounts of choline, inositol, and methionine.  Try reducing oil, margarine, and butter use to 2 tablespoons per day as a first step.

## ESSENTIAL FATTY ACIDS

Primary Uses in the body--collectively known as vitamin F, the essential fatty acids are needed for growth, healthy skin, blood, arteries, nerves, fertility, good functioning of cell and sub-cell membranes, and for producing prostaglandids, which are similar to hormones.

Intake and Metabolism--the body needs linoleic acid, arachidonic acid, and linolenic acid, but can synthesize the last two from linoleic acid.  While unknown except from experimental or intravenous diets, deficiency can cause eczema and poor growth.

Tips for efficient use--Linoleic acid comes from plant sources such as seeds, nuts, and soybeans, and can replace the need for arachidonic acid which comes from animal fats.  Filberts, sunflower seeds and peanuts are particularly good sources.

## AMINO ACIDS

Primary uses in the body--properly mixed amino acids build body tissue. Histidine helps infants grow, methionine and threonine help digest fats, methionine also helps supply sulfur and synthesize choline. 60 mg of tryptophan allows the body to form 1 mg of niacin.

Intake and metabolism--the sufficiency of amino acids is determined by both the content and digestability of the whole diet. If lysine, tryptophan, and sulfur-containing amino acids are sufficient, the others will be unless there are additional limiting amino acids.

Tips for efficient use--Mix different foods to improve amino acid mix. Sprout or soak seed foods. Use the slide rules in this book to check and fine-tune combinations. Cooking improves digestability, but if over 240°, as in pressure cookers, lysine is destroyed.

# Mineral    Nutrients

A study of the nutrients calcium, iron, iodine, and zinc requires more than an examination of the experimental data dealing with these nutrients.  We must consider the cultural and agricultural assumptions that have influenced the perceptions of our needs for these minerals.  It may be necessary to question some of these assumptions, and to make several personal decisions as to what to believe or not believe and what to do or not do.

Our nutritional need  for these nutrients is also difficult to understand.  Many of the complexities are, however, only relevant within the context of the drastic changes in diet and personal lifestyle within present day society.  Many of the important and more difficult to understand aspects apply to several minerals.  Once these are understood for one mineral, mineral nutrition in general will begin to make sense.  It will be important to continue the learning process on this complex subject.  Work is still needed to find good answers.

These minerals may be among the most difficult nutrients to supply within a minimal area diet.  We must try to include food in the diet that  is especially efficient in supplying these minerals, but our efforts must not stop here!  It is important to plan into our gardens provisions for healthy soil, for if the soil is deficient in minerals, or if they are in unavailable forms, then the food we grow may also be deficient.  We must carefully consider how we will prepare and process the foods we grow.  The presence or lack of other nutrients in our diet may affect our body's ability to use the minerals we take in.  Other factors may also limit our absorption of minerals.  We may even need to consider strange and unusual foods to help us get an adequate supply of minerals.

Yet the complexities of the problem, particularly those that have been generated by modern day changes in diet and the treatment of our soil and environment, need not obscure the fact that the solution may be relatively simple.

*                *                *

Imagine being required to drive cars designed to prevent all accidents. Before you could start the engine, you would have to breathe into a tube so that the on-board computer could make sure that you were not intoxicated. Your body would be monitored by sensors so that if you became drowsy alarms would go off to waken you. Thousands of dollars of special safety equipment would have to go into every car so that the small percentage of the drivers who pursued life recklessly or who were naturally more accident prone could be properly protected. The cars would be built according to government standards and the design would be heavily influenced by the interests of the companies that built the cars. The costs would be outrageous, and while quite safe, such a car would not perform well in other aspects such as comfort, convenience, and fuel consumption.

Consider the way many of the standards of nutrition are set by the U.S. government. The imbalanced and excessive eating habits of Americans are assumed in the setting of the standards. The standards are also set high enough to provide for the small percentage of the population whose special needs are the greatest. The influences, both direct and indirect, of the various lobby groups of the food industry must also be questioned. We are told that we must drink milk to get our calcium, eat considerable amounts of red meat or take pills to obtain our iron, use iodized salt to get our iodine, and eat large amounts of animal protein to get our zinc. Such recommendations are not an accurate reflection of our needs. If we bring all of our diet into balance, take steps to improve our absorption, care for our soil, and choose carefully from whole, nutritious foods, we should have no difficulty in getting all the minerals that we need from a diet which requires much less land and other resources to produce.

Calcium requirements have been a matter of controversy for a number of years. Calcium needs vary considerably among individuals. Our ability to absorb calcium is strongly affected by such cultural factors as our intake of protein, and our accustomed level of calcium intake. Americans who consume large amounts of protein and who are used to a high calcium consumption need considerably more calcium than many peoples around the world who are accustomed to more efficient diets. A closer examination of how we use calcium is necessary in order to understand calcium requirements.

We have two kinds of calcium needs. About 99 percent of the calcium we consume is combined with phosphorous to build bones and teeth. The other one percent is used in a variety of chemical reactions throughout the body.

Calcium accumulation is most rapid during the body's growth periods, and calcium absorption is highest during pregnancy and early growth. Fetuses and infants accumulate calcium rapidly. Over time, the soft bones of the infant take on a crystalline structure and become hard. This process is not completed until the early 20's. Both soft and hardened bones are made primarily of calcium phosphate.

Our phosphorous intake can affect our calcium balance. While the ideal ratio of calcium to phosphorous, the Ca:P ratio, should be between 2:1 and 1:2, excessive phosphorous intake, particularly from meat, has resulted in an average ratio in the U.S. of 1:3. Excess phosphorous can cause calcium deficiency, even if calcium is otherwise adequate. Sufficient vitamin D, however, is thought to extend the acceptable range for the Ca:P ratio.

Our bones are a living material, with calcium constantly being added and taken away. We are able to store calcium in crystal structures at the end of bones called trabeculae. When we have no reserves, bones can be borrowed from, with the pelvic bones and the vertabrae being borrowed from first. We also tend to lose more calcium at night due in part to the horizontal position of sleep. Astronauts lose more calcium during weightlessness.

The other one percent of our calcium, that used by the rest of the body, is maintained at a much more constant level. When more is needed it is taken from the bones, and when it is in excess, it is excreted through the kidneys. This tiny amount of calcium, the one percent, is critical for the nerves, muscles, blood, for the passage of nutrients through cell membranes, in the utilization of iron, and in the activation of enzymes in metabolism.

To understand calcium requirements, we must examine the factors of calcium losses, absorption, and deficiency. We lose calcium mostly through the feces and urine.  For the typical American adult, 70-80 percent of the calcium we take in is not absorbed and is excreted in the feces.  Urinary calcium excretion is nearly constant for each individual, but varies considerably from one individual to another.  Increased protein intake causes calcium excretion to increase.

There are a variety of reasons for our low absorption of calcium.  Probably the biggest reason is our high customary intake of calcium.  Our body adjusts the absorption rate according to our intake.  If we are used to taking in a large amount then we will use calcium less efficiently than if we were used to taking in a smaller amount.  If we switch to a diet lower in calcium, it may take our body several weeks or even months to readjust to our new intake level, but we will then be able to absorb calcium more efficiently and will need less of it.

To get the best use of calcium, we must get adequate amounts of magnesium, phosphorous, and vitamins A,C, and D.  We must also not get too much phosphorous. Vitamin D, which we can produce for ourselves with adequate exposure to sunlight, is particularly important.  Exercise can help calcium absorption and stress can interfere with it.  Lactose, protein, and butterfat--all of which are present in milk--can help in calcium absorption.  Excess protein and fat, however, can have a negative effect on our calcium balance.  High fiber content can speed the passage of food through our small intestines and thus decrease calcium absorption.  Acids such as fruit juice help to dissolve and make more available the calcium in food, and might be taken after a meal for this purpose. Grinding grains with a stone mill, or adding wood ashes to grains, as is traditionally done in making corn tortillas, can supplement the calcium in the grains, for both the small amounts of dust from the mill stone and also the ashes tend to be high in calcium.

Two naturally occurring acids, oxalic acid and phytic acid, can decrease the available calcium in the foods in which they are present.  Oxalic acid is found in some of the foods highest in calcium such as beet greens, purslane, spinach, New Zealand spinach, and Swiss chard.  This is not thought to be as big a problem as it once was, but you can also choose from a number of greens that are high in calcium and low in oxalic acid, such as dandelion greens, turnip greens, kale, mustard, and collards (see chart).  Oxalic acid is probably not a problem unless a low intake of calcium and a low level of vitamin D are combined with a high level of oxalic acid.  Young plants may be lower in oxalic acid, and cooking may help to nullify the effects of the oxalic acid.

44

| Kind of Leafy Greens | Oxalic Acid in Grams per Pound | Calcium in Grams per Pound |
|---|---|---|
| Beet greens | 4.16 | 540 |
| Purslane greens | 4.13 | 468 |
| Spinach | 4.05 | 422 |
| New Zealand spinach | 4.04 | 263 |
| Swiss chard | 2.93 | 399 |
| Parsley | 0.86 | 922 |
| Dandelion greens | 0.11 | 849 |
| Turnip greens | 0.07 | 1117 |
| Kale leaves | 0.05 | 1130 |
| Collards | 0.04 | 1135 |
| Mustard greens | 0.04 | 831 |

Phytic acid is associated with grains, and particularly wheat, but it is also present in moderate amounts in potatoes and sweet potatoes. It also tends to bind minerals such as calcium, iron and zinc into salts that are unavailable to the body. There is another naturally occurring substance called phytase which acts to neutralize phytic acid. It is found in grains, and rye contains a more active phytase than other grains. Including ten percent rye flour in bread may help reduce the phytic acid problem. Yeast is also a source of phytase, and an unlevened bread may contain 50 percent more phytic acid than a yeast bread. Laurel's Kitchen recommends a number of steps for minimizing the phytic acid content of home baked breads. It helps to use a moderately moist dough that is allowed to rise two or even three times at a warm but not too hot temperature. The use of acidic ingredients such as fruit juice, yoghurt, and sour milk also helps. Soy yoghurt or sour soy milk should also work. Rhyzopus mold in tempeh also produces phytase, so that using wheat tempeh instead of bread is another way to get more calcium from grains. Sprouting grains produces enzymes that chelate with the minerals by attaching the mineral molecules to easily absorbed organic molecules. This minimizes the binding effects of the phytic acid. As with oxalic acid, phytic acid is probably a significant concern only when calcium and vitamin D are marginal.

One symptom of calcium deficiency is the condition tetany, which involves muscle cramps and tingling and numbness in the limbs. Joint pains, heart palpitation, slow pulse, tooth decay, insomnia, impaired growth, and irritability of nerves and muscles are also signs of possible deficiency.

Osteoporosis is a disease caused by the loss of calcium in the bones, and results in brittle bones that break easily. This disease effects older people more, especially older women. Calcium losses in women begin to accelerate after menopause, and osteoporosis has been estimated to affect 80 percent of elderly American women. It was once thought that high intakes of calcium could help, which was part of the basis for the high RDA for calcium. We now know that high calcium intake does little to help osteoporosis, and that a more important factor is protein intake.

Recommended Daily Allowances states that "Calcium losses can be substantial when protein intake is high." Rather than recommending a reduction from our country's excessively high protein intake, this publication sets a calcium requirement of 800 milligrams per day that assumes the customary level of United States protein intake as well as the low absorption caused by our high customary calcium intake.

This is in spite of the fact that it is understood that people who take the recommended amount of protein will not need nearly this amount, in spite of the fact that both the World Health Organization of the United Nations and Great Britain have adopted a lower recommendation of 400 to 500 milligrams per day, and in spite of the fact that large doses of calcium may limit our absorption of manganese, iron, and zinc. Many peoples around the world have calcium intakes in the range of 200-400 mg per day with no adverse side effects. Again, we must wonder if these recommendations are being made to protect our health or to support the interests of certain segments of the food industry.

Five hundred milligrams per day, the upper end of the range of recommendations set by the F.A.O. and Great Britain is used in the design of the minimal area diet in this book, and can be met by including liberal amounts of leafy greens.

Iron exists in every cell in the body, and is found combined with protein. A single iron atom is found in the center of each giant hemoglobin molecule. These molecules are part of our red blood cells and carry oxygen throughout our body. It is the ability of iron to take on and give up oxygen that makes it so important.

Iron is also found in myoglobin, which supplies the oxygen needed by the muscles for contraction. Iron is also important in certain enzymes involved in protein metabolism. The body stores iron in the liver, spleen, bone marrow, and blood.

Our iron balance is regulated by adjusting the absorption rate--we have no good way of getting rid of excess iron, but will absorb it less efficiently if we have too much. It is this complex and poorly understood process of

46

absorption that determines most of our iron needs. The body is quite efficient at conserving iron, but since it is assumed that only ten percent of the iron we take in is absorbed, it is supposed that we need to take in at least ten times as much iron as we lose. Thus 90 percent of our iron needs are generated by our low absorption.

The average iron loss in men is about one milligram per day. Added to this for women are the menstrual iron losses which are estimated to be about 0.5 mg per day when averaged over a one month period. There is much variation among women, however, and the RDA's have been set to cover a broad range, with menstrual iron losses being set at a figure corresponding to 0.8 mg per day. Women have a tendency to be deficient in iron. Between 15 and 58 percent of women of child-bearing age have insufficient iron stores, and in a study of college women, two-thirds of them had iron problems. One possible source for the increased iron deficiency in women is the switch away from cast-iron cookware that can add considerable quantities of iron to our diets.

The body reuses its iron, with the iron in red blood cells being recycled by the liver or spleen when the cells wear out after about 100 days. While we do have some iron reserves, restoration of these reserves, even with iron supplements, can take about six months. Diarrhea can decrease iron reserves as can various blood parasites such as hookworm. These problems help explain why iron deficiency is such a problem in many parts of the Third World. It is also good to have a reserve of iron in case of blood loss.

Iron deficiency (almost all of which occurs in women) is cited by some as the most common nutrient deficiency both in this country and world-wide. One of the most common problems associated with iron deficiency is anemia, or the shortage of red blood cells. Other deficiencies and health problems can also produce various types of anemia which are unrelated to iron deficiency. Deficiency symptoms for iron include pale skin, abnormal fatigue, constipation, brittle nails, and difficult breathing.

The iron intake recommended for women is so high that it is commonly asserted that they can only be met through the consumption of large amounts of red meat or through the use of iron supplements. The question of how to supply a woman's iron needs is a difficult one. Since 90 percent of these needs are to make up for the low absorption rate, it is important to ask what can be done to increase absorption.

Iron is absorbed in the upper part of the small intestine, just after leaving the stomach.  The acidity of the gastric juices has a lot to do with regulating the solubility and availability of the iron in our food.  Perhaps the advice given for protein foods--to eat them early in meals, preceded by perhaps a little apple cider vinegar or wine--should also be applied to foods high in iron.

We get our iron through the intestinal mucosa, the mucous membranes of the small intestine.  When iron intake has been insufficient, the intestinal mucosa can increase absorption from the average for a normal American of about ten percent to between twenty and thirty percent.  In cases of anemia, absorption may increase to between 45 and 64 percent.

If the food going into the body is low in iron, there will be less to be absorbed.  Variations of as much as 500 percent can occur for a given food, so that one sample of a food might have only twenty percent of the iron of another sample.  Alkaline soils are often deficient in available iron.  Kelp meal and wood ash can help supply iron to an alkaline soil or a  soil that is otherwise deficient in iron.  The ash of oak is especially high in iron as well as calcium.  Plants capable of acumulating iron, which could make good supplements to a compost pile, include stinging nettle, goosegrass, bedstraw, sweethearts, parsley, spanish moss, salsify, parsnips, beets, and radishes.

The use of cast-iron cookware is an important and simple way of supplementing your iron intake--it is also cheaper than buying iron pills.  Acidic foods and longer cooking times increase the amount of iron added to food cooked in cast-iron cookware.  A 100 gram serving of spaghetti sauce that has been cooked in cast iron for three hours will pick up about 84 milligrams of iron just from the cast iron.  This is more than four and a half times a woman's daily needs.

Another important aspect in iron absorption is chelation.  By becoming loosely bound to an enzyme, vitamin, or certain other organic molecules, iron is more readily absorbed.  It is also less likely to get bound up with either phytic acid or oxalic acid and become unavailable.  Chelated iron is easily absorbed, whereas iron bound to molecules of either phytic or oxalic acid is excreted.  Vitamins C and E, the sulfur-containing amino acids, and enzymes released by sprouting and fermentation can all help in iron absorption through chelation.

Having adequate intake of calcium and copper helps iron absorption, whereas excess phosphorous can hurt.  Combining high quality protein foods with plant foods rich in iron can help in the absorption of the iron from the plant sources. High fiber intake or the consumption of coffee or tea can hinder iron absorption. Phytic acid can reduce iron absorption from the normal ten percent to between two and five percent. Fructose (fruit sugar) can help iron absorption, as can citric acid. A diet high in potatoes could provide substantial amounts of citric acid and thus help iron absorption.

| Food | Citric Acid Content g per 100 grams edible portion |
|------|---------------------------------------------------|
| Lemon | 3.84 |
| Strawberry | 1.00 |
| Orange | .95 |
| Potato | .51 |
| Tomato, ripe | .38 |
| Kale | .35 |
| Parsnip | .13 |
| Sweet potato | .07 |

If you can increase iron absorption, your needs for iron intake should be less. We must consider that these savings cannot be accurately accounted at this time--more research is needed. The iron losses of women and the iron content of foods both also vary considerably. While it is not advocated or advised, it would be possible for individuals to test for themselves--given their body and the food they consume--to see if they could achieve an adequate iron balance, with less iron intake, through better absorption. If iron absorption could be raised from ten percent to twenty percent, then, in theory at least, iron intake needs would be cut in half. Regular blood tests would be needed to monitor your iron status.

For a simple, inexpensive way to help your iron intake, eat iron-rich greens steamed in a little vinegar in a cast-iron pan.

The green leafy tips of sweet potato plants are also very high in iron and may prove to be an important iron supplement. They are not poisonous, as are the leaves and stems from Irish potatoes, and are an important food in many areas of the world. One pound of sweet potato greens can provide an amazing 49 milligrams of iron. In tests in tropical countries, yields of the greens have been about half the yields of the tubers, but the cutting of the greens may cause significant decreases in the tuber yield. More research will likely prove sweet potato greens to be an important part of a minimal area diet for the humid tropics.

Iodine was first identified by Courtois when he isolated this mineral in the seaweed kelp. The relationship between iodine and goiter, a condition of the thyroid, was suspected by the late 1800's and was firmly established in 1919 when the iodine containing enzyme thyoxine was isolated by Kendall. It was found that the thyroid glands combine iodine with the amino acid tyrosine to form thyroxine. Iodine is also used in the formation of triiodothyronine. Both enzymes are important in metabolism. Iodine helps in growth, speech, hair, nails, skin, teeth, the conversion of carotene into vitamin A, and the development of reproductive organs. A deficiency may have an influence on the incidence of breast cancer in women, and possibly lead to hardening of the arteries, sluggish metabolism, slower mental reactions, restlessness, and irritability.

Goiter, the most well known iodine deficiency symptom, includes in its symptoms the enlargement of the thyroid glands. Starting in the 1920's, the connection between iodine and goiter led to a series of surveys to determine the iodine concentration of plants, water, rocks, and soils. In this country and world-wide, the incidence of goiter was found to correspond to soils deficient in iodine. Today with foods being transported world-wide, iodine deficient foods are also being transported world-wide.

In the United States, soils deficient in iodine are found in the Great Lakes and Pacific Northwest regions and in Vermont. Around the world, iodine deficient soils can be found in Switzerland, Central America, New Zealand, the Himalayas, and mountainous areas of South America.

Iodized salt has generally been supposed to have solved the iodine problem, but in many parts of the world, iodized salt is not in general use. Even in this country, as recently as the 1960's, goiter was found in 6.6 percent of those surveyed in Michigan, and enlarged thyroids in 5.4 percent of those surveyed in Texas.

Since iodine is not necessary in plants, and iodized salt is thought to have solved the problem in humans, iodine is not considered to be much of a soil problem. The soil chemistry of iodine is similar to that of chlorine. Among the trace minerals, chlorine's availability is the least affected by pH. One would suspect, then, that the use of kelp meal (see page 27 of the 1982 edition of How to Grow More Vegetables), which is extremely high in iodine, could correct iodine deficiencies in most soils in the course of a few years. The only way to be certain, however, is to have foods grown in your garden tested for iodine. *Remember that compost made from plant materials grown in deficient soils will probably not help very much in improving the iodine content of your soil.* Goosegrass and bedstraw are iodine accumulators and might help concentrate iodine from your subsoil. They could be added to your compost pile, and thus possibly help enrich your topsoil.

If you do not wish to use iodized salt, kelp is also an excellent supplement. Be aware that excess iodine can also be a health problem. A tablet containing eight and a half grains of kelp will supply one day's iodine needs, and a pound of kelp is enough for over two years.

The amount of iodine needed to prevent goiter is considered to be about one microgram per kilogram of body weight. The RDA is 130 micrograms for the average man and 100 micrograms for the average woman.

Goitrogens are chemicals which can interfere with the use of thyroxine and thereby increase our needs for iodine. They are found in rutabaga, kale, turnip skins, and cabbage, and in the red skins of peanuts. Their effects can be negated by cooking. It might also be wise to remove the peanut skins. The synthetic estrogens in birth control pills can also rob the body of iodine.

The most important question relative to iodine in a minimal area diet, is whether or not your soil is providing your plants with enough iodine. If soil iodine is adequate, it should be possible to provide your iodine needs from a minimal area diet without supplementation.


Zinc is a nutrient that needs the careful scrutiny of a nutritional science capable of tracing the connection between the food in front of us, the affects of our modern society, and the planet upon which we live. Zinc cannot be understood by an equation that states our needs as being this much, and our intake as equaling the sum of the zinc content of the foods that we eat.

Zinc's importance in human nutrition has only been recognized in recent times, and many of the difficulties concerning zinc are also products of our modern times. To understand zinc nutrition, we must consider the excesses and imbalancs of modern diets, the birth control pills of the sexual revolution, the polluting of our environment by heavy metals, and the problems of depleted soils artificially bolstered up by chemicals. For the answers, we may have to step in to complete and repair the circle of life by taking better care of ourselves, our soils, and our planet.

Zinc is critical to the chemical communications within the body. At least 25 different enzymes contain zinc, many of which are critical in triggering the processes of digestion and metabolism. Zinc is found in nucleic acids, and in relatively high concentrations in the RNA and DNA molecules that carry the blueprint of life. The role of zinc in RNA and DNA is not well understood.

In digestion, zinc-containing enzymes help break down incoming proteins, carbohydrates, and alcohol. Zinc is important in making use of vitamins, particularly the B vitamins. It is also important in the metabolism of phosphorous. Zinc-containing enzymes help in the re-synthesis of proteins from amino acids that is necessary for the growth and repair of tissues. Zinc is a component of insulin and is needed in men to keep the prostate gland functioning properly. Sperm is high in zinc. Zinc is also needed to enable the body to complete the processes of metabolism by transferring its waste product, carbon dioxide, to the lungs so that it can be passed out of the body in each out-going breath.

Zinc is absorbed in the upper part of the small intestine. The complex relations between zinc and other nutrients are enough to make one fear that balanced nutrition might be impossible to achieve. High amounts of protein, calcium, copper, iron, vitamin A, sugar, phosphorous, and phytic acid may all tend to raise our need for zinc. Vitamin D can improve our absorption of zinc. Too much zinc can cause a need for increased amounts of Vitamin A, and can interfere with the utilization of copper which can prevent good iron metabolism. Alcohol and oral contraceptives tend to flush zinc from the body. Cadmium, even in very small quantities, can greatly increase our needs for zinc. The interrelationships between zinc and the other nutrients are as complicated as a soap opera, but the solution may be as simple as a return to a healthier diet and lifestyle.

Wheat is an interesting crop in relation to zinc. Zinc is concentrated in the germ and the bran, so that most of the zinc is removed to make white flour. At the same time, the zinc-binding phytic acid is also found mostly in the bran of the wheat. Steps to minimize the effects of the phytic acid were given in the calcium section and would also help with zinc. In that most of the phytic acid is in the outermost part of the bran and most of the zinc in layers below that, it might be possible that a light milling could remove most of the phytic acid while leaving most of the zinc.

The zinc to cadmium ratio in wheat can also be a problem. Cadmium is a heavy metal that is located just below zinc in the periodic table of elements. In chemical reactions, it tends to react similarly to zinc, and if both are present, it tends to replace zinc. This makes it necessary to have much more zinc than cadmium or the cadmium will take the zinc's place in the reactions of digestion and prevent the body from absorbing enough zinc. Cadmium is highly toxic and has invaded the biosphere only in modern times. Most of the cadmium we take in comes from our food and water. In wheat, cadmium is absorbed by the starchy inner grain. If we eat whole wheat, the zinc to cadmium ratio is about 100 to 1. When wheat is milled, much of the zinc is removed and all of the cadmium remains, resulting in a zinc to cadmium ratio in white flour of about 17 to 1. This makes it harder for us to get enough zinc--not just from the white flour, but also from the other foods eaten at the same time whose zinc will have to compete with the cadmium from the white flour for absorption.

Wheat is also vulnerable to soil deficiencies in zinc. While the _health_ of a field of wheat--in terms of its ability to produce a profitable harvest-- is not greatly affected by the levels of zinc deficiency common in soils in this country, the _healthiness_ of the wheat--in terms of its ability to produce healthy animals and people--may be considerably affected by these zinc deficiencies. The addition of zinc fertilizer to deficient soils can double the zinc content of wheat grown on those soils.

As of 1961, zinc deficiency in the United States had been reported in 32 states. The problem is considered to be getting worse. While the major soil deficiencies are east of the Rockies, zinc deficiencies can be found from coast to coast, both north and south. A call to your county agricultural agent should reveal if soils in your area are known to be deficient.

While the nutritional content of many crops may be affected, the crops whose economic yields are the most affected are corn, field beans, sorghum, and potatoes. World-wide, zinc deficiencies can be found in Canada, Brazil, Denmark, Germany, Greece, Ireland, Israel, the Netherlands, Spain, Sweden, Switzerland, the United Kingdom, Australia, New Zealand, east central Africa, southern Africa, Guinea, the Camaroons, and Chad.

Sometimes zinc deficiency is a problem of availability resulting from cool wet weather early in the growing season. Agricultural practices are probably the more important, and certainly the more correctable problem. It used to be that annual manure applications renewed the zinc in soils. Now zinc is depleted unless economic necessity causes zinc fertilizers to need to be applied--fertilizers in which zinc is often less available than the zinc found in manures. More importantly, the use of "conventional commercial fertilizers can reduce the available zinc in the soil by half."* The applica-

* Diet and Nutrition, Rudolf Ballentine, M.D.

tion of lime, chemical nitrogen and phosphorous fertilizers, and mercury fungicides have all been shown to cause or worsen a zinc deficiency by altering the chemical availability of the zinc. Today's high-input agriculture depletes zinc from the soil more rapidly through its higher yields, does not replace the zinc with manure as agriculture once did, and tends to make what zinc there is in the soil unavailable.

Since livestock need zinc, their feed is frequently supplemented to make up for deficiencies in the grain. Manure from grain fed animals or animals whose pasturage is not deficient in zinc, then, may still be a good source of zinc for the soil. Pig manure is particularly high in zinc, having about twenty times as much as cow manure. Bone meal, fish meal, and kelp meal are all good sources of zinc. Corn, ragweed, horsetail, vetch, alfalfa, poplar and hickory leaves, and peach tree twigs are all plant materials that accumulate zinc. Alfalfa cover crops have been shown to be effective in reducing and preventing zinc deficiency in orchards. A build-up of organic matter helps hold and thus accumulate zinc that is added to the soil, or brought up from the subsoil to be concentrated in the topsoil through the use of cover crops and composting. Alkalinity can tie up zinc and make it unavailable, but a composting program can help considerably with this problem. An organic soil building program that includes: composting; the addition, if needed, of composted manure, bone meal, fish meal, or kelp meal; and the build up and preservation of organic matter, should, over a period of years, take care of a zinc deficiency or availability problem.

Is your soil deficient in zinc? Diagnostic Criteria for Plants and Soils* states that "Growth characteristics and leaf symptomatology of acute zinc deficiency are so well defined that supplementary leaf and/or soil analysis tests are unnecessary." Citrus and corn are considered good indicator plants for zinc deficiency. Diagnostic Criteria for Plants and Soils gives the following deficiency symptoms for citrus:

leaves become chlorotic; this is known as "mottle leaf" in California and "frenching" in Florida. Irregular green bands develop along midribs and lateral veins; leaves become small and narrowed; small green dots often appear in chlorotic areas; twigs tend to die back; fruit quality and quantity vary with severity of deficiency.

*Diagnostic Criteria for Plants and Soils, Homer D. Chapman, ed., University of California, Division of Agricultural Sciences, 1960.

Those for corn are:

Older leaves have light yellow streaks or chlorotic striping between veins; this may show as a broad band of white or yellow tissue between the midrib and the edge of the leaf, occurring mainly in the lower half of the leaf, and is visible when the young leaf is coming out of the whorl. Silking and tassling are delayed. Severely deficient plants are also stunted, and have short internodes.

The average zinc intake in a mixed U.S. diet is given as between 10 and 15 milligrams. Recommended Daily Allowances states that 8-10 milligrams of zinc is adequate to maintain equilibrium, but recommends an RDA of 15 milligrams per day for an adult. Robin Hur* argues that it is the high protein, calcium, calorie, sugar, and phytic acid levels in our diets that raise the need for zinc from eight to fifteen milligrams per day.

It is difficult to produce the fifteen milligrams per day level of zinc in a minimal area diet. Potatoes and turnip greens are important sources. The mineral concentration in turnip greens is reported to increase as they grow, so it may be important to allow them to mature. The missing zinc data for sunflower seeds and collards, both probably good sources of zinc, should also help solve the problem once their zinc contributions can be correctly accounted for. It may also be important to investigate special foods with high zinc concentrations that could be used as supplements. At 5.2 milligrams per 100 grams, Chinese taro could provide all of one's daily needs in a serving of just a little over ten ounces. In Angola, moth and weevil larvae are eaten that could provide all of one's zinc needs in just a little over two ounces per day. If we begin to investigate the question with an open mind, there are probably a variety of exciting solutions to meeting our zinc needs.

The problems involved with zinc are admittedly complex, but the solutions are probably quite simple. A balance among the minerals and other nutrients can generally be accomplished by eating a simple diet of whole foods. To ensure that our plants can get enough zinc, we must take better care of our soil. There are probably many unusual and tasty zinc-containing foods just waiting to be discovered. While more research is needed, there is no reason to believe that there will be any difficulty in getting enough zinc from a minimal area diet.

*Robin Hur, Food Reform: Our Desparate Need, Heidelburg Publishers, Austin Texas, 1975.

## Vitamin Nutrients

Vitamin A was the first of the fat soluble vitamins to be discovered. While research in this vitamin goes back to 1912, a U.S. government study done between 1968 and 1970 showed that significant deficiency in this vitamin still existed in the U.S.

We really need to deal with two groups of substances when we speak of vitamin A. Retinol compounds, which come from animal products, are the "active vitamin A" and are already in the form needed by the body. Carotene compounds, which come from plant sources, are the "provitamin A", and must first be converted to vitamin A before they can be used. Both carotene and retinol are commonly called vitamin A, but it will be important later, in discussing requirements, to distinguish between the two.

Vitamin A is important for growth--it helps in the formation of healthy bones and teeth, and in the general growth and repair of tissues throughout the body. It is also important for the mucous membranes--it helps protect the mouth, throat, nose, and lungs from both infection and air pollution. It helps provide protection to similar tissues in the linings of the kidneys, bladder, and digestive system. In the stomach it stimulates the production of gastric juices and thus helps maintain the acidity necessary for the proper digestion of protein and many vitamins and minerals. Vitamin A is needed for healthy skin and blood. Its role that is probably most familiar to us is as an aid to good eyesight.

Children are often told that to have good vision they must eat their carrots. Vitamin A does indeed play an important role in sight. A mild deficiency can produce what is called night blindness. This term refers to the eyes' slow adjustment to dim light after having been exposed to bright light. You walk out of a brightly lit house and it takes a while for your eyes to adjust--to be able to see the stars and the trees and to walk around comfortably. You are driving at night and a car passes you from the other direction with its brights on. For a brief but frightening moment you can not see the road very well. These are both probably examples of night blindness.

Severe vitamin A deficiency has not been found in this country, but has been a significant problem in India. Children there suffer particularly from eye problems that result from deficiency. Deficiency can cause styes in the eyes, skin problems, loss of smell and appetite, fatigue, diarrhea, and increased susceptibility to certain respiratory or other infectious diseases such as tuberculosis, pneumonia, emphysema, salmonella, and polio.

Diabetics may not be able to convert carotene into vitamin A, but for others, this conversion happens either just before or during absorption which takes place in the small intestine. For the vitamin A to be effective we need to get enough iodine, because thyroxine, the iodine containing enzyme from the thyroid gland, is needed for the conversion of carotene into vitamin A. Only about one quarter of the carotene in carrots is converted, whereas half the carotene in leafy vegetables is.

Conversion of carotene into vitamin A is one link in the chain, and absorption is another. Heavy activity within four hours of eating can limit absorption, as can inadequate amounts of fat, protein, and vitamins D and E. Vitamin E protects both retinol and carotene from oxidation and loss. Cold weather can hurt both transport and metabolism of vitamin A. Barring gastrointestinal, liver, or bile duct problems, enough A can be stored to last for months or even years. Some 90 percent of the vitamin A storage is in the liver and requires zinc for release back into the blood.

With so many seemingly weak links in the chain that provides for our vitamin A needs, one might think that recommendations for our daily intake would include a substantial safety factor in addition to the minimal needs. The problem with this is that, as with other fat soluble vitamins, active vitamin A, or retinol, can quite easily accumulate and reach toxic levels. In humans, overdoses can occur at 100 times the RDA from a single dose, at 20 times the RDA over many doses, and at only six times the RDA as a daily regimen.

At the same time in tests on rats, the individual rat that needed the most for its minimal needs needed at least 40 times as much as the rat with the lowest needs. The possibility suggests itself that what might be a toxic dose for one individual might not be enough to meet the needs for another. There is an escape from this dilemma. Carotene does not accumulate to toxic levels the way retinol does. Thus, by getting our needs filled through the consumption of plant foods high in vitamin A we can take in larger quantities of vitamin A without worry. It has been found that many healthy traditional cultures had daily intakes of about 20,000 I.U. per day, or about four times the old RDA. This generally came from plant sources.

In the old standard, the RDA had been 5,000 I.U., or International Units, with the assumption that half came from retinol and half from carotene. The problem with this is that only about one third of the carotene is absorbed, so that instead of two micrograms of carotene being worth one microgram of retinol, as had been assumed, six micrograms of carotene are needed to provide the same nutritional value as one microgram of retinol.

The new system measures the RDA in what are called retinol equivalents.  One retinol equivalent is equal to one microgram of retinol or six micrograms of carotene.  In terms of the old International Units, one retinol equivalent equals 3.33 I.U. of retinol or ten I.U. of carotene.  The 2500 I.U. of retinol that had been assumed (in the old RDA) would therefore equal 750 retinol equivalents, and the 2500 I.U. of carotene would equal 250 retinol equivalents for a new requirement of 1,000 total retinol equivalents or RE.  This can be met by all carotene, all retinol, or an appropriate mixture of the two.  There are several foods in the diet that are excellent at providing vitamin A.

Research into <u>riboflavin, or vitamin B$_2$</u>, has been underway since 1879 when a yellow-green pigment containing it was isolated in milk.  It was first synthesized in 1935.  Today, riboflavin deficiency is thought by many to be the most common vitamin deficiency in the United States.  The health hazards of this deficiency are generally not that serious, however, and extreme deficiencies are rare.

Riboflavin works in enzymes that metabolize fat, protein, and carbohydrates.  It helps release the energy stored in these calorie containing substances and also helps in the recombination of protein substances for protein synthesis.  Riboflavin is important for the growth and repair of tissues, cell respiration, and the maintenance of healthy eyes, skin, nails and hair.

A common symptom of deficiency is cheilosis, in which cracked, sore skin develops at the corners of the mouth.  Other deficiency symptoms include lip lesions, scaley skin around the nose, mouth, forehead, and ears, swollen mouth and throat membranes, and a sore, red or purple tongue.  A wide variety of other deficiency symptoms are possible.

Riboflavin is a water-soluble vitamin.  It is sometimes synthesized by micro-organisms in the small intestine.  Riboflavin synthesis may be dependent on diet.  The body's ability to absorb and utilize synthesized riboflavin is unknown.

Over the years the requirements for riboflavin have at different times been set relative to protein intake, body size, or calorie intake.  The current RDA is 0.6 milligrams per 1,000 calories.  Robin Hur argues that this includes 0.3 milligrams per 1,000 calories minimum requirements and a 100 percent safety margin.  The RDA assumes a normal American level of activity (very light), and states that riboflavin should not be increased because of <u>extra</u> calories that might be needed for a more strenuous level of activity.  A simple chemical test of the urine can determine if our riboflavin intake is adequate.

While riboflavin is not broken down easily by heat, oxidation, or acidity, it breaks down readily in the presence of alkaline substances and light. Milk left in direct sunlight can lose most of its riboflavin in just a few hours. Stress can increase one's need for riboflavin. Sprouting can increase the riboflavin content of grains.


Pellagra is a disease of <u>niacin</u> deficiency. While its name means "rough skin", it can cause not only skin problems, but also mental illness and even death. Pellagra was probably first described in 1771 by Francis Grapoli of Italy, and at about the same time by Gaspar Casal of Spain. Over the years, it has been a problem in various parts of the world, including Yugoslavia, parts of southern Africa, India, and the poorer areas of the southeastern part of the United States. The general pattern is that niacin deficiency has followed the spread of corn.

This is not really the fault of corn as a food. The nutritional worth of a plant cannot be reduced to its chemical analysis alone, and corn is a good example of this. While there are a number of variations on the basic method, corn was traditionally ground with a little lime water--water mixed with a little wood ash--which helped release the niacin. Among native American peoples using this method, niacin deficiency was not a significant problem. To gain the full nutritional worth of corn, you have to not only have the seed, and know how to grow it, you must also know and practice the proper preparation techniques.

In the early part of this century, pellagra was a major health problem in the areas of the South where corn grits and corn meal dishes were common in the diet. This scourge that was affecting poor people in many southern states was at first thought to be an infectious disease, but in 1915, Dr. Joseph Goldberg made a major breakthrough by showing that the disease could be cured through nutritional means. By the late 1930's niacin had been isolated and identified as the source of the prevention and cure of pellagra. The other major piece of the puzzle fell into place in 1945 when Dr. Willard Krehl showed that tryptophan, an amino acid in which corn is low, could be used by the body to produce niacin.

Besides pellagra, other deficiency symptoms generally involve the skin, digestive system, or nerve tissues. Early symptoms include skin eruptions, indigestion, loss of appetite, fatigue, and weakening of the muscles.

The niacin in food includes both nicotinic acid and nicotinamide. The most important role of niacin is as a component in 2 coenzymes which act with thiamine and riboflavin in the metabolism of fats, carbohydrates, and proteins. One of these is called coenzyme I, or diphosphopyridine nucleotide, or DPN. The other coenzyme is called coenzyme II, triphosphopyridine nucleotide. or TPN. Niacin also plays an important role in maintaining mental health, providing good circulation, reducing cholesterol, and synthesizing sex hormones.

The milling of grains causes the loss of 80-90 percent of the niacin. Much of the niacin in cereals is also in a bound form. The role of lime water in the preparation of corn is to make the bound niacin more available. Niacin is absorbed in the small intestine. Some niacin can be stored in the liver, but a daily supply is needed because the body's storage supply is limited, and any excess is excreted.

For every sixty milligrams of tryptophan that is eaten, we are able to make one milligram of niacin. This does not mean that the sixty milligrams of tryptophan are used up in making the one milligram of niacin--only a small percentage of the tryptophan we take in is converted into niacin --but that the body regulates its niacin production at this rate. Vitamin $B_6$ is necessary for the conversion.

The transformation of tryptophan to niacin is stated to "complicate" the setting of the RDA for niacin. It is assumed that this implies that some extra safely factor may be involved. Besides this complication, the other problem in setting the RDA has been the lack of studies, with the bulk of data used in setting the RDA coming from work done at two research centers over 30 years ago.

The most accurate way of expressing our need for niacin would be in niacin equivalents, with either one milligram of niacin, or sixty milligrams of tryptophan being equal to one niacin equivalent. The average American gets between 16 and 33 niacin equivalents per day. The two main studies found needs to range from 9.2 to 13.3 niacin equivalents. The RDA has been set at 6.6 mg per 1,000 calories, with the additional recommendation that intake not go below 13 milligrams, no matter how low the calorie intake. This includes a 50 percent safety factor.

Niacin is moderately soluble in hot water, and only slightly so in cold water. It is considered stable in the presence of alkali, acid, light, oxidation, and boiling. Intestinal bacteria are able to synthesize it in a process separate from the transformation of tryptophan. Vegetarian diets are more favorable to synthesis than some meat diets. Taking in too much sugar or starch, or using antibiotics can deplete niacin supplies. It should be remembered that herbs such as golden seal and certain foods such as garlic are also antibiotics. Niacin is not a major problem in a minimal area diet.

The name pantothenic means "that which is everywhere", or "from everywhere". Pantothenic acid is one of the more recently discovered nutrients, with the scientific literature for it beginning in the late 1940's. While no RDA has yet been set, this is indicative of our limited knowledge about it rather than its nutritional significance.

Pantothenic acid is almost everywhere--or at least in all living cells. In humans it plays a central role in the metabolism of fats, carbohydrates, and proteins. It is part of coenzyme A which is needed for acetylation. In order for the energy in foods to fulfill the body's needs, the substances containing this energy may either have to be recombined to make more complex compounds or broken down to make simpler ones. Coenzyme A plays an important role in this process.

Pantothenic acid helps form sterols, steroid hormones, cholesterol (which is needed by the body in proper quantities), fatty acids, and antibodies. It can be important in dealing with stress. Through its stimulation of the adrenal glands, pantothenic acid enables the body to produce more cortisone and other adrenal homones.

Deficiency in humans can be artificially induced, but has never been proven to occur under natural conditions. A deficiency may be possible with a diet that is high in processed foods. Deficiency symptoms include problems with the gastrointestinal system and the adrenal system. A healthy gastrointestinal system may be extremely important in improving the absorption of other nutrients which may be marginal in a minimal area diet.

While there is no RDA for pantothenic acid, Recommended Daily Allowances suggests that 5-10 milligrams per day may be adequate. The average American gets 5-20 milligrams per day. Robin Hur suggests 3 milligrams per 1,000 calories per day may be adequate.

Some pantothenic acid is lost at low cooking temperatures, and up to a third at the higher temperatures of baking. It can be destroyed either by acids or by alkali. As with many of the other vitamins, pantothenic acid is produced by bacteria in the intestine, but the usefulness of this synthesis and the factors governing it still need further research.


Vitamin $B_6$, or pyridoxine, is not a single substance, but includes pyridine, pyridoxal, and pyrdoxamine. It was first isolated in 1936. Vitamin $B_6$ deficiency due to poor nutrition is not a serious problem anywhere in the world. It does, however, play many important roles in the body, several of which help in making the best use of other nutrients.

Vitamin $B_6$ is needed for absorption of vitamin $B_{12}$. It helps make the best use of linoleic acid. It is necessary in the conversion of tryptophan to niacin. $B_6$ also helps in the production of hydrochloric acid for the gastric juices in the stomach. In all these uses, this vitamin helps maintain an adequate balance of other nutrients which are more likely to be marginal or deficient. In a minimal area diet it is important to consider the many factors relevant to the efficient use of critical nutrients.

Vitamin $B_6$ also plays roles in the metabolism of protein and fat, and in the production of red blood cells and antibodies. It provides energy for muscles by converting glycogen to glucose. A deficiency can bring on certain nervous conditions through its role in the chemistry of the brain and nervous system. $B_6$ also helps maintain the body's sodium and potassium balance.

While a deficiency in $B_6$ is not naturally found in people, for purposes of research it can be chemically induced. Because of the many important roles it plays in the body, there is a huge and diverse array of possible symptoms, which resemble deficiency symptoms for many of the other B vitamins.

Pyridoxine is highly soluble and comes in both free and bound forms. It can be synthesized in the intestine and some may even be absorbed. Such synthesis probably depends in large part on one's diet.

Vitamin $B_6$ is generally excreted in the urine within eight hours of ingestion. There is however some storage within the body, but even this has a half life of only about 15-20 days.

A high protein diet is stated to "complicate" the setting of an RDA for vitamin $B_6$. This appears to be a way of indicating that the RDA has been set especially high to allow for the large amounts of protein consumed by the average American. In one study, those on a low protein diet needed between 1.25 and 1.5 milligrams per day. In another study, 0.6 milligrams per day was sufficient in a diet providing 54 grams of protein daily, but was insufficient when the protein level was raised to 150 grams per day. Hur stated that when our protein intake is not excessive, that our vitamin $B_6$ needs should be about 20 micrograms per gram of protein. This is equal to one milligram for a diet containing 50 grams of protein. The RDA for adults is two milligrams, or about double this amount.

Besides avoiding excessive protein intake, there are other ways you can help your vitamin $B_6$ balance. Three-quarters of the $B_6$ in wheat is lost in milling. Many processed foods also have lost most of their $B_6$. Both alcohol and radiation increase the need for the vitamin. Having sufficient choline, linoleic acid, biotin, and pantothenic acid all help. While vitamin $B_6$ deficiency does not appear to be a problem in a minimal area diet, $B_6$ may be important in the efficient use of other nutrients.

Vitamin $B_{12}$ is a collective term for all the cobalt-containing corrinoids. It is present in every cell in our body. The soil is rich in $B_{12}$, for it comes originally from bacteria and fungi which are abundant in a healthy, living soil. Some algae such as seaweed also produce $B_{12}$. Animals can get significant amounts of the vitamin directly from the soil, as can we, when we nibble on a not-to-thoroughly-washed carrot from our garden. Concerns over pathogens make soil a questionable $B_{12}$ source for humans.

Plants do not need $B_{12}$, and while roots may pick up minute quantities from the soil, or leaves may pick up small quantities on their surface, plant foods are generally rejected as a source for our $B_{12}$ needs. All animals except humans synthesize part of their $B_{12}$ needs through the presence of microorganisms in their intestines. Actually, *we can* synthesize the vitamin, but there are complications that cause this route to be ruled out by most as a source for our $B_{12}$ needs. The routes generally thought to be left open, then, are through animal foods, such as milk, meat, and eggs, and through factory foods such as pills, or the crystalline $B_{12}$ that is sometimes added to soy milk and nutritional yeast.

In this context, vitamin $B_{12}$ and calories appear to be the two limiting factors in the design of a resource-efficient diet. Just as protein foods and protein combining have been used as the basis for designing diets, it is also tempting to design diets around their $B_{12}$ source. Laurel's Kitchen, one of the best works on vegetarian cookery and nutrition, comments that in the beginning of their search for an understanding of nutrition they thought of milk as the basic food in their diet. It still plays a central role in the sort of diet advocated in the book. The Farm's Vegetarian Cookbook relies heavily on $B_{12}$-supplemented soymilk and nutritional yeast in many of their recipes. In The Book of Tempeh by William Shurtleff and Akiko Aoyagi, tempeh, which is an excellent $B_{12}$ source, is referred to as the "Backbone of a Meatless Diet". Other diets have been advocated that have been built around comfrey, sprouts, or seaweed as the $B_{12}$ source. It appears that those seeking to avoid animal products are over-emphasizing vitamin $B_{12}$ in a pattern similar to what has happened with protein and amino acids. There are many indications that our understanding of vitamin $B_{12}$ will change in a few years in such a way that it will no longer be such a problem.

Buckminster Fuller, the creator of the geodesic dome, designed with an extensive knowledge of the materials with which he worked. Just as an artist might look at a block of marble and see a sculpture suggested in it, Fuller would consider the qualities of some of the new materials becoming available and see how they suggested new and innovative designs. The geodesic dome was suggested in part by some of the aluminum alloys then being developed. Fuller had an excellent knowledge of metallurgy and used this knowledge to create designs that anticipated the development of new and better aluminum alloys that he accurately predicted would be available within a decade or two.

We face a similar challenge with vitamin $B_{12}$. At present there is no simple, efficient solution ready for dissemination. At the same time, if we start down a path of research and development that assumes, for example, that milk is the answer to our $B_{12}$ needs, then we may find ourselves burdened with assumptions that will slow our progress towards more efficient answers to the question of how to produce a minimal area diet. It is important that we act with vision, as Fuller did, and begin designing with elements of the puzzle which may not be available yet, but can be expected to be available as simple and elegant answers in the not too distant future. We must also, of course, deal with our present need for an adequate vitamin $B_{12}$ balance.

Vitamin $B_{12}$ helps form a variety of enzymes including ones involved in the formation of nucleic acids such as RNA and DNA, which are necessary for cell division. $B_{12}$ plays an important role in the functions of most of the cells in the body. It is involved in our use of four of the amino acids, including methionine, and in our use of pantothenic acid, vitamin C, and iron. Vitamin $B_{12}$ also works with folic acid in the synthesis of choline.

Deficiency of vitamin $B_{12}$ can come either from having too little in the diet or from not absorbing enough from the foods that we do eat. In order for it to be absorbed, the $B_{12}$, which is called the extrinsic factor, must join with a substance secreted by the stomach, which is called the intrinsic factor. The intrinsic factor helps the $B_{12}$ move to the small intestine and attach itself to the wall of that part of the intestine called the ileum. There, but only in the presence of a calcium ion, the $B_{12}$ is absorbed by the mucosal cells in the wall of the ileum. After absorption, the body stores $B_{12}$ in the liver. It is the only B vitamin that the body can store in a significant way. It has a half-life of about 400 days, and enough can be stored to last for two or three years or even longer.

Most of the $B_{12}$ in foods is in a form that is easily absorbed if the absorption process is functioning properly. At low intake levels, below 0.5 micrograms, our absorption rate is about 70 percent. Absorption decreases with intake, but even at the RDA level of 3 micrograms, the absorption rate is still assumed to be at least 50 percent.

Serious absorption problems generally appear later in life and are probably inherited. Such people suffer from what is called pernicious anemia, which must be treated by injections of $B_{12}$, since ingested $B_{12}$ is not absorbed. Absorption gener-ally decreases with age, and can be limited by inadequate gastric acidity--too little

64

hydrochloric acid in the stomach. Deficiencies in iron, calcium, $B_6$, and folic acid can all limit absorption. If we consume large amounts of $B_{12}$ all at once, the absorption--even among people with no absorption problems--will be limited by the limited amount of available intrinsic factor.

Dr. Rudolf Ballentine states that "In cultures where food is grown organically and processed little or not at all, deficiencies in $B_{12}$ are uncommon, even where there is no meat, milk, eggs, or other animal foods in the diet." The subject of $B_{12}$ deficiency in vegans--people who do not consume animal products--has been a matter of considerable research and controversy. In an exhaustive review of nearly 20 studies on this subject, Dr. Alan M. Immerman* concludes that vegans usually have a normal $B_{12}$ status, and that "...pure dietary $B_{12}$ deficiency in all classes of vegetarians is the exception rather than the rule." A problem in many of the studies is that when deficiencies did occur, the studies could not adequately rule out the possibility of other explanations. The complex chain of requirements for proper absorption, storage, and retrieval suggests many possible alternative causes. Dr. Immerman gives criteria for more accurate diagnoses of dietary $B_{12}$ deficiency.

Deficiency symptoms can take five to ten years, or even as long as twenty years to appear. They can be extremely serious, especially the later symptoms. Since $B_{12}$ is needed for the production of RNA and DNA, which are needed for cell division, the first deficiency symptoms are usually associated with tissues in which there is rapid cell division, such as the bone marrow or the alimentary canal. Problems in the production of red blood cells in the bone marrow can cause a form of anemia called megaloblastic anemia, in which immature, oversized red blood cells are produced. The problems in the alimentary system can include an unhealthy tongue, indigestion, abdominal pains, constipation, and diarrhea.

The more serious, and generally later occurring symptoms involve the nervous system. Nerve damage due to deficiency is exhibited by symptoms such as numbness of the extremities and shooting pains. Such damage to the central nervous system can be extremely serious. Even if the deficiency is corrected, it takes the nervous system a long time to repair itself. It is possible for psychiatric symptoms to preceed anemia, but it may be that these are a cause rather than a symptom of deficiency. Some emotional distresses can reduce gastric acidity and possibly thus reduce $B_{12}$ absorption.

The average American takes in between five and fifteen micrograms per day, but the range of intake runs from one to one hundred micrograms. For those more accustomed to thinking in pounds, there are 454 grams in a pound, and one million micrograms in a gram. *The RDA is three micrograms, the F.A.O. recommends two micrograms, and Robin*

*Vitamin B12 Status on a Vegetarian Diet, <u>Wld. Rev. Nutr. Diet.</u> vol. 37, pp35-54, 1981.

*Hur suggests that 0.5 micrograms may meet our needs.* There is still considerable disagreement as to what our needs for $B_{12}$ are.

There is even more controversy concerning possible sources for the vitamin. $B_{12}$ has been reported as being contained in root vegetables, mung beans and sprouts, garbonzo bean sprouts, comfrey, peas, whole wheat, peanuts, lettuce, alfalfa, rice polish concentrate, legume root nodules, turnip greens, and fermented soy products such as tempeh. The presence of $B_{12}$ in all these foods is not constant, for it has not always appeared when some of these foods have been retested. More reliable sources, known to be rich in $B_{12}$, such as insects and snails, may be controversial because of people's food preferences and biases. Certain seaweeds are thought to be reliable sources. Healthy, organically cared for soils are a known source, and in India, well water is sometimes found to contain $B_{12}$.

| SOME JAPANESE SEAWEEDS HIGH IN VITAMIN $B_{12}$ | |
|---|---|
| Seaweed | Vitamin B12 content in mcg/100g edible portion |
| Cambarns clarkii - dried | 6.7 |
| Caulerpa racemosa - dried | 14.9 |
| Euphausia sp. - dried | 17.8 |
| Neomycic intermedia - frozen whole | 13.9 |
| Sergestes lucens | 10.1 |

An Australian study claiming to discredit comfrey as a useful source found that the average $B_{12}$ content of 100 grams of fresh comfrey leaf was 0.63 micrograms. In a study of tempeh made and sold in North America, the $B_{12}$ content ranged from 1.5 to 6.3 micrograms per 100 grams. The bacteria needed to produce the $B_{12}$ is not found in the pure tempeh starter that can be purchased commercially. It is, however, common in the environment, and can easily enter a batch of tempeh, especially if tempeh from one batch is used as starter for the next. Klebsiella is one of the bacteria, and has been isolated and found to produce sizable amounts of $B_{12}$. When klebsiella was added to a tempeh starter, the tempeh thus produced contained 14.8 micrograms of vitamin $B_{12}$ per 100 grams.

Assuming the FAO recommendations of 2 micrograms per day, and a tempeh starter containing klebsiella, whose tempeh could produce 14.8 mcg of $B_{12}$ per 100 grams of tempeh, you could get your $B_{12}$ needs from about 13.5 grams of tempeh, which you could produce from about half that weight of dry soybeans. *For a year's supply of vitamin $B_{12}$, this would amount to about 5.4 pounds of dry soybeans, which at Good biointensive* *yields could be produced in about 68 square feet.* Further research in both tempeh and soybean production will probably bring this area down still further. Tempeh can also be made using other legumes, grains, and sunflower seeds. Research is also underway in the use of sweet potatoes--which could greatly reduce the area required for the production of one's $B_{12}$ needs. Our needs might also be lower than two or three micrograms.

Another controversial possibility is to achieve $B_{12}$ adequacey through its production by the bacteria in our own intestines. For a long time it was thought that such $B_{12}$ producing bacteria existed only in the large intestine, well "downstream" from the site of absorption in the ileum in the small intestine. Still, vegans have persisted in showing adequacy in $B_{12}$, and none of the many possible explanations for this have been able to gain general acceptance.

In research presented in 1980*, it was found that significant amounts of $B_{12}$ were produced by bacteria in the small intestine. An important piece in the puzzle has fallen into place. In affluent parts of the world, our small intestines are inundated with any number of food additives, chemicals, and drugs which might destroy or interfere with a healthy population of intestinal flora. Antibiotics, which would directly kill $B_{12}$ producing bacteria, enter our bodies not only through prescribed drugs, but also in a steady trickle through almost all commercial animal products, which come from animals which have been grown from birth on feeds containing antibiotics. We must also consider that goldenseal and garlic have antibiotic properties that might interfere with the $B_{12}$ producing bacteria. More research is needed.

The intestines of most people in the Third World are under frequent attack from disease and parasites. Some intestinal parasites are known to destroy B vitamin producing bacteria, and many of the parasites of the tropics have not yet even been named and identified. If intestinal production of vitamin $B_{12}$ requires a healthy intestine which has not been inundated by chemicals, drugs, disease, and parasites, there are probably few such intestines around. Perhaps in a few years there will be a time-release pill that could "reseed" our intestines with healthy flora so that we could get a second chance at being self-sufficient in vitamin $B_{12}$.

Such possibilities certainly do not solve the present question of $B_{12}$. After his lengthy review of the subject, Dr. Immerman writes:

---

*Vitamin B12 Synthesis by Human Small Intestine Bacteria, M.J. Albert, V.I. Mathan, S.J. Baker, Nature 283: 781, 1980.

It is advised that physicians may be of valuable service to vegetarians by instructing such individuals to avoid factors which may cause $B_{12}$ deficiency (deficiencies of folate, $B_6$, or iron; use of alcohol or certain drugs; smoking); to be aware of the early signs of $B_{12}$ deficiency and to see their doctor in case these occur;  and check hematology and serum $B_{12}$ levels every 4-5 years. In the unlikely event that signs snd symptoms of deficiency occur, lactovege-tarians sould be advised to increase their consumption of dairy products, and vegans could be advised to consume seaweed, a reliable source of $B_{12}$, or $B_{12}$ supplements.

To this should be added that laxatives and oral contraceptives also deplete $B_{12}$. While an exact answer to the question of vitamin $B_{12}$ can not be given, neither should we allow the lack of sufficient research to dictate a focus on $B_{12}$ producing foods in the design of a minimal area diet.

# CALORIE NUTRIENTS

| Nutrient | RDA Women | RDA Men | Basis/Comments | Recommendations From Other Sources | Targets Women | Targets Men |
|---|---|---|---|---|---|---|
| Calories | 2000 | 2700 | Based on U.S. average: Man - 5'9", 154 lbs. Woman - 5'4", 128 lbs. | Use Calorie worksheet to determine your own personal needs. | 2000 | 2700 |
| Protein | 46 | 56 | .08g/kg (.363g/lb) body weight, 30% safety factor, and 52.5% efficiency in use assumed. | Needs may be less. | 46 | 56 |
| Amino Acids mg/kg body weight. | | | | Set at 150% of RDA due to lower digestability of vegetable proteins. Some sources suggest 100% increase. | | |
| Isoleucine | 12 | | | | 1044 | 1260 |
| Leucine | 16 | | | | 1392 | 1680 |
| Lysine | 12 | | | | 1044 | 1260 |
| Cystine+ Methionine | 10 | | | | 870 | 1050 |
| Phynalalanine+ Tyrosine | 16 | | | | 1392 | 1680 |
| Tryptophan | 3 | | | | 261 | 315 |
| Threonine | 8 | | | | 696 | 840 |
| Valine | 14 | | | | 1218 | 1470 |
| Histidine | No Adult RDA | | | | none | |
| Carbohydrates | none | | | 60% of calories as an aid in design. | 300 | 405 |
| Fat | none | | 15 to 25 grams needed for fat-soluble vitamins and essential fatty acids. | 10% of calories may ease transition to new diet. | 0/22g | 0/30g |
| Linoleic acid | 1-2% of calories | | | 1½% of calories | 3.33g | 4.50g |

# MINERAL NUTRIENTS

| Nutrient | RDA Women | RDA Men | Basis/Comments | Recommendations From Other Sources | Targets Women | Targets Men |
|---|---|---|---|---|---|---|
| Iodine, mcg | 110 | 130 | Iodized salt assumed to deal with our needs. | Soil iodine level is critical. | 110 | 130 |
| Zinc, mg | 15 | 15 | | Hur says high protein, calcium, calorie, sugar, and phytic acid levels raise need from 8 to 15 | 10 | 10 |
| Calcium, mg | 800 | 800 | Typical U.S. high protein diets require more calcium. | FAO/WHO + U.K. recommend 400-500 milligram. | 500 | 500 |
| Iron, mg | 18 | 10 | | Absorption is a major factor | 18 | 10 |
| Phosphorous, mg | 800 | 800 | | Excess can make calcium a problem. | 800 | 800 |
| Potassium, mg | none | | Healthy adults need about 2.5g/day. | | 2500 | 2500 |
| Magnesium, mg | 300 | 350 | | | 300 | 350 |
| Copper, mg | none | | | | 2 | 2 |

# VITAMIN NUTRIENTS

| Nutrient | RDA | | Basis/Comments | Recommendations From Other Sources | Targets | |
|---|---|---|---|---|---|---|
| | Women | Men | | | Women | Men |
| Vitamin A, RE | 800 | 1000 | See section for conversion of IU to RE | Diets of healthy traditional cultures high in Vitamin A. | 800 | 1000 |
| Thiamin, mg | 1.0 | 1.4 | 0.5mg/1000 calories. | | 1.0 | 1.4 |
| Riboflavin, mg | 1.2 | 1.6 | 0.6mg/1000 calories | | 1.2 | 1.6 |
| Niacin, ,g | 13 | 18 | 6.6mg/1000 calories and at least 13 mg. | Count 1 mg per 60 mg of tryptophan | 13 | 18 |
| Vitamin $B_6$, mg | 2.0 | 2.0 | Set high due to extra high U.S. protein level. | May be important in a diet marginal in other nutrients. | 2.0 | 2.0 |
| Vitamin $B_{12}$, mcg | 3.0 | 3.0 | | 2.0mcg recommended by FAO/WHO. | 2.0 | 2.0 |
| Folic Acid | .4 | .4 | | | .4 | .4 |
| Pantothenic Acid, mg | none | | 5-20 mg per day is typical | | 5 | 5 |
| Vitamin C, mg | 45 | 45 | Larger doses may be beneficial to health, reduce colds. | | 45 | 45 |
| Vitamin D | none | | normal adult needs met by sun exposure. | | none | |
| Vitamin E, IU | 12 | 15 | The minimum adult need when fatty acids are minimum are probably not more than 3-6IU | | 6 | 6 |
| Vitamin K | none | | Synthesized in intestine. | | none | |

# SELECTED ANNOTATED BIBLIOGRAPHY

Ballentine, Rudolf, M.D., <u>Diet and Nutrition</u>, The Himalayan International Institute, Honesdale, Pennsylvania, 1978 - an excellent overview of wholistic nutrition, integrates Eastern and Western medical perspectives.  Much interesting history as well.

Devore, Sally and White, Thelma, <u>The Appetites of Man</u>, Anchor Book, Anchor Press/ Doubleday.  Garden City, New York. 1978 - Health is viewed in many dimensions as the diets, environments, and cultures of nine healthy society's are examined.  Includes recipes, and broad lessons from these groups.

F.A.O./W.H.O. Expert Group, <u>Calcium Requirements</u>, World Health Organization, Geneva, 1962 - Includes information on groups with very low calcium intake.

Food and Nutrition Board, National Research Council, <u>Recommended Dietary Allowances</u>, 8th ed. National Academy of Sciences, Washington, D.C. 1974 - Gives explanations of the setting of the RDA's.  Should definitely be read if you are considering using different standards than the RDA's.

Heritage, Ford, <u>Composition and Facts about Foods</u>, Health Research, Mokelumne Hill, California, 1968 - Covers aspects of nutrition other sources don't--oxalic acid content of foods, digestion times, etc.  Mostly tables and charts, including food composition charts listing foods in order of concentration.

Hur, Robin, <u>Food Reform: Our Desparate Need</u>, Heidelburg Publishers, Austin Texas, 1975 - A somewhat radical examination of modern diets, disease, and nutrition.  Advocates a diet based around sprouts, greens, algae, and a calorie source such as potatoes. Extensively researched and well argued.  Covers problems of excess protein.

Labine, Pat; Burrill, George; and Nolfi, James, <u>The Home Grown Vegetarian</u>, Center for Studies in Food Self-sufficiency, Burlington, Vermont - An excellent effort in designing a home grown diet (complete diet takes 1½ acres).  Emphasizes protein, and problems of short-season climate.

Nutrition Search, Inc., John D. Kirschmann, dir. <u>Nutrition Almanac</u>, McGraw-Hill Book Company, New York, 1975 - Detailed examination of individual nutrients, including deficiency symptoms; nutrient content tables cover more nutrients than most other sources.  Based on extensive review of scientific literature.  Worth buying.

Robertson, Laurel; Flinders, Carol; Godfrey, Bronwen, <u>Laurel's Kitchen</u>, Bantam Books, New York, 1976 - Contains an excellent and readable explanation of nutrition as part of a vegetarian cookbook.  Excellent bibliography. A good place to start.

Shurtleff, William and Akiko Aoyagi, <u>The Book of Tempeh</u>, Harper and Row, New York, 1979 - Preparation and nutrition of tempeh.  A beautiful book.

U.S.D.A. <u>Food The Yearbook of Agriculture 1959</u>, The U.S. Government Printing Office, Washington D.C. 1959.  - While dated in some areas, it gives in depth yet readable coverage on most nutrients and is generally readily available in libraries.

# The Crops

By Cindy Gebhard

# INTRODUCTION

Some of the 14 crops selected for the initial minimal area diet are probably familiar to you, and you may already have a good sense of how to grow them, and may even have collected some baseline data for each. Others, like wheat, filberts, or sweet potatoes, you may never have grown before. Or, you may never have thought of growing a crop like parsley with the aim of maximizing yield. Whatever your background in food-raising, like most gardeners, you take pleasure in raising plants and are curious about them.

Your desire to learn from your plants and soil is your greatest attribute as you launch into growing your own food in a serious way. What one book says about turnips may contradict a second source, and your neighbors may do something completely different in growing their turnips. How then do you know the best way to proceed?

The answer is that you <u>observe</u>. Perhaps this sounds too passive. Conscious of the resources and space that you use in your gardening, you prepare your soil, transplant your seedlings, water, and then watch closely. The more contact that you have with your garden (and the fewer automatic devices that you employ to occupy <u>your</u> place in the garden), the more you will learn, and the better your yields will

become.  The crop-specific information that follows is only to get you started.  Though
I have tried to collect some of the more objective information available in the
literature, you will hopefully sift through the crop sections that follow, pick up
an idea or two, or possibly a revised "approach," and return to your garden.

Whether your garden is a spiritual retreat or a living laboratory, <u>experiment</u>.
The way to experiment is to try to alter just one variable in each trial.  Say that
you prepare your soil the same way, use the same mix and quantity of ammendments,
the same variety and apparent quality of seedlings, and the same watering methods.
Then, for example, for three years in a row you try planting collards at three different spacings in a 100 square foot bed, perhaps like this:

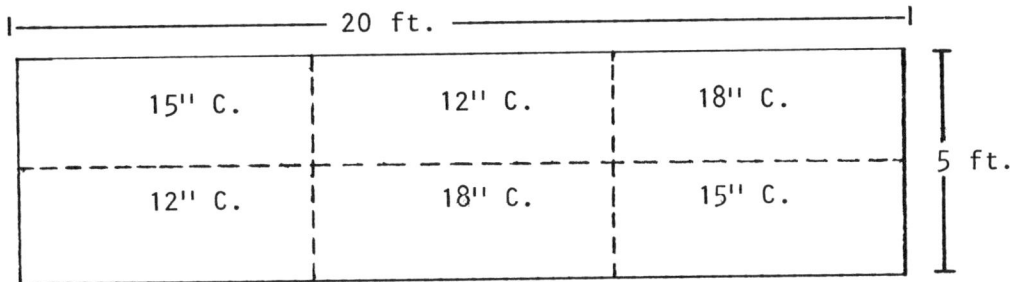

```
|———————————————————— 20 ft. ——————————————————|
 ┌────────────────┬────────────────┬────────────────┐   ⊤
 │                │                │                │   │
 │    15" C.      │    12" C.      │    18" C.      │   │
 │                │                │                │   │
 ├────────────────┼────────────────┼────────────────┤   5 ft.
 │                │                │                │   │
 │    12" C.      │    18" C.      │    15" C.      │   │
 │                │                │                │   │
 └────────────────┴────────────────┴────────────────┘   ⊥
```

The first year your highest yields may occur on the lower spacing.  The following
year you might modify your plan and plant the collards on say 10, 12, and 14 inch
centers.  Your best yields that year might alternate between the 12 and 14 inch
centers.  Planting on 12, 13, and 14 inch centers the following year would then be
a good approach.

In ten years you will have begun to focus in on an optimal spacing for collards,
and will also have learned a great deal about how your soil has changed over time,
and about collards in general!  By staying focused in your observations of the garden
as a whole, being consistent in your record keeping, and staying with a set of
standardized techniques for all your crops, you can learn much more than the limited
size and number of your replications might suggest.

Besides testing the spacing of your plants, you can eventually compare double-
dug versus U-barred beds, large transplants versus small transplants, or frequency
and quantity of watering, for example.  Remember that the biointensive method is an
entire system.  Changing one piece often produces unforeseen (and sometimes unex-
plained) results!  Rather than looking at different elements as good or as counter-
productive techniques, realize that the whole works as an integrated system.  For
instance, for close spacings to work, extra compost, deep digging, and frequent light
watering may be required.  Similarly, frequent light watering may not work without

the close spacings which create a dense special mini-climate; and too close or too wide a spacing will probably not work well at all.  By learning to view your garden as a system, you will better be able to trouble-shoot, and increase your garden's overall health and yield.

When you refer to the literature, it is important to keep in mind the frame of reference of the author(s).  Many agricultural books written before the 1920's, for example, come from an era in which farming was still small-scale and without the influence of mechanization or chemical fertilizers.  The ingenuity from these times may be just what you are needing now.  Modern works addressing the needs of small-scale, subsistence farmers (such as some materials from the Asian Vegetable Research and Development Center) can also be of great value.

Have patience during what may seem like endless trial and error.  Be conservative in making changes.  You have an important objective in mind--to provide for yourself.  Enjoy gardening, and above all, feel proud of your new or renewed attempt at "sustainable" living!  By providing for yourself in a sustainable way, you create a path that may also help others.  Welcome to the world community.

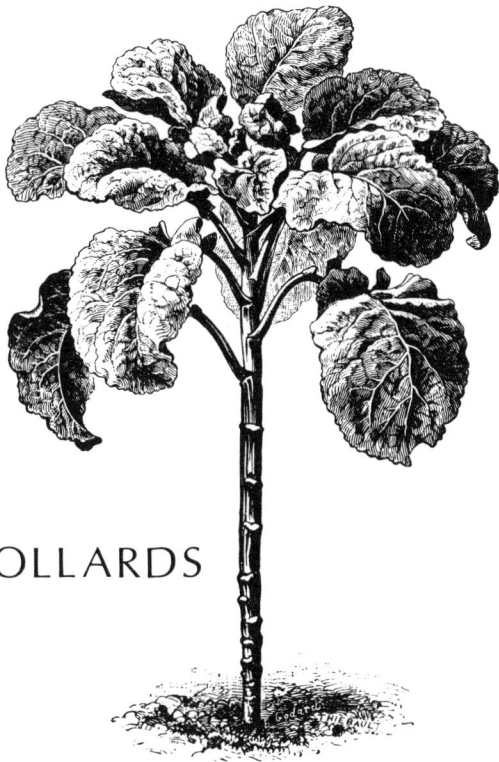

COLLARDS

Because they are a non-heading form of the cabbage family, collards, along with its very close relative kale, are often referred to as "primitive cabbages." Thought to be native to the eastern Mediterranean region or Asia Minor, collards are among the earliest cultivated cabbages known to the Greeks and Romans. Collards have been eaten by Europeans since the days of Pliny the Elder, a Roman writing in the first century A.D. No one knows when they arrived in this country, but they have become popular, particularly in the South where their heat-tolerant nature proves valuable.

USE:

Collards are often tossed in salads or cooked as steamed greens. They are rich in vitamins A and C and in minerals, particularly calcium. Compared to milk, raw collards contain 3% more protein and 72% more calcium on a pound for pound basis. Among collard eaters in the American South, collards cooked with a little vinegar is a favorite. One of the national dishes of Ethiopia, *yegomen kitfo,* is composed of buttermilk curds and collard greens. Collards are useful in soup and soup stock. Another common dish is to combine collard greens with salt pork or a hambone.

PLANT PHYSIOLOGY:

Most collards are biennials which are grown as annuals. While they are taller than kale, and the leaves are of a different color and shape, botanically both kale and collards are known as *Brassica oleracea var. acephala.* Where they are adapted, they will commonly reach a height of 3 to 4 feet. "Tree collards," which can act as perennials, can grow even taller.

CULTURE:

Collards are heat-tolerant but also winter-hardy in regions that have first frosts around October 30 or later (roughly Virginia and southward). They do best in a slightly acidic soil with a pH of 5.5 to 6.5.

The seeds can be sown early in protected flats and transplanted out about 4 weeks before the last frost date. Rapid growth is said to favor more tender greens. Growers need not be limited as to when to plant collards except where very high temperatures will cause bolting. Sown early in the summer, collard greens can be harvested at a time when other *Brassicas* and green leafy vegetables are few and far between. In the South, collards are also sown in the fall. The seeds should germinate in 3-10 days. Plant in biointensive beds on 12 inch centers. Once mature, the harvest period for biennial collards can last up to 24 weeks. If the collards start to bend and fall over, be sure to stake them for the best results.

## VARIETIES:

Georgia, Southern, Vates, and Louisiana Sweet are all common, heat-tolerant varieties. Vates is somewhat shorter in height. Here at the Ecology Action research site in Willits, California we have been very impressed by a perennial collard known as "Tree collards." We are currently testing them on 12, 15, and 18 inch centers. The advantages of these tall (up to 6 feet!) elegant collards are that: they can be harvested year-around; they generally grow without bolting, even in extreme heat or moderate cold; they are sweeter than the biennials, even in hot weather; and preliminary yields indicate that they may produce two times that of biennial collards, and possibly more. The leaves are often highlighted with red or purple, making them especially attractive. Several more years of testing will better define their yield potential and their nutritive value.. At some point we hope to make seeds for them available through the Bountiful Gardens seed catalog.

## POTENTIAL PROBLEMS:

The forces which affect collards are similar to those affecting other *Brassicas*. If bolting is a problem, try planting smaller seedlings. Cabbage loopers, blister beetles, and cabbage webworms can all be handpicked. Older or stressed plants can especially suffer from aphids. An aromatic companion such as garlic or mint may help as will a blast of water on the leaves. A good approach is to minimize stress as an integral part of your gardening.

## HARVEST:

Collards should be harvested about once a week. The rate at which you harvest can have an important effect on yields, with the correct rate stimulating growth and an excessive rate stunting it. Optimally, cut the leaves where they join the main stem when they are full-sized but not yet woody. Keep the main stem and the central

growing tip on the plant uncut so that each plant will continue to produce.  The flavor
is sweeter and better in cold weather, particularly after a frost.

STORAGE:

    Storing collards is normally not necessary, especially if a perennial variety
is grown.  Also, storage results in some vitamin loss.  If the leaves must be picked
ahead of time, keep them in a cool dark place.  The leaves can be dried.  In drying,
vitamins A and C are lost, but the minerals remain intact.

``Collard  Soup?``

## FILBERTS

The scientific name for filberts, *coryllis*, comes from the Greek word, *koris*, or helmet, which refers to the leafy covering of the nut that resembles a helmet. There are some 15 species of *coryllis* that might be called filberts, but some of these might also be called hazelnuts, wild hazelnuts, American filberts, or European filberts. The four relevant species in a discussion of food production are *C. maxima* and *C. avellana,* the European filberts, and *C. americana* and *C. cornuta,* the American filberts, also called hazelnuts or wild hazelnuts. Sometimes only *C. maxima* is being indicated in a reference to the filbert, but most cultivated filberts are a result of hybridization between the two native European filberts. *C. americana* is native to the eastern forests of North America, and *C. cornuta* is a native to the maritime northwest of North America.

Following the last ice age, filberts were probably the most important food plant in Europe. While pollen profiles suggest that people of the time may have helped in the distribution of the plant, stone age man did not domesticate the filbert. When the Saxons arrived in England around the fifth century A.D., they used filberts as a part of the hedgerows which they began, some of which have been maintained continuously since then. In hedgerows they thrived in a semi-wild state and were used in a number of ways by later groups who tended and expanded the hedgerows started by the Saxons. Today, the main filbert producers in Europe are Italy, Spain, and Turkey.

American filberts have been found in archeological sites in the Pacific Northwest dating back to the last ice age. 'Barcelona', a European filbert which is the principle cultivated variety in the U.S. today, was first introduced into this country just before the turn of the century. The earliest introduction into the Pacific Northwest came at about the same time. Today, some 98 percent of the U.S. filbert harvest comes from the protected inland valleys of the Willamette and Columbia rivers in Oregon and Washington. In the East, improved hybrids between American and European filberts are bringing hopes for increased home filbert production in that region.

USE:

    *C. avellana* was such an important part of the traditional hedgerow in part because of the many uses that could be made of the plant. Besides the nuts, which fed wildlife as well as people, the branches, or *hazel rods*, were woven into the hedges to give

80

strength to the *dead fence* that was part of the living hedge; the slender shoots, or suckers, were used for making crates and baskets; and branches were also used as water-finding dousing rods.  The nut meats can be boiled to extract an edible oil that has industrial as well as culinary uses.  The nuts themselves can be eaten alone or as part of other dishes.

PLANT
PHYSIOLOGY:

European filberts are winter hardy, and in fact have a fairly high chilling requirement, but they are also among the earliest flowering of all plants, making their nut production vulnerable to the ravishes of late winter and early spring weather.  Trees put  out both female flowers called pistillates, and male flowers called catkins, which look similar to the catkins on birch trees.  While there are male and female flowers on the same tree, the female flowers of one tree are generally not receptive to pollen at the same time that its catkins are ready to spread pollen.  More than one variety is needed, then, so that good pollination and good nut production can be achieved.

catkins

Filberts begin to bear at about four years of age, go through a phase of rapidly increasing yield between the ages of six and about ten or twelve, and then slowly continue to increase yields as they add bearing wood.  Filberts bear on wood added the previous season.  They have a relatively short life expectancy of only 50 years and are recommended for U.S.D.A. zones four to eight.

CULTURE:

To grow filberts from seed, the nuts should be gathered as soon as available and then stratified.  To do this, place the nuts in a moist growing medium such as peat, sand, or sawdust, and keep them overwinter at a temperature of between $32^{\circ}$ and $41^{\circ}$ F to break the nuts' natural dormancy.  They can be planted in a nursery bed in the spring.  Filberts can also be propagated vegetatively by layering.  In the spring, bend a sucker down and peg it firmly to the ground.  Cover the middle of it with three to six inches of soil.  This should root and put out more shoots to which can be added more soil to promote more roots.  In the fall or following spring, these new shoots can be cut into separate plants and grown in a nursery bed for a year before being planted in their final location. Growing a tree from seed will produce considerable variation, so better to use layering when trying to propagate from a high-yielding tree. Neither method will produce trees similar to the parent plant if it is a grafted tree. See the VARIETIES section for suppliers.

Filberts appreciate a deep, well drained soil, and may gain from a site protected from cold winter winds. Plant more than one variety for good pollination. The best mix is one pollinator per eight heavy bearing varieties. Single trees are used in the sample diets, but a cooperative effort among several families will produce better results. In larger plantings, it is good to mix early, medium, and late pollinators.

Filberts can be trained as trees or bushes. For a tree, prune the young plant to a single trunk with four to six main branches. For a bush, train to three main trunks and periodically thin out some of the large branches. Either way, good filbert maintenance should include the removal of suckers three to four times a year for good nut production. Since the nuts come from last season's wood, a light pruning each year can encourage new growth and thus higher yields.

Filberts need to be kept from drying out. In hot climates, white latex paint on the trunks has been recommended to protect young plants from sunburn. In areas where catkins are damaged by cold winter winds, it has been suggested that inexpensive coverings placed over individual catkins could provide the needed protection. Tubes of waxed paper might work. Particularly for intensive production, this could be a worthwhile procedure, and might only need to be done for the pollinator trees.


VARIETIES:

A discussion of varieties is complicated by the fact that there are four different species that have also been crossed to form hybrids. *C. avellana* produces a smaller tree than *C. maxima*, which produces larger, thin-shelled nuts. *C. cornuta* is quite hardy and is adapted to a wide variety of soil types. *C. americana* is resistant to Eastern filbert blight, a serious problem in many areas. While most commercial varieties are hybrids of the two European filberts, the term "hybrid filberts" is often used to refer to crosses of an American and a European variety. Much work was done on this during the 1940's, but many of the varieties have been lost. Most European varieties are generally grown only in the West, due to their susceptibility to Eastern filbert blight. Descriptions of these are given below:

Barcelona - this is the most successful and widely available filbert for the West, but is highly vulnerable to Eastern filbert blight. It is slow growing, but reaches a height of 18 feet and an even wider spread. Its best pollinator is Daviana, but it is also pollinated by Du Chilly and Royal.

Royal - Royal is a good pollinator and also produces an early crop of large, thin-shelled nuts. It grows to 18 feet with a similar spread. It is the result of a cross between a Barcelona and a Daviana and is best pollinated by Daviana.

Du Chilly - produces high quality, large, long nuts that need to be knocked from the tree and husked. It has a height and spread of 15 feet and is pollinated by Daviana.

Daviana - This is the superior pollinator. It is pollinated by Barcelona or Hall's Giant to produce a light crop of long, medium-sized nuts of good quality.

Hall's Giant or Bolwyer - Has large nuts, pollinated by Barcelona, Royal, or Daviana.

Ennis - Developed at Oregon State University at Corvallis. Has higher yields and a higher percentage of filled nuts. It is pollinated by Butler or Hall's Giant.

In the East, Italian Red is the most productive variety, while Medium Long and Gosford are the hardiest. Two important native varieties are Rush, which is a good bearer, and Winkler, a native of Iowa, which is hardy to thirty below and also produces decent sized wild hazelnuts. These natives have been used to produce hybrids that have some resistance to Eastern filbert blight, such as Bixley and Buchanan. Bixley is a cross between Rush and Italian Red and is hardy, a good bearer, and suitable for the East. Sources, including those for hybrids, are listed below.

Al Bacharach Inc., 17490 Westview Rd., Lake Oswego, OR, 97305 - carries Butler and Ennis, wholesale only.

Burnt Ridge Nursery, 432 Burnt Ridge Road, Onalaska, WA, 98570 - grafted varieties.

Burpee Seed Company, Warminster, PA, 18991.

California Nursery Company, Niles District, Fremont, CA 94536 - carry Royal.

Fowler Nurseries, Inc., and Garden Center, 525 Fowler Road, Newcastle, CA, 95658 - free pricelist, catalogue $1.

Grimo Nut Nursery, R.R. 3 Lakeshore Road, Niagara-on-the-Lake, Ontario, Canada, LOS IJO - carries hybrid filberts that are especially hardy.

John H. Gordon Jr., 1385 Campbell Blvd. N. Tonawanda, NY, 14120 - carries hybrid filberts.

Louis Gerardi Nursery, R.R. 1 Box 143, O'Fallon, IL, 62269 - carries a large selection of grafted filberts.

Northern Nut Growers Association, R.R. 3, Bloomington, IL, 61701 - $10 membership, can help locate specific needs through newsletter.

St. Lawrence Nurseries, R.D. 2, State Route 56A, Potsdam, NY, 13676 - hybrid filberts.

Waynesboro Nurseries, Waynesboro, VA, 22980

The Wayside Gardens Company, Hodges, SC, 29695 - catalogue, $1--refunded with order.

Willis Stribling Nursery Company, 1620 W. 16th street, Merced, CA, 95340.


## POTENTIAL PROBLEMS:

Eastern filbert blight is the filbert's most serious disease.  In the East, it seriously limits the varieties that can be grown, and in the West, it was discovered in southwest Washington about 15 years ago.  It can kill young trees and cause severe die-back on older ones.  It is not a serious problem to *C. americana,* and some of this resistance can be inherited in hybrids.  In commercial operations in the Pacific Northwest, bacterial blight and powdery mildew can also be problems.

Both young and old plants can be attacked by mice and rabbits in the winter, and protection may be advisable.  Squirrels and chipmunks may take the nuts if the trees are not protected from them.  Winter damage to early catkins can hurt nut production.  Research has suggested that it is not the cold itself that damages the catkins as much as the cold, dry winds that dry them out and kill them.  The English hedgerows may have provided the ideal protected environment for sheltering the catkins.


## HARVEST:

Nuts should be gathered frequently, and those from the Du Chilly variety should be knocked from the tree.  If rain splatters dirt on the nuts, they should be cleaned.


## STORAGE:

In the shell, filberts will store for several months in a cool location.  They can also be shelled and sun-dried to extend their storage period.  The meats are sufficiently dry if they snap when bitten.

# ONIONS, LEEKS, and GARLIC

Onions, leeks, and garlic are all members of the *Allium* (Lily) family and are similar in many ways. Each is started in cool, damp weather and to mature, requires drier, warmer weather. Historically, all three have been used as vegetables since ancient times. Onions (*A. cepa*) go back as far as 5000 B.C. when they were used by Chaldeans. Native to western or central Asia, onions are mentioned in the Bible as something for which the Israelites longed for in the wilderness. Leeks (*A. porrum*) are thought to have originated in Switzerland. During the Middle Ages in Europe, leeks were quite popular and remain so today. In England in 1726, Townsend said that "leeks are mightily used in the kitchen for broths & sauces." Garlic (*A. sativum*) has a long history as well. Over the years it has been valued for its superb "burning" flavor, its antibiotic and repellent qualities, and among various peasant peoples, for its alledged aphrodisiac qualities. Though they disliked the odor, the Romans must have appreciated garlic's food value, having fed it to their laborers "to strengthen them" and to their soldiers "to excite courage."

USE:

Onions, leeks and garlic can all be used cooked or raw, in salads, in soups, in casseroles, or in almost anything. They are a favorite with potatoes in soup. Onion juice is said to be effective on bee or wasp stings. Leeks are milder than onions and are delicious braised whole. Save the greener tougher upper leaves of the leek for soup broths. Standard recipes are much too conservative in their use of garlic. The cloves can be lightly fried or steamed and eaten whole. They are great in stews or cooked with other vegetables. Some like to rub a salad bowl with raw garlic before mixing the salad to impart the garlic flavor throughout. Garlic, more so than other *Allium* family members, contains sulfide of allyl, which has been used as everything from a mole repellent to a disinfectant.

PLANT PHYSIOLOGY:

Onions:   Onions are a biennial and sometimes a perennial. Their form, color, and size vary greatly with variety but all possess a prominent "storage" bulb that we commonly eat as the onion.

Leeks:   Leeks, a true biennial, are eaten for both their small bulbs and also for their sheath of flat leaves, mistakenly called a stem.

Garlic:   Garlic is a smaller, perennial plant that forms a bulb which can be broken into separate, thinly skinned components called cloves. Individual cloves are propagated to grow new garlic plants.

CULTURE:

Onions:   Like garlic and leeks, onions do best in a friable, somewhat sandy soil, or in an organic soil, so that their bulbs can adequately develop. It is cheaper and safer (in terms of bringing in pests and diseases) to start seeds in flats rather than planting sets. Depending on the climate, you can plant onion seeds in either late summer or mid-winter. Where winters are mild, plant flats between August and October. In colder climates, seeds are normally started in a greenhouse in February or approximately 10-12 weeks before they are needed for outdoor beds. Optimum germination occurs at 60-65° F but the range is 50-75° F. The general wisdom is to plant as early as possible for higher yields since the cooler, moister conditions of spring promotes greater top growth before the longer daylengths and heat of summer initiate bulbing. The seeds can be planted as close together as is manageable in the flats. Much further apart than ½ inch and you will be tripping over the large number of flats needed. The flats are normally set outside after the last hard frost (light frosts are not damaging), hardened off slightly, and then transplanted. The seedlings will hopefully be about 6 inches tall and between 1/4 and 3/8 inches in diameter. The biointensive spacing for onions is 3-4 inches. The seedlings should be set about 1 inch deep and the soil tamped firmly around each one. Some clip the onion tops by as much as a third before transplanting. Plant them where they will get plenty of sun.

If you use sets instead of seed (you can grow your own sets), plant directly in the bed at the time you would otherwise transplant seedlings. Soaking the sets in water or compost tea prior to planting may give them a boost. Stick the bulbs about ¼ inch into the soil, leaving the tip exposed. Firm the soil around the bulb. Whether you are buying sets or growing your own, aim for bulbs about 1/2 to 3/4 inches in diameter. Bulbs which are too large are likely to bolt and the smaller ones will never take off. If you store sets, cold (32° F) temperatures are best to prevent bolting. To grow your own sets, plant a section at very close spacing, less than an inch, and harvest as you would for larger onions.

After the planting-out stage, onions need relatively little care, only timely observation. Because of their shallow and condensed root systems, onions are fairly sensitive to weeds. It is best to pull weeds when they are small to avoid damage to the onion roots, which will in turn reduce bulb growth. Another thing to watch out for is flowering. Onion flower stalks should be pinched as soon as you see them because they intercept energy that would otherwise go to the bulb. Once having flowered, the bulbs should be harvested soon afterward before their inner core becomes tough.

Leeks:

Start leeks from seed at about the same time as onions in mid- to late winter, or in spring if you choose. The common advice is to plant out leeks when they are 6 to 8 inches high and perhaps 3/8 inches thick. Knott, in his Handbook for Vegetable Growers, recommends planting out leeks in June or July when they are 1 to 2 inches in diameter! Whether or not to blanch your leeks is a matter of preference. Green leaves will be higher in vitamin A. The leek seedlings can be placed in 6 inch deep holes and allowed to fill in naturally over the season, which effectively blanches the lower leaves; or they can be planted so that just the bulb of the leek is buried and the plant stands erect. Trimming the roots and the tops just before planting out is also an option. As with onions, the formation of the flower stalks may toughen the edible portion. In the biointensive system, leeks are planted in the bed on 4 to 6 inch centers. One source recommends double transplanting leeks, once when they are 3 inches high and then to the bed when they are 5 inches high. We suspect that thicker transplants may produce higher yields.

Garlic:

Unlike onions and leeks, garlic is almost always propagated from the cloves which are the bulblets composing the mother bulb. Plant the cloves in flats at the same time as onion seed, at 1 inch centers, with the sharp ends up and sticking out of the soil or just barely covered with soil. In mild winter areas, garlic is planted in the fall for an early summer crop. Also, like onions, garlic is weed-sensitive and needs good sun exposure in the beds to produce bulbs. The bulk of the garlic bulb weight is put on in the last 45 days of growth. If you save your own bulbs for planting be aware that they ideally need a chilling period of 1 to 2 months at $32^{\circ}$ F to $50^{\circ}$ F before planting in order to induce bulb formation. More than a hundred years ago, Vilmorin Andrieux in The Vegetable Garden said that "gardeners are in the habit of twisting the fully-grown stem into a knot, in order to increase of size of the bulb." This practice may be analogous to bending over the tops shortly before the plants are pulled out of the ground.

VARIETIES:

Onions:

Popular onion varieties that also store well include Early Yellow Globe, Yellow Globe Danvers, Southport Yellow Globe, and White Portugal. When choosing an onion variety, remember that the formation of the bulb is determined by the length of daylight so that, like soybeans, each cultivar is adapted over a limited range of latitude, which is noted in terms of hours of sunlight per day. For example, Red Wethersfield needs 14 hours of sunlight/day in its maturity period whereas Yellow Bermuda

needs only 12. A favorite in the Common Ground garden in Willits, CA.
are the Red Torpedo onions.

Leeks:

Leek cultivars vary in their size, winter-hardiness, and earliness.
Check the latest catalogues for varieties that match your needs.

Garlic:

Garlic is generally of two types: common, such as California White,
and giant, such as the Elephant varieties. Biointensive yields in How
To Grow More Vegetables... and the standardly available nutritional information on garlic that is presented in this book are based on common
garlic varieties.

## POTENTIAL PROBLEMS:

Thrips and onion maggots can bother onions. Healthy plants, occasional rotation,
and the use of seed or homegrown bulbs should minimize the chance of these insects in-
festing. Garlic and leeks are quite hardy and pest-resistant but can be prone to the
same problems that affect onions.

## HARVEST:

Onions
&
Garlic:

Onions and garlic both are harvested when their tops die back.
Once die-back begins, bend over all the tops to hasten their ripening.
After the tops have died back substantially, loosen them with a fork
and let them lie in place for a few days. Then pull up the plants to
lie in the sun for about two weeks to dry or "cure" them. If the
weather is rainy, take them off the ground and place under a cover.

Leeks:

Leeks take a good seven months from seed. Harvest just before the
freezing weather unless the varieties you plant can overwinter. Dig
around the plants if necessary to facilitate harvesting them without
breakage.

Onions
&
Garlic:

Once the bulbs are cured, store by either braiding and hanging them, or by clipping the tops ½ inch above the bulb and storing in mesh bags or in trays made from screen or hardware cloth. In either case the room should be ventilated, cool, and dry. Damaged bulbs will rot and cause other bulbs to rot; use these early on rather than storing. Seymour's The Self-Sufficient Gardener illustrates the onion braiding process well.

Leeks:

Store the leeks unwashed. Any soil around the roots will help to keep them from wilting. Stored in bunches, with the roots grouped together and occasionally moistened, in a cold ($32^{\circ}$ F) location, leeks will keep for 2-3 months. Another method is to pack them or "heel" them in soil in a root cellar.

# PARSLEY

Parsley has been a common ingredient in the diet since at least the first century A.D.  A frequent seasoning is salads and sauces, this pungent herb was thought to absorb the intoxicating fumes of wine, thereby preventing drunkenness.  During the Middle Ages, parsley was grown for medicinal purposes in monastic and other herbal gardens, with its beneficial effects coming perhaps from its high content of minerals and vitamins A and C.  Probably native to southern Europe, it was not until 1806 that the first documented use of parsley occured in the U.S.

## USE:

Though frequently seen on dinner plates, parsley is quite often used only sparingly in each dish--most often as seasoning or decorative garnish.  Low in calories, but concentrated in vitamins and minerals, parsley is a good nutritional complement to foods like potatoes.  Fresh parsley adds a good edge to salads.  Middle Eastern tabouli (see Lappe's _Diet For A Small Planet_ for a recipe) even uses fresh parsley as a main ingredient.  The herb is also frequently added to soups, stews, tomato sauce, vegetable pies, and to dishes containing members of the onion family (parsley is a natural breath sweetener).

## PLANT PHYSIOLOGY:

There are five species of parsley.  The plain-leaved _(Petroselinum hortense)_ and the curly-leaved _(Petroselinum crispum)_ forms are most commonly grown.  The plain-leaved type is thought to be more flavorful.  The curly-leaved type is probably chosen as a garnish because it stays fresh-looking longer.  Other forms include the celery-leaved or Neopolitan, the fern-leaved, and the turnip-rooted (which is grown for its parsnip-like root).  The plain-leaved and celery-leaved types are both sometimes confusingly called "Italian" parsley.  All varieties of parsley are biennial and are usually replaced in the second year when the flower stalk appears.

## CULTURE:

Because it is aromatic and may help in insect control, parsley is thought to be a companion plant to most other vegetables. For this reason consider spreading your parsley throughout the garden--in odd corners or at the ends of beds where it can be left for a full year without being disturbed. Partial shade is desirable. The seed is sown shallowly in flats, usually in the early spring but up until late summer, and is quite slow to germinate (expect to wait a month at least, maybe two). Various tricks are described in getting the seeds to germinate more quickly. Most involve chilling the seeds while keeping them moist for up to a two week period before planting.

Parsley roots are sensitive to transplanting so take extra care that the roots remain intact and are only minimally exposed to the air. The highest parsley yields using the biointensive method are acheived with plants spaced 4 to 10 inches apart, probably at the closer end of the range. The plain-leaved species will withstand frost but will not produce foliage during prolonged freezing weather.

## VARIETIES:

The plain-leaved type of parsley may be more cold and wet-tolerant than the curly-leaved . The main distinctions between available parsley varieties are species-distinctions, and are covered in the Plant Physiology section.

## POTENTIAL PROBLEMS:

Parsley is relatively free from diseases but watch for insects like cabbage loopers, parsleyworm, celery leaftier, carrot rust fly, and strawberry mites. Gophers seem to enjoy parsley and will gnaw clean through the root just at the base of the plant.

## HARVEST:

It is best to harvest parsley continually, picking the outer leaves singly just as they mature. Harvesting in this manner probably optimizes yield and possibly nutrition although more study on this is needed. Any flower stalks should be cut off unless seed is desired.

## STORAGE:

Fresh parsley is best used immediately after picking when it is crisp and green. In many areas, with well-timed plantings, fresh parsley can be kept available year-around. Store at cool temperatures if necessary. Parsley for drying can be picked and hung in bunches, however, unlike other herbs, it is difficult to dry parsley thoroughly in this manner except possibly under hot, dry conditions. Instead, parsley can be dried in a 100$^{\circ}$ F oven over a 12 hour period, or at 400$^{\circ}$ F in 15 minutes. Watch the plants carefully if the latter method is chosen so they will not scorch or burn. Once dry the leaves and stems can be crushed to reduce their volume and then placed in small airtight containers.

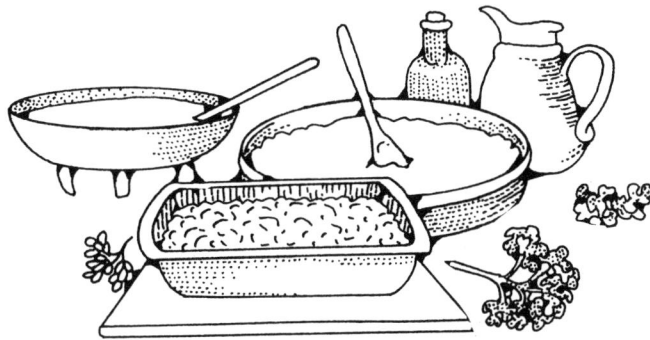

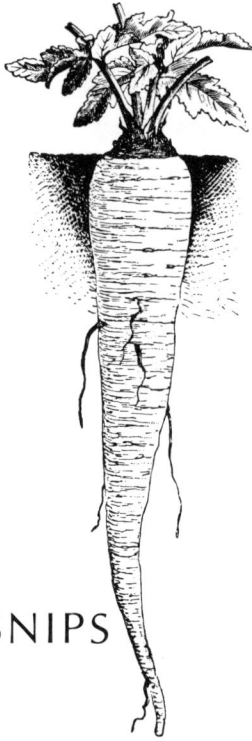

# PARSNIPS

The cultivated parsnip (*Pastinca sativa*) was first recorded by Columella in the first century A.D. and is a native of Europe, probably northeastern Europe. It seems that the parsnip was more popular prior to the 18th century than it is today. Waverly Root, in his book Food (1980), speculates that the acceptance of the potato in Europe led to a decline in parsnip consumption, since both were starchy vegetables and the potato had a more popular flavor. In 1552, parsnips and the European broad bean were said to have been staple foods during Lent (when meat was abstained from). Parsnips and salt cod were also a favorite combination.

## USE:

In Roman times, parsnips were used both medicinally and also for their food value. The foliage, however, is indigestible. Parsnips are frequently served boiled, sliced, and lightly fried, and are used in soups and soup broth. One writer admits to eating raw parsnip sandwiches!

## PLANT PHYSIOLOGY:

Parsnips are a hardy biennial with a large swollen tap root. The seeds are short-lived and normally lose their viability after one year of storage. You should be sure to start with fresh seed each year.

## CULTURE:

Just as with parsley, due to their slow germination, parsnips are planted early--in late winter or early spring. A soil temperature of 60-70° F is best for germination. Planted later in spring, the crop yield may be smaller but the roots can be more tender. Parsnip flavor is improved by cold weather and is therefore less commonly grown in the deep South. If grown in the South, plant in the fall and let it mature through the winter. Be sure to harvest before the warm weather. Though generally hardy, parsnips are said to be sensitive to weeds during their early growth.

VARIETIES:

Widely available parsnip cultivars include Harris Model (120 days), All American (105 days), and Hollow Crown (105 days).

POTENTIAL PROBLEMS:

Parsnips are affected by some of the same insects that bother parsley--the carrot rust fly and the parsleyworm (also called the celeryworm)--as well as the parsnip leaf-miner and the parsnip webworm. Canker, a fungal disease, can be a problem in cool, wet soils.

There has been some concern over psoralens, a group of chemicals found in parsnips. Most evidence concerns their use as a tanning agent on the skin. No toxic effects have ever been reported from people eating parsnips, but skin problems have resulted among vegetable handlers and processors. In one scientific article, four to five milligrams is cited as being an effective tanning agent when applied to the skin and exposed to light. Another article cites this information to assert that this amount "might be expected to cause some physiological effects under certain circumstances." A book uses this information to state that 5 mg, the amount found in 3 ounces of parsnips, is a toxic amount. Scary reports about food help sell books, but there are genuine concerns that parsnips may be carcinogenic. Check the literature for yourself. There is as yet no definitive answer.*

HARVEST:

For the best flavor, leave the roots in the ground until after the first few frosts and then harvest as needed.

STORAGE:

Parsnips can be left in the ground if they are harvested before the leaves start to grow again. They may also be put into clamps like potatoes and turnips (see Turnips), or put into a trench, laid flat, and covered with about six inches of soil.

---

* These journal articles can probably be found in any small college library and in many public libraries:

M. Berenbaum, Science, vol.201 (1978), p.532.
M. Ashwood-Smith, et.al., Nature (London), vol. 285 (1980), p. 407.
I.G. Wayne, et.al., Science, vol. 213 (1981), p. 909.

# PEANUTS

Peanuts, groundnuts, and goobers are common terms for this below-ground pea so popular in the world diet. Native to the South American tropics, peanuts were carried by early slave ships to Africa, and then again to the U.S. where they were introduced during colonial times. Leading regions of peanut production today are in China, India, West Africa, and the U.S.

<u>USE:</u>

Before the advent of peanut butter, peanuts were first used in the U.S. for fattening animals, particularly turkeys, pigs, and chickens. The peanut plant is still fed to animals. It is high in protein and fat, yet low in minerals. Hogs fed too much peanut in their diet will produce flabby meat known as "soft pork." Today 63% of U.S. peanuts go into peanut butter, a product first discovered in 1890 by a St. Louis physician who began prescribing peanuts to his elderly patients as a nutritious high-protein, low-carbohydrate food easy to digest. Peanuts are also eaten whole either raw, dry-roasted, or parched. One method of roasting peanuts is to bake them in the shells at 300° F for 20 minutes, allowing them to cool while still in the shell.

Processing affects both the nutrition and the shelf-life of peanuts. Heat generally improves the flavor, aroma, and texture of the peanut, but decreases its thiamin content and reduces the shelf-life of the oil component by destroying natural antioxidants. Blanching or removing the skins also reduces the thiamin content since the vitamin is concentrated in the skins. Other vitamins in peanuts remain stable in the roasting process.

Peanut recipes include such diverse items as peanut soup, peanut flour bread, peanut desserts, peanuts cooked with vegetables, and peanuts as a coffee substitute, which was drunk by Americans during World War II.

<u>PLANT PHYSIOLOGY:</u>

The cultivated peanut (Arachis hypogaea) is a low, annual legume. Peanut pods (they are not a true nut) contain as many as 1 to 6, but usually only 1 to 3, seeds (peanuts). Two types are distinguished: one in which the peanuts are clustered at the base of the plant--the bunch type, and the other in which the peanuts are strung along the prostrate branches--the runner type. The runner types have a seed dormancy period in which they will not germinate of up to two years, whereas the Spanish peanuts, a bunch type, have none.

The bright yellow flowers are staminate and obvious, whereas the productive pistillate flowers are inconspicuous. After self-fertilization, the latter bury themselves to form peanuts. Loose raised soil around the plants will help the neophyte peanuts, commonly called pegs, to easily bury themselves.

Unshelled peanuts contain 25% protein and 33% fat. Shelled they contain 25-30% protein and 40-48% oil. They are rich in thiamin, riboflavin, and niacin.

CULTURE:

Peanuts are a long (110-140 days) hot-weather crop, therefore commercially their production has mostly been limited to the Southeast and Southwest. Healthy peanut plants can withstand a light spring or fall frost, and with season extenders, have been grown as far north as Michigan, Massachusetts, and South Dakota. A light textured (i.e. sandy), fairly acidic soil (pH 5-6.2) is usually recommended for growing peanuts, but a heavy soil that is made friable, such as by the addition of organic matter and cultivation, can accomodate peanuts. Peanuts are planted shelled, with skins intact, after the danger of late spring frost has passed, or when the soil temperature has reached 65-70$^{\circ}$ F.

Experiments show that most peanuts, especially the Spanish type, benefit from innoculation. Of course the conditions of testing may be very different from those of your garden so you might experiment. Peanuts are reputed to be capable of using nutrients not available to other crops, an observation which usually reinforces the advice that extra fertilizers will not improve yields. On the other hand, peanuts "mining" ability is what allows them to easily deplete a soil. The following Virginia rotation uses peanuts once every three years:

>     1st year--corn followed by crimson clover as a winter cover
>     2nd year--early potatoes followed by cowpeas
>     3rd year--Spanish peanuts followed by rye as a winter cover.

Peanut kernels are usually planted 1½-4 inches deep, the more shallow depth in cool, wet regions. Under optimum conditions, the seed can germinate within 8 days. In less than optimal conditions, the process may take up to 2 weeks. In cool climates especially, peanuts are often started under glass and transplanted after frost danger. How To Grow More Vegetables... recommends starting peanuts in flats and transplanting out on 9 inch centers. Before blossoming, and in the last month before harvest, peanuts need only 50-60% of the water required just after blossoming.

## VARIETIES:

American peanuts are of three main groups:  Spanish, a bunch type, Valencia, a bunch type, and the collection of runner varieties which include the traditional Virginia peanut.  The runner type is sometimes called the Virginia type.  Also, some of the runner varieties have been bred to be semi-erect, such as the Virginia bunch and the North Carolina bunch.  Spanish peanuts have the shortest growing season (100-120 days), are small-kerneled, and are the most widely distributed peanut.  Another short-season type, Valencia (120 days), is large-kerneled, often 3-seeded, and grown chiefly in New Mexico.  Virginia peanuts take 120-140 days to mature, have large pods, and are grown mainly in southeastern Virginia and northeastern North Carolina.  Other runner types take 140+ days and are grown commercially in Alabama, Georgia, and Florida.  One of the quickest maturing peanut varieties is Pronto, a Spanish type, which can take only 90 days.  An abbreviated list of peanut varieties and sources from Richard & Shirley Flint's article on peanuts in the April 1981 Organic Gardening follows:

| TYPE | VARIETY | DAYS TO MATURITY | SOURCES |
|------|---------|------------------|---------|
| Virginia | Early Bunch | 120 | Geo W. Park |
| Virginia | Jumbo (Vine) | 120 | Burpee |
| Virginia | NC 17 | 112 | Gurney |
| Spanish | Early No 1 | 100 | Gurney |
| Spanish | Unidentified | 110 | Burpee |
| Spanish | Unidentified | 110 | Geo W. Park |
| Valencia | Tennessee Red | 120 | Geo W. Park |

The authors note that longer-season varieties, given adequate maturing time, generally are higher yielding.  Experimenting with the tradeoffs of long and short season peanuts in terms of yield and in-ground time might be especially important for someone attempting to grow a minimal area diet.

## POTENTIAL PROBLEMS:

Insects which affect soybeans, such as the leaf hopper and the velvetbean cater-pillar, may also bother peanuts.  Leaf spot diseases, indicated by small brown spots on the leaves, can decrease yields and are worst in very hot weather.  Rotation can minimize root rots.  Peanut growers should be aware of a yellow-green mold called *Aspergillus flavus* which sometimes freckles or covers the surface of shelled peanuts. This mold can produce the carcinogen aflatoxin.  Infected nuts and shells should be discarded.

## HARVEST:

The best yields will be gained when the harvest is timed just right.  Picked too early, the peanuts significantly shrink in size after drying.  The Spanish type, if left too long in the ground, can sprout. You can loosen the soil slightly, reach under, and pull off a pod or two each day as the crop nears completion to check for ripeness. You want to wait to harvest the plants until the peanuts are fully mature.

When immature, the peanut shells are soft, white, and spongy, and the kernels are watery and bland-tasting. As they mature, the kernels grow plumper and develop a distinct texture and color in their skins characteristic of the variety. The inside of the shell should begin to show color and darkened veins. In areas where frost threatens, it may not be possible to leave the peanuts in the ground until full develop-ment. Some say to harvest just before the first frost (unless you are able to protect the plants). Others say to leave the plants in the ground until the foliage is com-pletely damaged. If picked and left on the vine to dry, some additional ripening will occur. Remove the peanuts from the plants when they rattle and continue to dry them in their shells in an airy place. Save the nitrogen-rich vines and shells for the compost pile!

## STORAGE:

Adequate drying is necessary to prevent mildew and rot. The USDA recommends not more than 8% moisture for unshelled peanuts and 6% if shelled. Rancidity, a problem especially for the shelled crop, is best controlled through a low moisture content. Commercial storage rooms are kept at about 60% relative humidity. The traditional way to cure peanuts is in stacks 6 to 8 feet high, placed 1 foot off the ground. The peanut vines are stacked around a single pole with pods placed to the center. The stack is then topped with grass or canvas and left for 3-6 weeks before threshing. It is probably best to dry small quantities in a protected place, either removed from the vines and placed in trays, or hung upside down from rafters or some similar warm airy location. If you are saving seed, choose the larger, riper, healthier pods from the higher-yielding plants and store them in the shell. Be sure to protect all peanuts from rodents! Any moldy peanuts should be removed from food supplies and the garden as they may be carcinogenic.

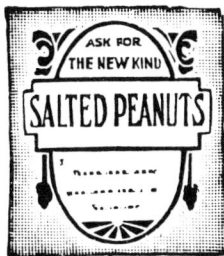

ASK FOR
THE NEW KIND
SALTED PEANUTS

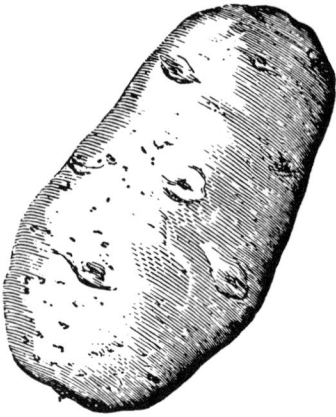

## POTATOES

When the potato was first carried from its homeland in the Andes Mountains of Chile and Peru and introduced into Europe in the 16th century, it was frowned upon as an "evil food." In France it was thought to be "unhealthy," and at best suitable only for livestock. Grudges are still held against this high-yielding, nutritious tuber, despite the fact that it is one of the most widely consumed vegetables in the world today, grown in 130 of 167 independent countries. The Soviet Union produces 33% of the world crop, Poland 15%, and the U.S. 5%. Worldwide it is a major source of nutrition, producing large amounts of calories, protein, and many vitamins and minerals from a relatively small area.

Peruvian indians have collected wild potatoes since before 6000 B.C. The Inca civilization was largely supported by potatoes. There are still some 3000 varieties of potatoes cultivated in the Andes, and more than 5000 worldwide.

In Europe the potato is said to be responsible for everything from the existence of absentee landlords to the population expansion which fueled the industrial revolution. Until the 1700's, the potato was scarcely known among the upper classes of England, though as early as 1663, the Royal Society of England recommended growing potatoes as a safeguard against potential famine. In France, even as late as 1749, Raole Combes in his book Ecole du Potager calls the potato "the worst of all vegetables."

By the 1800's, the story had changed, and the potato was accepted almost universally as an important foodstuff. Before the potato blight tragedy in Europe, the average Irish adult ate 9 to 14 pounds of potatoes a day according to a National Geographic article (this is about double what the authors of One Circle believe to be the maximum amount that one person can comfortably consume). The Irish population had exploded to over twice what it is today.*

---

* Robert E. Rhoades, "The Incredible Potato," National Geographic 161(5), May, 1982.

## USE:

According to Waverly Root, a minor result of the potato dependence in Ireland was that the people forgot how to cook most everything but a boiled potato! The potato is actually one of the most versatile vegetables in our diets today. Besides being eaten it is processed into starch, paste, and dye, distilled into whiskey and vodka, and converted into gasohol. Potato chips, invented in 1853, and french fries, unfortunately are the major forms in which Americans consume potatoes. Baked whole, most of the potato nutrients are preserved. When cut, some vitamin C will be lost (this can be minimized if the potato is first chilled). Potatoes are often steamed, hashed, or fried, and tend to complement other more pungent vegetables. Indians of the Andes sometimes make *chuño,* a dried potato product, **cabable of being stored up to four years,** which they use in soups, stews, and desserts (Rhoades, 1982).

## PLANT PHYSIOLOGY:

As its Latin name, *Solanum tuberosum,* implies, the potato is a tuber, or swollen root. It is also a member of the nightshade or *Solanaceae* family, the members of which contain a poisonous glycoalkaloid called solanine (a fact which may have contributed to the potato's early unpopularity in Europe). The potato plant is propagated by the tubers which multiply. Potatoes are planted deeply in part because the new tubers grow above the seed potato. Potatoes exposed to the above-ground environment don't grow as well and will, at the very least, turn a green color from the production of chlorophyll. This green portion contains the solanine. Most potatoes never produce seeds and some do not flower at all.

## CULTURE:

Potatoes ideally prefer an acidic soil in the pH 5-6 range, which helps prevent scab, but they grow well in a wide range of soil types. They are a cool-weather plant, growing best where the mean July air temperature is $70^{\circ}$ F or lower. According to Martin and Leonard (1949), the young sprouts develop best at $75^{\circ}$ F soil temperature, but later growth is best at $64^{\circ}$ F. Tuber production is inhibited at $68^{\circ}$ F and completely retarded at $84^{\circ}$ F, above which point respiration exceeds photosynthesis in terms of the carbohydrate balance. The plants can withstand light frosts and the first crop is often planted anywhere from 10 days to 6 weeks before the last killing frost date--the warmer the locale, the earlier since cold periods in the South do not normally freeze the ground as deeply. Some sample approximate planting dates are:

Gulf Region: winter
South Georgia ($31^{\circ}$ latitude): Jan 20-Feb 1
Aroostook County, Maine ($46^{\circ}$ latitude): May 10-20.

One general rule is to alter the planting date by one day for each eight miles or 1/8th degree in latitude, and then to add an extra day for every 100 foot rise in altitude.

A potato crop takes 3-4 months to mature. With careful timing, two crops of potatoes can be grown in a year, the second crop being planted sometime between July and September in time to mature before the freezing weather. The microclimate created by a biointensive plant canopy may also allow potatoes to be produced in warmer weather. Be sure to plant a second crop from stored tubers and not from the first crop since potatoes undergo a dormancy period lasting from one to five months after harvest.

Potatoes are normally allowed to sprout in a dark place before planting. The optimal size of the sprout is disputed among potato growers. In the biointensive system, in which potatoes are planted at 9 inch centers and 6 inch depths, 24¼ to 31 pounds of seed potatoes (of about 2 ounce size each) are needed per 100 square feet of growing area. Large vigorous sprouts are sometimes an indication that the crop will be quick to emerge and early-maturing. A minimum temperature of 40° F is needed for sprouting; warmer temperatures will hasten sprouting. Only after moisture and a protective medium such as soil is provided will the potatoes form roots.

The length of the sprout, the size of the seed potato, and the depth of planting are important variables to consider when you start to fine-tune your potato growing to achieve maximum yields. William Blackman in his article "Long Shoot Potatoes" in the Henry Doubleday Research Association Newsletter says that a 6-8 inch long sprout can provide up to 30% greater yield. The theory is that it allows the plant to complete some of its growth before it is planted in the ground, thereby saving in-bed time and allowing one to plant after frost danger is past. Perhaps this technique would be useful in short-season areas or where it would allow two crops instead of one.

The size of the seed potato is recommended to be anywhere from 1¼ to 2½ ounces in weight, relatively chunky in shape, and containing 1 to 3 eyes. The use of smaller-sized seed potatoes will save seed costs, but if they are too small (or too large), they may not produce as well. The eyes are what produce the lateral branches or sprouts that lead to the above-ground growth of the potato plant. The ideal number of eyes per potato will vary with the quality of the tuber, the growing conditions, the density at which the potatoes are planted, and the size of harvested potatoes desired.

As for planting depth, probably the deeper that you can successfully plant potatoes, the higher the yield. One problem that can arise in deep planting is that the potato may rot, especially in a compacted, heavy soil. Another is that temperatures lower down may be too cool for sprouting to initiate. Another is simply that the potato sprout has too far a distance to go, particularly if conditions are less than optimal. Loosening and aerating your soil and pre-sprouting will help prevent these problems.  Deep planting, when successful, allows more vertical space for tuber growth and is less likely to produce sun-exposed, solanine-containing potatoes.  Another technique is to plant potatoes not quite so deeply and then to hill them after the top growth has formed.  For well-shaped, heavy tubers, keep the plants uniformly watered, especially up through the flowering stage.

## VARIETIES:

Your preference and growing conditions will govern which of over 5000 potato varieties that you choose (though not all 5000 will be available to you).  If scab is a problem, you might try one of the Russett Burbanks or other scab-resistant culti-vars.  In extreme cold areas, Alaskan Frostless, for example, has proven useful down to 27°F.  Many of the varieties now grown in the U.S. have been dereived from sources in Britain and from sources in Bogotà, Columbia and Chile in the mid-1800's.  A list-ing of potato varieties from six major seed companies can be found in John Jeavons' and Robin Leler's The Seed Finder (1983).  A listing of low-solanine varieties of potatoes (and of all the other nightshade family garden plants including tomatoes, peppers, eggplant, and paprika) is available from the American Medical Association. Examples of potatoes low in solanine are Red Pontiac, Irish Cobbler, Norgold Russet, Penobscot, and Shurchip.

## POTENTIAL PROBLEMS:

The first way to prevent potato problems is to plant healthy seed.  L.H. Bailey in Hortus Second says this is the best way to control disease.  Aphids sometimes intro-duce viruses into potatoes which stay with potatoes season after season if you continue to use seed from an infected potato plant.  If this is a problem, buy certified seed or obtain seed from someone who is producing healthy seed.  Diseases can often be avoided by rotating potatoes (but not with other Solanaceae), by having clean storage areas, by not planting damaged potatoes, by planting in a sufficiently acidic soil (organic matter helps to acidify basic soils), and if necessary, by planting resistant varieties.

One insect pest which eats potato leaves (this in itself is not necessarily harm-ful) and can also spread disease is the Colorado Potato Beetle.  Strong plants are less susceptible to damage by this insect.  Handpicking and an abundant bird population can keep them under control.  Bean flowers and onion family members are said to repel them.  Inadequate boron levels in the soil are said to encourage them.

Other difficulties encountered by potato growers include yellowing or browning of the leaves, which may indicate that the plants are needing more water (or have been overwatered); too much top growth and not much tuber growth, which sometimes happens in too warm a season or when too much nitrogen fertilizer is used; dead tissue in the tubers, which can be avoided by getting the potatoes out of the ground more quickly after the tops have died back; and the production of small, marble-sized potatoes grown directly from the potato eye, which is more likely to occur if the potatoes are planted too early in the season.* The solanine content of potatoes has been associated with arthitis, gout, and bursitis. Planting pototoes deeper and using low-solanine varieties will help.

HARVEST:

Though potatoes could be harvested anytime after blossoming, there are at least two good reasons to leave them in the ground until they are fully mature. One is that they gain a significant amount of weight at the very end of the growing period. Another is that immature potatoes tend to shrink, bruise easily, and do not keep well. Handle all newly-dug potatoes with care until the surface has dried or cured for a few days. Some recommend leaving the potatoes on top of the ground for a day or two, although beware of not over-exposing them to sunlight. They can also be cured in darkness. Potatoes are probably ready to dig when the tops have turned brown and fallen over. Unless the ground is wet or frozen, it will not hurt the potatoes to remain in the ground for a short period of time, even a month or so.

STORAGE:

After potatoes have been allowed to dry at warmer temperatures (around 60° F) for a few days up to two weeks, store potatoes in a dark, ventilated place at 36-40° F if possible. Low temperatures serve to keep potatoes from sprouting. Potatoes for immediate or early use can be stored in a dark place at warmer temperatures (50-70° F). Sprouting will be inhibited if apples are stored in the same container. Another method, for large quantities, is to store them in a clamp--a soil and straw covering well described in John Seymour's The Self-Sufficient Gardener.

---

*Duane Newcomb, RX for Your Vegetable Garden, L.A.: J.P. Tarcher, Inc., 1982.

# SOYBEANS

Soybeans have been given much attention in the last forty years, as a "meat substitute" and particularly as an animal filler. The U.S. leads the world in soybean production but almost certainly not in direct human consumption. Native to China, soybeans have been grown at least since 2838 B.C. when the emperor Sheng Nung first recorded their use. Soybeans were one of the "five sacred crops" of China along with rice, wheat, barley, and millet. It has been known in Europe since the 17th century and in the U.S. since 1804.

USE:

Soy foods have long been a staple in many East Asian cultures. Tofu, or bean curd, is usually made from the yellow soybean varieties. One of the most nutritious ways to prepare the beans is to ferment them and to make tempeh. Instructions for making tofu and tempeh are in Shurtleff and Aoyagi's The Book of Tofu and The Book of Tempeh, respectively, and in The Farm Vegetarian Cookbook. The beans can be cooked and fried in patties, prepared as baked beans, made into dip, soymilk, or soy ice cream, ground into flour or grits, roasted as "nuts," or sprouted like adzuki beans. Soy oil is of course a main commercial product of soybeans. The meal and oil both are processed into all sorts of industrial products such as glue, plastics, celluloid substitutes, candles, enamels, oil cloth, paints, rubber substitutes, varnish, and soap. Even alcohol is made from the bean to fuel automobiles in Brazil.

PLANT PHYSIOLOGY:

Certainly part of the soybean's attraction is that it contains all the essential amino acids needed for human (and animal) nutrition. The beans contain about 40% protein and about 20% oil on a dryweight basis. This will vary depending on variety and growing conditions. Also, not all of the protein is digestible unless the beans are specially prepared. In general, soybean cultivars with a low oil content are high in protein and those higher in oil are lower in protein. The beans make up 41 to 57% of the above ground weight of the plant and contain over 50% of the total plant nitrogen.

An annual plant, soybeans are erect and bushy, and their seed is normally self-fertilized since pollination occurs as soon as or even before the flower opens. This makes for little natural crossing among varieties--much less than one percent. Another characteristic of soybeans is their sensitivity to the photoperiod, or the length of time it is exposed to light during the day. As a result, no one cultivar is high-yielding over a wide range in latitude, and so proper variety selection is important.

## CULTURE:

Soybeans are a warm weather crop. Some sources list it as being tolerant of a light frost. Others say it is intolerant of any frost. The dispute may be varietal. The time to plant depends on at least three factors: variety, soil temperature, and (when dry-farmed), moisture supply and distribution. You need to fit your variety within its growing season. Sucessful Farming (Jan. 1975) states a general rule for soybean growing: that "for highest yields, plant the latest-maturing variety that will ripen before a killing frost." It also recommmends that if you are planting more than one variety and hoping to get successive harvests, plant the short-season varie-ties first so that they all don't finish at the same time. This advice was intended for those needing to schedule their harvesting equipment, but is also applicable for succession harvesting of immature beans.

You can probably start planting soybeans two or three weeks after the last frost date, but a better way to optimize your planting time to check your soil temperature. Best germination will occur when the soil temperature has surpassed 50$^{\circ}$ F. Another factor, particularly in dry-farming, is to anticipate possible moisture stress. A full-season soybean variety, if planted in mid-May for example, will be in its re-productive stage from late July to early September, and this is the stage in which its water needs are greatest (see graph). If you can time the planting to avoid dry periods at this stage you are that much better off. The germination and seedling stages are also moisture-sensitive periods. The amount of water is not so critical as the constancy of supply. One final note on planting: old wisdom says to plant when the apple trees are in full bloom.

Innoculation is also important in soybean culture. The majority of sources recom-mend seed innoculation with the nitrogen-fixing bacteria Rhizobium japonicum (availa-ble from Johnny's Selected Seeds, Albion, Maine, among other places). Some say that the lack of this bacteria is the most important cause of poor soybean yields.

Though heat-loving, soybeans have their limits, and extended periods of above 100$^{\circ}$ F will probably be detrimental to yields. A high temperature/low moisture com-bination is the most unfavorable. Under high temperatures, the beans tend to develop less oil of a lower quality. A mean mid-summer temperature of 75-77$^{\circ}$ F is thought to

106

## Characteristic Growth and Water Use Pattern of Soybeans
### (Full Season Varieties)

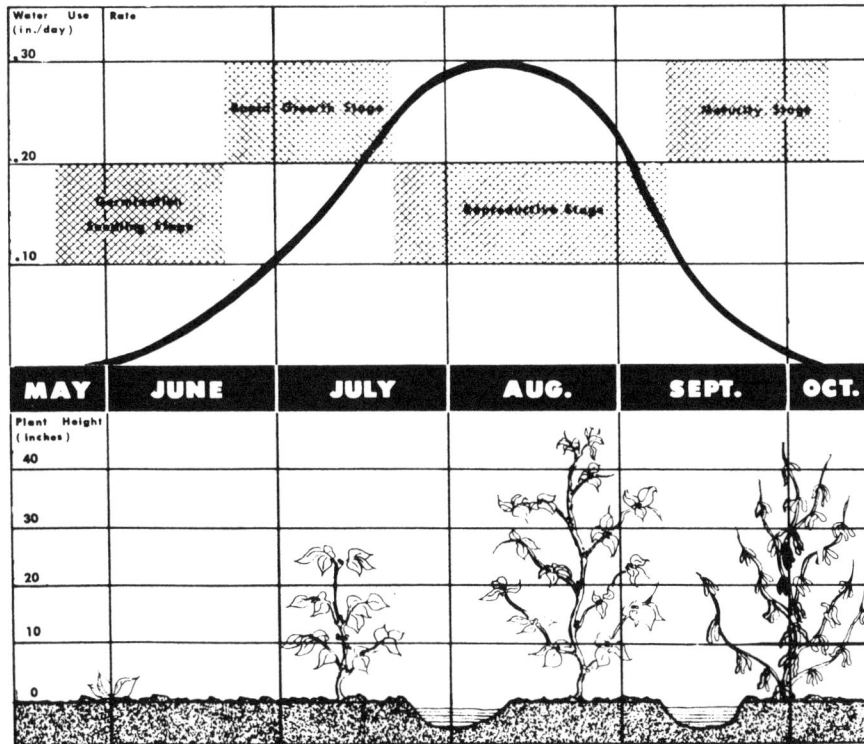

be optimum for most varieties. Lower temperatures tend to delay flowering. Recommended planting depth is 1 inch, or twice the size of the bean, and the biointensive spacing is 6 inches. If you are late in getting your soybeans in, your yield may be improved by closer spacing. Soybeans give a similar yield over a wide range of spacings, and this closer spacing may be to allow for the expected lower germination of plantings late in the season.

VARIETIES:

It may be difficult to pick the best soybean variety for your local conditions and you will probably need to try several. Your local agricultural extension agent can get you started. "A New Look at Soybeans," an Ontario government publication, indicated that mixtures of varieties sometimes give higher yields than one cultivar grown alone. It goes on to say that "most blends, however, yield less than the best variety in the blend." This may be saying that certain varieties do best in different years and that you can more consistently get good yields by planting more than one variety. Planting more than one variety also allows you to get successive harvests of green beans. The beans will mature in anywhere from 75 to 175 days depending on the cultivar and growing conditions. Some of the cultivars intended for earliness are: Fiskeby V, Okuhara, Envy, Altona, and Frostbeater. Johnny's Selected Seeds notes that the black varieties of soybeans are the more popular dry bean in the Orient and that they are generally easier to cook. In their 1983 catalogue they carry Black Jet (104 days) and Panther (120 days), along with yellow types. Altona is also a full season variety (105 days) as is Hokkaide. Note that some varieties are intended for silage and others for the dried or green bean.

## POTENTIAL PROBLEMS:

Soybeans are hardy as a rule. They sometimes suffer from fungal diseases which can mostly be avoided by good crop rotation. The Japanese beetle can bother soybeans, as can the Velvetbean caterpillar in the South. Watch your plants and hand pick the latter. Rabbits prefer soybeans over many other garden plants. A fence or possibly a solid hedgerow will check them.

## HARVEST:

Ideally, soybeans are harvested when they are fully mature and dry (about 14% moisture). At this point the leaves have dropped and the pods are crisp. This is also the stage at which shattering (splitting open of the pods) occurs and so it is usually necessary to harvest earlier. Shattering loss may be minimized somewhat by harvesting the beans after a light rain or dew. Normally the soybeans mature at different rates and so harvesting when some of the pods are dry and most of the others have turned yellow should allow you to catch most of them. Harvesting seed as it matures may be even better but will be more work. If green beans are desired, harvest some of the pods before they turn yellow. The beans should be mostly mature but not yet dry. The harvest period in this stage is usually 7 to 10 days.

## STORAGE:

To store dried soybeans, the moisture content should be no more than 13%. Shurtleff notes that a well-dried soybean will split in two if tapped lightly with a hammer on a hard surface. Craig Dremann of Redwood City Seed Company says to slit the pods and to dry them whole for 1 to 2 weeks in full sun before shelling, then to shell the beans and allow them to dry an additional 2 to 3 weeks before storing. If storing large quantities, or for a long time, or if the weather becomes warm, aerate the beans.*

* Craig Dremann, "Vegetable Seed Production in the San Francisco Bay Area of California and Other Warm Weather Areas of the United States," 1974.

# SWEET POTATOES

Sweet potatoes, probably originally from tropical America, are today an important food crop in the tropics and subtropics throughout the world. The vines and root both are valued for their very high iron, carotene*, and B vitamin content. Widely eaten in West Africa but less well known as a food source in this country, the <u>vines</u> are especially concentrated in these nutrients. The sweet potato was grown in Virginia as early as 1648 and was grown extensively for dehydration in the U.S. during World War II.

## USE:

The sweet potato root is often eaten fresh like potatos, either baked, steamed, browned, fried, stuffed, scalloped, hashed, pureed, or candied. Mashed and cooked, the fleshy root is often formed into pies, breads, muffins, and puddings. The vines, often used as silage in this country, can be harvested for the shoots or "tips," which make an extremely nutritious green vegetable stir-fried or steamed. One author relishes sweet potato tips stir-fried with garlic and tofu, to which a little soy sauce and vinegar is added. Sweet potato roots can also be dried and ground into flour. In <u>Sweet</u> <u>Potato</u>: <u>Proceedings</u> <u>of</u> <u>the</u> <u>First</u> <u>International</u> <u>Symposium</u>, there is mention of commercial interest in tempeh produced from the sweet

---

*Carotene content can vary widely with variety. Philip L. White and Nancy Selvey in their book <u>Nutritional</u> <u>Qualities</u> <u>of</u> <u>Fresh</u> <u>Fruits</u> <u>&</u> <u>Vegetables</u>, 1974, list the carotene concentrations of several common sweet potato varieties: (note that paler varieties have less carotene)

| Variety | $\beta$-carotene mg/100g | Variety | $\beta$-carotene | Variety | $\beta$-carotene |
|---|---|---|---|---|---|
| Julian | 18 | Heart O' Gold | 6 | Porto Rico | 6 |
| Centennial | 18 | Georgia Red | 6 | White Star | 0 |
| Goldrush | 12 | Kandee | 6 | Pelican Processor | 0 |

potato.  Just as carotene concentration varies with each variety, so may protein content.  L. Li in the above Proceedings found a positive correlation between orange-
colored flesh and higher protein content.

## PLANT PHYSIOLOGY:

The sweet potato (*Ipomoea Batatas*), as is characteristic of the morning glory, or
Convolvulaceae family, has trailing vines and heart-shaped leaves.  Unlike the morning glory, the sweet potato rarely flowers.  It is a perennial, even though is grown
as an annual in most parts of the U.S. where cold weather eventually kills the heat-
loving vines.  The vines are 4 to 16 feet long and range from green to red or purple
in color.  The below ground portion of the plant that we call the sweet potato is a
root and not a tuber like the potato.  The sweet potato root also has no eyes or buds
as do potato tubers.

## CULTURE:

Most critical to the successful culture of sweet potatoes is heat.  Most varieties
need a minimum, four month frost-free growing season, a sunny location, and warm
nights.  Maximum yields occur where the mean July and August temperature is greater
than $80^{\circ}$ F.  They are difficult to grow much farther north than southern Pennsylvania, Indiana, or Iowa, but with proper varietal selection and care, they have been
grown in Connecticut, Massachusetts, and Michigan.  A soil temperature of $70-85^{\circ}$ F
is ideal.  At $60^{\circ}$ the vines stop growing and at $50^{\circ}$ they die.  The plants do best
in a loose, somewhat sandy and acidic soil with a pH range of 5.2 to 6.7.

Propagation is somewhat tricky.  Usually roots are planted to produce slips
(rooted sprouts) which are then removed and transplanted.  Each root can produce up
to 20 to 50 slips.  Where the growing season is sufficiently long, vine cuttings can
be made from the first planting and then replanted, thereby requiring fewer seed potatoes.  When propagating slips, smaller roots will produce more slips per volume of
roots.  The slips should be placed approximately 3 inches apart, (or close together
but not quite touching), and 2-3 inches deep in flats filled with a light-textured
flat mix or sand.  The root may be left partially covered and filled in gradually as
the sprouts elongate.  Fifty to sixty pounds of sweet potatoes (1 bushel), rooted in
a 24 square foot nursery bed, can provide up to 1000 plants, or enough for a 400
square foot growing area of sweet potatoes planted on 9 inch centers, the recommended
biointensive spacing.  In cooler areas it will be necessary to start sweet potatoes
under glass, possibly in a hot bed.  Controlling temperature is tricky but important
if the young plants are to be strong and disease-free.  When they reach 6-10 inches

110

in length and are well-rooted and sturdy, pull the slips from the parent root sequentially while holding the parent root firmly. Keep slips moist during the period between pulling and transplanting.

Vine cuttings normally require fewer potatoes than slips and are less likely to spread disease, but take longer to produce and are therefore only used in areas with a long warm season. Martin and Leonard note that "any delay beyond the earliest practicable frost-free planting date results in marked decreases in yield." They add that "late planting also produces slender roots of low starch and carotene content." Cuttings are made when a vine is 3-4 feet long. Seven to eight-inch long pieces, each containing two joints, are cut, and are planted horizontally or obliquely with 1-2 inches of the stem sticking above the ground.

Sweet potatoes are relatively drought tolerant and two researchers, A. Sajjapongse and Y.O. Roan, note that root formation may be stimulated by an imposed water stress sometime during the growing period (Sweet Potato: Proceedings...). "Topping" the vines also may not only provide valuable nutrition in the form of edible greens but can improve root yields. P.U. Bartolini (Sweet Potato: Proceedings...) has obtained the highest root yields when the plants are "topped" twice between 1½ to 2 months from the transplanting date. Bartolini cautions, however, that after 2 months, root development and formation become key and that topping after this point may reduce yields.

VARIETIES:

There are two general categories of sweet potatoes: the dry flesh type (often grown in the North), which include the Big-Stem Jersey, Yellow Jersey, and Gold Skin; and the moist flesh type (often grown in the South), which includes the Nancy Hall, Porto Rico, and Dooley varieties. Some of the highest-yielding varieties fall in a different class altogether and are grown only for livestock. The Jersey or dry flesh types are actually higher in moisture content though the flesh appears drier. The moist flesh types are sometimes mistakenly called yams, a tropical plant of a different family, and which is not grown in the U.S. except for a few locations in southern Florida. The geographical division for commercial production of the two types falls roughly along an east-west transect through Virginia.

Several people are trying to develop sweet potato plants harvested especially for the tips, among them Ed Villareal, editor of Sweet Potato: Proceedings... . The Asian Vegetable Research and Development Center's (AVRDC) September 1983 issue of "Centerpoint" notes that a sweet potato variety developed for its tips is available for testing. The cultivar, called CN 1367-2, is so far only a medium-level yielder, but produces tender yellow-green tips, and rates high for consumer tastes.

Mike McGrath in the December 1984 issue of _Organic Gardening_ notes success in his cold Massachusetts location with two commercial varieties, Goldman and Redman. Next best, he says, and available to the home gardener were Jewell and Centennial.

## POTENTIAL PROBLEMS:

Insects cause few problems for sweet potatoes. The sweet potato weevil and the sweet potato gold bug can usually be controlled by crop rotation. Diseases are more of a problem both in the ground and during storage, but leaf diseases are generally unimportant. Rotation, good seed selection, careful handling, and clean storage areas help reduce disease problems. One author reports that sweet potatoes do best when they follow a leguminous cover crop.

## HARVEST:

You will sacrifice yield if you harvest sweet potatoes too early. Growers usually wait until the first frost, but in this case you must dig up the roots immediately or they are subject to decay. Dig carefully so as not to bruise the skins. Allow the roots to dry in the sun or some other dry place for a few hours. Collect the sweet potatoes in sturdy containers in which movement and bruising will be minimized.

## STORAGE:

A great advantage of the sweet potato is that it can be stored all winter long under the proper conditions. Most people recommend that sweet potatoes be cured. This means keeping the roots at 80-85$^\circ$ F and 85-90% relative humidity so that they can "sweat" for 10-14 days according to Martin and Leonard, or 4-7 days according to the Massachusetts Extension Service*. The curing stage heals cuts and reduces the moisture content so the roots will keep longer. After this stage, they are stored at 50-55$^\circ$ F and a relative humidity of 80-85% with occasional venting. Clean containers reduce the incidence of decay. In storage, starch is converted into sugar and the flesh softens. Both of these factors tend to improve cooking quality and flavor.

Sweet potatoes may also be dried, or canned, or stored uncured.

---

*Mike McGrath, _Organic Gardening_, December 1984.

# SUNFLOWER

More American than apple pie, the North or South American-borne sunflower *(Helianthus annuus)* is favored by some to be the U.S. national flower. During Dust Bowl days, wild sunflower (also *Helianthus annuus)* spread itself and protected against wind erosion before perennial grasses could re-establish the barren soil. Our favorite varieties actually descended from sunflowers cultured in Europe before 1600. From Europe the use of the seeds spread to the Middle East, to India, and to Russia. The czars are said to have fed soldiers two pounds per day as a staple. The American Indians, however, were probably the first to enjoy this hardy plant, and were noted to have sometimes interplanted sunflowers with maize.

## USE:

Most cultivated sunflower acreage is devoted to oil production, and the protein-rich by-product is often ground into meal for cattle fattening. Across the world nearly all parts of the sunflower are used: the petals for yellow dye, the dried leaves as tobacco, the ground seed as flour for baking and for thickening, the whole roasted seed as a coffee substitute, and the stem as a source of silk-like fiber. The seeds may also be sprouted before eating. Besides improving the nutritional value of the seed, sprouting helps to loosen the hull. There are at least two ways to enjoy sprouted sunflower. One is to rinse the whole seed in water, eating when the sprout is about the length of the seed and the hulls can be shaken free. Another is to plant the seeds in a flat and to eat the seedlings when they are 2-3 inches high.

## PLANT PHYSIOLOGY:

About 50% of the dry matter contained in the whole plant is contained in the head of the mature sunflower. Half the weight of dried heads is seed, including hulls. Fifty to sixty-five percent of the seed is kernel. Sunflower is one of the few plants that contains vitamin D.

## CULTURE:

Sunflower is said to need growing conditions similar to corn. A heavy-feeding crop, it is also tolerant of poor soil conditions. Seedlings with four leaves or less can withstand a light frost. Many books, therefore, recommend planting seeds two weeks prior to the last frost in order to maximize the growing period and yield. Conscientious placement of sunflowers in the garden will make the best use of their shading properties, and insure that they will have enough sun. Biointensive spacing between plants is 24 inches.

## VARIETIES:

The best known of the eating varieties is Mammoth Russian (80 days). Others include Sundak, Greystripe, and Manchurian. Oilseed varieties generally take longer to mature (95 to 120$^{+}$ days). Oilseed, Peredovik, and Sunbred Brand are some examples of cultivars grown for their oil.

## POTENTIAL PROBLEMS:

A chief enemy of the sunflower is the stem borer, a grub which tunnels its way into the main stem, killing top growth. If the tops of your plants start to droop, suspect the stem borer and look for its entry point. Once found, slit the stem in both directions to uncover the insect.

## HARVEST:

The seeds are mature when the back of the head is brown and dry with no trace of green. At this stage, however, the plant may shatter or be ravished by birds. Some growers remove the heads earlier and dry them in a protected place. If you will hang the heads to dry, leave a foot or so of stem attached to the head. Or you can lay the heads flat without overlap, screening from rodents if necessary.

## STORAGE:

Remove the seeds by hand or with a stiff brush, or by rubbing the heads on a screen. Continue to dry the seeds if they are still moist. The seed should not be stored with a moisture content greater than 8 or 9 percent. Small containers are best. If the seed is stored in large bins it may heat up and thereby suffer vitamin loss. Also, it is best to shell the seed only as needed to prevent loss of vitamins to the air.

# TURNIPS

Turnips are a wonderful seed for children to plant. They are extremely viable and quick to produce a multi-purpose food that is concentrated in almost all the vitamins and minerals. Nutritionally, the tops or greens of the turnip are the most important, but both the bolted seed-stalk (also called the raab or broccoli raab), and particularly the root, are also used. Like the potato the turnip root can be stored for winter use.

The origin of turnips (*Brassica rapa*), like many of the *Brassicas*, is unclear. Some say we can at least be certain that they originated in Europe or Western Asia. It's thought that turnips have been used as a food for 4000 years or more. Columella, writing in 42 A.D., reports the use of the turnip, especially in France, for both man and animals. "Turnip" Townshend popularized the turnip for agriculture in the late 1700's. It had previously been grown mainly as a garden crop but became an important crop of the agricultural revolution when it was discovered to make excellent feed for sheep and other animals. Its high nutritive productivity per acre allowed more animals to be fed per acre as well.

## USE:

The most common way to prepare turnip roots is to steam or boil them, or to bake them whole. For those who have trouble appreciating the distinctive turnip flavor, Organic Gardening writer Mark Kane suggests mashing them with potatoes. Turnip lovers can eat them raw. In Europe, turnip kraut is commonly made from the sliced roots. The greens are eaten raw in salads, steamed, and stir-fried. Turnips are also used quite efficiently as silage and directly as forage.

## PLANT PHYSIOLOGY:

The turnip is a biennial though it may go to seed the first year if conditions are unfavorable. The most versatile of the *Brassica* genus, every part of the plant is edible. Turnips are tastier in cool weather, and for a good reason. The sugar produced in the day accumulates in the roots on cool nights. In hot weather the leaves respire more, draining the roots of sugar.

## CULTURE:

Since turnips are quick to mature they are frequently sown at one month intervals for a continuous supply. Seeded directly outdoors 3 or 4 weeks before the last frost, or earlier if a cold frame is used. The young plants can withstand temperatures in the mid-20's but will be killed at $20^\circ$ F. Hot weather or water stress will create woody, bitter-tasting roots. Plant again in late summer and fall near the end of the heat as a catch crop in areas where you can harvest before the frost. Some varieties are ready for greens in 35 days.

The recommended biointensive spacing of turnips is 3-4 inches. This may be worth experimenting with. The roots are said to fill any space that they are given. Optimum root-yield spacing may not correspond to the optimum spacing for greens, and may also be variety-specific. Also consider interplanting turnips between slower growing plants with wide spacings. The turnips should mature and be harvestable before the other crop becomes crowded. Cabbages, brussel sprouts, broccoli and the like take time for their canopies to fill in when planted out as seedlings in late summer. The exposed soil could benefit from a quick crop of turnips between seedlings.

Biodynamic literature indicates turnips as a companion plant to peas. The natural insecticidal properties of turnip skins, along with nitrogen-fixing properties of peas, may in part responsible for this mutually beneficial relationship.

As mentioned already, cool weather and adequate moisture are critical for good tasting turnips. Soil type can also contribute positively or negatively to these factors. Well-developed soils rich in humus will hold moisture and insulate better against temperature extremes.


## VARIETIES:

Turnip varieties vary widely in maturity, physiology, and resistance to adverse conditions. Certain ones are chosen for their greens, for roots, for raab, or for a combination of uses. It is worthwhile to choose a combination of varieties which permit a succession of turnips throughout most of the year. An abbreviated listing of turnip varieties and their primary use(s) is given on the following page.


## POTENTIAL PROBLEMS:

Turnips are naturally resistant to some harmful insects and can usually avoid damage altogether if well-cared for and timed well (see CULTURE section). Heat and drought will weaken the plant and increase susceptibility to turnip aphids, flea beetles, and root maggot. Club root disease is sometimes a problem and is said to be encouraged by soil acidity. Varieties vary widely in susceptibility to club root.

Turnips and rutabegas are good indicator plants for boron deficiency. If the soil is low in boron, the turnips will develop a grayish brown area in the core which

| VARIETY | Days to maturity | For roots | For greens | For raab | For animal feed | Stores well | Overwinters well | Cold frame variety |
|---|---|---|---|---|---|---|---|---|
| Cowhorn | | | | x | | | | |
| Early Flat varieties (Round Croissy, Jersy Navet) | | x | | | | | | x |
| Extra Early White Ball | 25-30 | x | | | | | | |
| Gem | | x | | | | | | x |
| Golden Ball | | x | | | | | x | |
| Hardy Green Round | | | x | | | | x | |
| Jersey Lily | 40 | x | | | | | | |
| Just Right | 35-40 | | x | | | | | |
| Late Rapone | | | | x | | | | |
| Macomber | | x | | | x | | | |
| Orange Jelly | | x | | | | | x | |
| Purple Top, White Globe | 58 | x | x | | x | | | |
| Seven Top | | | x | | | | | |
| Shogoin | 25 | x | x | | | | | |
| Tokyo Cross Hybrid | 35-40 | x | | | | | | |
| Tokyo Market | 50 | x | x | | | | | |

will eventually rot, sometimes becoming hollow. One ounce of boron dissolved in water is enough to restore ¼ acre (over 10,000 square feet). Boron accumulator plants include soybeans, sweet potatoes, sunflowers, alfalfa, clover, vetch, and muskmelon.

HARVEST:

Greens can be harvested before the roots are mature. The time to start will vary with the variety. For best taste, harvest only the greens that are fully open but before fully grown. More mature greens, however, have a higher mineral content, even if they do not taste as good. Leave the emerging crown for later pickings. Harvest the roots before the first very hard freeze or when the tops have yellowed and withered, and probably before the roots are any bigger than 3 inches in diameter to insure good flavor.

STORAGE:

Turnips keep well if they are not damaged and are kept ventilated and moist. Some store turnips with soil remaining on the roots for moisture retention and protection. John Seymour in The Self-Sufficient Gardener has a good explanation and illustration of storing large quantities of turnips and potatoes in a "clamp," a simple mound-shaped pile covered with earth and straw. Whatever the method, clip the tops before storing, leaving a ½ inch stub.

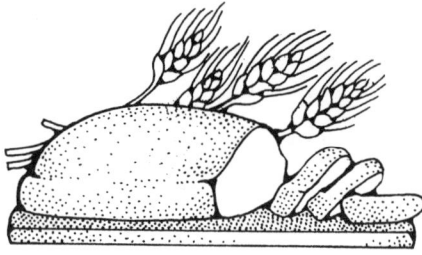

WHEAT

Wheat is the world's most widely cultivated cereal, with harvests occurring somewhere in the world every month of the year. Human consumption began some 10,000 to 15,000 years ago, in the Middle East, where it probably started as a weed in barley fields and slowly gained preference. Its first known use was as a parched cereal.

USE:

In Europe during the nineteenth century, bread was more of a staple than it is now, with laborers eating as much as two pounds per day--enough to supply most of their calories. Wheat is made up of 13-14 percent bran, 2-3 percent germ, and 83-84 percent endosperm. To make white flour, the bran and the germ, which contain much of the vitamins, minerals, and protein is milled off. In the endosperm, gluten is the primary protein. Gluten helps give wheat its light, attractive texture. Because wheat has more gluten than the other grains, it is the preferred grain for bread making.

Whole grains, also called wheat berries, may be soaked overnight and then lightly toasted to make an excellent breakfast food. They may also be sprouted. The sprouted grain may be ground, worked into a dough, and baked in the sun to make a simple bread. Sprouted wheat can be quite sweet. Wheat that has been sprouted and allowed to grow as a short grass for about a week can be juiced to produce a high chlorophyll, high vitamin drink.

PLANT PHYSIOLOGY:

Wheat needs more heat and a longer growing season than other small grains, and does not generally do well in warm moist climates. Most of the world's acreage receives between 15 and 35 inches of rain per year. Good growth is said to come from low temperatures and high light. For winter wheat, which accounts for about 75 percent of the world's acreage, a spring temperature averaging 60-75° F is ideal. High temperatures hasten maturity, preventing the grains from reaching maximum size. A high return of dry matter in the form of stalks requires a higher average spring temperature of about 72°.

Germination generally occurs in the 40 to 60° range, with the minimal temperature being 39° and the optimum being in the range of 68-72°. Significant root growth occurs early in the plant's life, and unlike some of the early roots in many other crops, these can continue to function throughout the life of the plant.  Its fibrous root system, which can be a great aid in improving the structure or tilth of your soil, can spread to about four feet wide and three to six feet deep.  Winter wheat has more roots than does spring wheat.

Tillers are the stalks which hold the grain heads.  Generally, the more tillers, the greater the yield.  Mild winters favor good tillering in winter wheats.  Overly rapid growth may decrease the number of tillers.

The first joint can occur within a week of germination.  The joints, or nodes on the tillers start close together and then later elongate rather rapidly.  In cold winter climates, this process doesn't start until spring, but growth rates of as much as ½ inch per day are possible.  In mild winter climates, growth can continue through the winter, but with enough moisture, plants may topple over or "lodge".

Later, heads appear out of the leaf sheaths on the tillers.  For winter wheat, it takes 40 to 50 days from heading to harvest.  Warm temperatures early in growth slow down heading, but warm temperatures later in growth can speed it up.  Spring temperatures of 60 to 70° are best.  Weather that is too warm will decrease the yields of both the grain and the total organic matter.

Flowering begins at the base or middle of the head and ends at the top.  Wheat is mostly self-pollinated, with cross-pollination occurring only between 0.5 and 4 percent of the time.  The grain goes through a series of ripening stages in which it gets less and less moist and eventually begins to dry out as the heads turn golden.  Wheat is one of the most beautiful plants you can grow in your garden.


CULTURE:

The approach of researchers in Henan province, in China, as expressed by Mr Liu Ying-Xiang* is to satisfy the plants needs at each stage of development--very similar to the philosophy of "working with nature" expressed by Aquatius, one of the people who wrote about the French Intensive system.  To apply this principle to the increasing of yields, you must optimize each of the three components of yield; the number of ears, the number of grains per ear, and the weight of each grain.  To design a sustainable agriculture may require a slightly different balance that will also maximize the yield of organic matter as well.

Most of the wheat grown in the world is winter wheat which is fall planted.  This

* Liu Ying-Xiang, "Agronomic Indices for High Yield-Low Cost Winter Wheat in Henan Province, China," pp. 40-48 in Hugh J. Roberts, editor, Intensive Food Production on a Human Scale. Palo Alto, CA: Ecology Action of the Midpeninsula, 1982.

represents an adaptation of the plant made by man. For an extra four to five months of in-ground time during the winter dormancy period, wheat can be harvested one or two months earlier in the spring. The milder weather during the heading period also allows longer and better heading and thus higher yields. In the United States, yields for hard red spring wheat are at the rate of about 3.7 pounds per 100 square feet, whereas those for hard red winter wheat are 4.3 pounds per 100 square feet.

Part of the question of winter versus spring wheat is what would you do with your garden in the winter otherwise. In mild, moist winters, fava beans are an effective winter cover crop, supplying organic matter and helping fix nitrogen.

Commercially, wheat seed is planted from one to three inches deep, with the deeper planting being appropriate for lighter soil, or where birds digging up the seed may be a problem. For maximum yields, transplanting may be an important technique. In the U.S., from the Great Plains eastward, planting dates for winter wheat are governed by the Hessian fly-free date. This ranges from around September 16 in Michigan to about October 27 in Georgia. The fly's disappearance with the coming of colder weather is close to the date wheat would normally be planted in these areas. In the West, for the colder winter areas, plant when the temperature is around $60^{\circ}$, and for mild winter areas, when the temperature is around $50^{\circ}$. Unlike barley, wheat will germinate even in wet, sticky ground. Spring wheat varieties may be fall-sown in mild winter areas as is done is some parts of India. It is possible that this helps prevent winter lodging in these areas.

If tillers emerge faster than the leaves, this overexuberant growth will in the end limit the total number of tillers and thus reduce yields. Growth can be slowed by compacting the ground or by root pruning the plants with a hoe. In Indiana, the yield of winter wheat was increased with a simulated grazing--the plants were clipped between April 1 and April 20. A similar grazing process earlier in the season might prove effective in preventing lodging in milder winter areas.

A weeding just prior to winter dormancy and then again when plants begin to leaf out again in the spring is recommended by Mr. Liu. High wheat yields are possible with little water if the water is properly distributed. Optimum rainfall according to American sources is 23-35 inches, with 4-6 inches during the two months just prior to harvest. It could be that more water could produce higher yields if healthier soil and plants could circumvent the potential problem of disease. Mr. Liu's wheat is irrigated at an average rate of between 4.5 and 5.3 gallons per 100 square feet per day over the growing season, but the average in the last two months is between 11.8 and 13.7 gallons per day per 100 square feet.

According to Mr. Liu, in Chinese intensive wheat production, both compost (at the rate of between 1.64 and 3.28 cubic feet per 100 square feet) and chemical fertilizers are used, with about 70 percent of the nutrients coming from the composted manure. Only 40 percent of the nitrogen fertilizer is applied initially with the rest being supplied in stages during the spring.*

The additional fertilizer applications of the Chinese, in terms of the rate per 100 square feet, were: .25 pounds nitrogen, .11 pounds phosphorous, and .19 pounds potassium.

The Chinese wheat was of two basic varieties, one with more tillers, and one with bigger heads and fewer tillers. The type with more tillers is planted at the equivalent of about 4 inch centers, and the one with bigger heads at about 3 inch centers. Yields can go as high as between 14.7 and 20.7 pounds per 100 square feet. The average on Mr. Liu's experimental farm is about 12.65 pounds per 100 square feet. The total dry matter harvested per bed, including grain, was optimally about 39.4 pounds. Mr. Liu recommends against having more than about 1.5 pounds of straw per pound of grain if maximum yields are sought. Higher moisture is known to contribute to increased straw per pound of grain.

Here, at the Ecology Action test site, wheat is planted at 5 inch centers. We have fewer plants per area, but get more heads per plant than the Chinese, who only average about two heads per plant. We also grow spring wheat, whereas they grow winter wheat. Our wheat is transplanted instead of direct-seeded. Ecology Action tests have indicated that wheat on five inch centers produces higher yields than wheat on either four or six inch centers. Broadcasting an amount of wheat that would be appropriate for producing five inch centers will probably set more plants closer to four or six inch centers than at five. Transplanting lets you get an even stand at five inch centers, lets you reject weak plants, and lets you get a slight jump on the season. For spring wheat, it appears that the earlier you can plant, the better.

VARIETIES:

There are three branches of the wheat clan, and these divide along the lines of the number of chromosomes. Diploid wheat has seven pairs of chromosomes, and includes *T. monococcum*, or einkorn wheat. One kind of einkorn, *einkorn var. Hornemanii*, also known as "early stone age" wheat, has performed well in regards to both yield

---

* Along similar lines, American studies have found that late nitrogen applications prolonged the period of photosynthesis in wheat, and thus increased yields. Acres USA reported in July 1976 that the spraying of one quart per acre of diluted fish and seaweed emulsion was able to stimulate the production of 25 percent bigger wheat heads.

and protein content, but is difficult to thresh. It could be important in the design of a minimal area diet for a goat, cow, or chickens. Tetraploid wheat contains 14 pairs of chromosomes, and includes emmer and durum wheat. Durum requires less water than common wheat and is used in making spaghetti. Hexaploid wheat contains 21 pairs of chromosomes and includes common wheat, *T. vulgare*. Common wheat includes some 20,000 cultivars worldwide.

In the U.S., most of the wheats, with the exception of limited areas of durum, are common wheats of the hexaploid type. Wheat production has gradually shifted westward, with New York having once been the leading U.S. wheat area, and Kansas not reaching great importance as a wheat state until around the turn of the century. Today, the East grows soft spring wheat, the Great Plains hard red winter wheat, the West, soft red winter, hard red winter, and white wheats, and the north central states hard red spring and durum wheats. For home production, you may have more leeway in the variety that you use.

Varieties have been developed that are resistant to sawfly, greenbug, Hessian fly, and other pests, but a specific variety referred to in the literature may no longer be available due to the rapid turnover among wheat varieties. The genetic diversity in wheat has been drastically reduced over time, and attempts to induce mutations through the use of chemicals and radiation have generally failed.

Red winter wheat is lower in protein than red spring wheat. You may find it interesting to experiment with growing varieties at times other than those for which they are intended. The optimum wheat for small-scale, intensive production has probably not even been developed for your area, or at least is not easily available. Also, most cultivars have been developed under near optimum irrigation conditions, and may not prove to be the best wheats for situations where water stress is likely. Wheat varieties in quantities appropriate for the home gardener are available from Bountiful Gardens*.


POTENTIAL PROBLEMS:

Lodging, in which plants topple over can be a problem. Fencing the perimeter of the bed with twine can help, as can a winter or early spring grazing--cutting the plants back to about 6 inches. Mice can be a problem, as can birds, with the former having to be trapped, and the latter being able to be kept out of the wheat with bird netting. It may be important to protect flats planted with wheat seed from both these pests. Soybeans planted near wheat can help repel cinch bugs. Controlling Hessian

*For a catalogue, write Bountiful Gardens, 5798 Ridgewood Rd. Willits, CA, 95490.

fly is mostly a matter of attention to planting dates.

Moist growing conditions favor disease. Most wheat diseases are fungus parasites such as rusts or smuts, but they can also be attacked by powdery mildew and mosaic, a kind of virus. Einkorn wheats such as "early stone age" wheat are somewhat resistant to stem rust. Diseased plants should be burned or removed from the garden.


HARVEST:

It takes 40 to 50 days for winter wheat from heading to harvest. The seed is mature at 35 percent moisture, but commercial harvesting methods require a moisture level of about 14 percent. You can hand harvest wheat when it is at 25 to 35 percent moisture, when the plants have turned from green to gold. This is 7 to 10 days earlier than is done commercially, but you will still need to reduce the moisture level before storing it. This can be done by letting it sit in paper bags in a warm dry place (like a high kitchen shelf) for about 2 weeks. The following procedure for threshing wheat is given in The Backyard Homestead:

> ...separate the seeds from the chaff and stems by placing them on the plywood digging board and shuffling thoroughly across them wearing a pair of shoes with smooth or slightly corrugated soles (or whatever method you are used to); separate the seeds from the rest by tossing the material into the air in a light breeze. And then pick out any stems that remain with the seeds.


STORAGE:

Wheat should be stored in a rodent-proof container in a cool, dry place. Put a bay leaf in the container to help control grain weevils. Well-stored seed can remain viable for as long as 30 years.

# APPENDIX 1

## NUTRIENTS PER POUND OF FOOD*

| | Collards | Filberts | Garlic | Leeks | Onions | Parsley | Parsnips | Peanuts | Potatoes | Soybeans | Sunflower Seeds | Sweet Potatoes | Turnip greens | Turnip roots | Turnips with .35# roots/1# greens | Wheat |
|---|---|---|---|---|---|---|---|---|---|---|---|---|---|---|---|---|
| Calories | 182 | 2878 | 622 | 236 | 173 | 198 | 341 | 2579 | 422 | 536 | 2542 | 640 | 127 | 136 | 129 | 1092 |
| Protein | 16.3 | 57.2 | 28.1 | 10.0 | 6.8 | 16.3 | 7.7 | 119 | 11.8 | 44.5 | 109 | 9.5 | 13.6 | 4.54 | 11.3 | 43.6 |
| Isoleucine | 508 | 6642 | -- | 795 | 91 | -- | -- | 4459 | 345 | 2859 | 2883 | 218 | 481 | 100 | 382 | 1398 |
| Leucine | 917 | 6606 | -- | 1362 | 168 | -- | -- | 8517 | 549 | 4891 | 4331 | 322 | 953 | 163 | 748 | 2858 |
| Lysine | 849 | 3133 | -- | 1276 | 286 | 2411 | -- | 4703 | 436 | 4015 | 2433 | 204 | 713 | 77 | 548 | 1227 |
| Cyst.+ Meth. | 477 | 1312 | -- | 908 | 73 | 82 | -- | 3196 | 173 | 1630 | 2288 | 163 | 259 | 50 | 205 | 1732 |
| Tyro.+ Phen. | 1249 | 7768 | -- | 1022 | 173 | -- | -- | 11818 | 613 | 5082 | 4281 | 368 | 1035 | 141 | 803 | 3216 |
| Tryptophan | 227 | 1194 | -- | -- | 91 | 336 | -- | 1385 | 150 | 805 | 917 | 100 | 218 | -- | 161 | 456 |
| Threonine | 518 | 1884 | -- | -- | 91 | -- | -- | 3759 | 359 | 6828 | 4136 | 386 | 568 | 114 | 450 | 1739 |
| Valine | 817 | 6810 | -- | 1535 | 136 | -- | -- | 5557 | 422 | 3019 | 3423 | 268 | 617 | 100 | 483 | 1893 |
| Histidine | 395 | 1308 | -- | -- | 63.6 | -- | -- | 3400 | 132 | 4136 | 2660 | 163 | 154 | 32 | 122 | 1230 |
| Carbohydrate | 32.7 | 75.8 | 140 | 50.8 | 39.5 | 38.6 | 79.5 | 79.9 | 95.8 | 45.9 | 90.3 | 149 | 22.7 | 30.0 | 24.6 | 233 |
| Fat | 3.2 | 283 | .9 | 1.4 | .5 | 2.7 | 2.3 | 220 | .5 | 23.2 | 215 | 2.3 | 1.36 | .9 | 1.24 | 6.56 |
| Lino. Acid | -- | 45.4 | -- | -- | -- | -- | -- | 63.6 | .26 | 13.6 | 135 | .77 | .23 | -- | .17 | 2.19 |
| Vitamin A | 4918 | 81 | -- | 30 | 30 | 6432 | 23 | -- | -- | 22.7 | 38 | 6129 | 5751 | -- | 4260 | -- |
| Thiamin | .91 | 2.09 | 1.14 | .50 | .14 | .54 | .36 | 4.49 | .45 | 1.41 | 8.90 | .41 | .95 | .18 | .75 | 1.87 |
| Riboflavin | 1.41 | 2.42 | .36 | .27 | .18 | 1.18 | .41 | .59 | .18 | .41 | 1.04 | .32 | 1.77 | .32 | 1.39 | .39 |
| Niacin | 7.7 | 4.1 | 2.27 | 2.3 | .9 | 5.45 | .9 | 71.7 | 7.7 | 2.7 | 24.5 | 3.2 | 3.63 | 2.7 | 3.39 | 14.1 |
| Vitamin B$_6$ | .89 | 2.59 | -- | .91 | .29 | .73 | .41 | 1.32 | 1.06 | 2.91 | 5.64 | .99 | .44 | .41 | .43 | 3.06 |
| Folic Acid | .46 | .30 | 4.54 | -- | .32 | .16 | .12 | -- | .07 | 1.02 | -- | .07 | .19 | .03 | .15 | .19 |
| Pant. Acid | 2.0 | 5.15 | -- | -- | .08 | 1.38 | 2.72 | 10.9 | 1.65 | 7.63 | -- | 3.72 | .31 | .91 | .47 | 3.55 |
| Vitamin C | 417 | -- | 68 | 77 | 45 | 781 | 73 | -- | 91 | 77.2 | -- | 100 | 631 | 163 | 510 | -- |
| Vitamin E | 13.6 | 152 | .07 | 19.4 | 1.34 | 21.1 | 6.8 | 52.5 | .20 | 34.7 | .07 | 44.0 | .5 | -- | 11.1 | 8.2 |
| Iodine | 77 | 9 | 12.3 | -- | 64 | -- | 16.3 | 90.8 | 68 | -- | -- | 50.0 | 350 | -- | 259 | 3.28 |
| Zinc | -- | 13.9 | 6.05 | 1.41 | 1.60 | 4.1 | -- | 15.1 | 2.72 | 3.03 | -- | .35 | 15.9 | -- | 11.8 | 7.93 |
| Calcium | 922 | 949 | 132 | 236 | 123 | 922 | 227 | 268 | 41 | 331 | 545 | 182 | 1117 | 177 | 873 | 135 |
| Iron | 4.5 | 15.4 | 6.8 | 5.0 | 2.3 | 28.1 | 3.2 | 9.1 | 3.2 | 12.3 | 32.2 | 4.1 | 8.2 | 2.3 | 6.67 | 10.8 |
| Phosphorous | 286 | 1530 | 917 | 227 | 163 | 286 | 350 | 1857 | 295 | 867 | 380 | 263 | 263 | 136 | 230 | 1257 |
| Potassium | 1821 | 3196 | 2402 | 1575 | 713 | 3301 | 2456 | 3060 | 2284 | -- | 4177 | 1362 | -- | 1217 | 316 | 1214 |
| Magnesium | 259 | 835 | 163 | 104 | 54 | 186 | 145 | 935 | 154 | 602 | 173 | 141 | 263 | 91 | 218 | 513 |
| Copper | -- | 6.05 | -- | .41 | -- | 1.62 | -- | 4.35 | .82 | 5.31 | 8.04 | .68 | .19 | -- | .14 | 1.97 |

*See pages 69-71 for standard units and information on needs. Form of food on next page.

## ADJUSTED ANNUAL YIELDS

| CROP | Form as Consumed: same assumptions are made for nutrient contents. Vegetables may be lightly steamed with only slight to moderate changes in nutrient concentration. | A. Weeks to Maturity | B. Weeks of Harvest | C. Safety Factor=2 wks | D. Total Time in Ground | E. H=half season crop / F=full season crop | F. Good Yield, lbs per 100 square feet* | G. Consumption Factor | H. Season Factor H=2 / F=1 | I. Adjusted Annual Yield/ 100 sq. ft. | J. Adjusted Yield per day/ 100 sq. ft. |
|---|---|---|---|---|---|---|---|---|---|---|---|
|  |  | A | + B | + C | = D | E | F | x G | x H | = I | ÷365=J |
| Collards | Raw leaves including stems. Yield is for tree collards.* | -- | -- | -- | 52 | F | 300* | 1 | 1 | 300 | .822 |
| Filberts | Raw, shelled. | -- | -- | -- | 52 | F | 12.4 | 1 | 1 | 12.4 | .034 |
| Garlic | Cloves, raw. | 24 | -- | 2 | 26 | F | 120 | 1 | 1 | 120 | .329 |
| Leeks | Bulb and lower leaf portion, raw. | 19 | -- | 2 | 21 | F | 240* | 1 | 1 | 240 | .658 |
| Onions | Mature, raw. Yield figure for torpedo variety. | 17 | -- | 2 | 19 | H | 400 | 1 | 2 | 800 | 2.19 |
| Parsley | Flat or curled leaf, raw. | 11 | 6 | 2 | 19 | H | 35* | 1 | 2 | 70 | .192 |
| Parsnips | Raw. | 15 | -- | 2 | 17 | H | 238 | 1 | 2 | 476 | 1.30 |
| Peanuts | Raw without skins. | 17 | 1 | 2 | 20 | F | 10 | 1 | 1 | 10 | .027 |
| Potatoes | Baked in skins. One lb. raw = .94 lb. baked. | 17 | -- | 2 | 19 | H | 200 | .94 | 2 | 376 | 1.03 |
| Soybeans | Mature, dry seed; cooked & drained. 1 lb. raw=1 lb. baked | 17 | 4 | 2 | 23 | F | 8 | 3 | 1 | 24 | .066 |
| Sunflower Seed | Hulled, mature, dry seed. | 12 | -- | 2 | 14 | H | 5 | 1 | 2 | 10 | .027 |
| Sweet Potatoes | Baked in skin. One lb. raw = .83 lb. baked. | 17 | 1 | 2 | 20 | F | 82* | .83 | 1 | 68 | .187 |
| Turnips | Raw. "For greens"variety is assumed. .35 lb. rt./lb. lf. | 10 | -- | 2 | 12 | H | 200 lf +70 rt / 270* | 1 | 2 | 540 | 1.48 |
| Wheat | Wheat flour figures used to estimate nutrients in simple bread. 1 lb. flour=1.38# bread | 17 | -- | 2 | 19 | H | 10 | 1.38 | 2 | 27.6 | .076 |

*Good Yields have been modified from: annual collards, 191# (382#/year); leeks, 480#; parsley, 52# (for whole year); sweet potatoes, 164#; turnips, 200# (400-600#/year).

# SELECTED ANNOTATED BIBLIOGRAPHY

Jeavons, John. 1982. How To Grow More Vegetables... Berkeley, CA: Ten Speed Press.

   An essential manual of biointensive techniques, covering 181 vegetables, fruits, nuts, grains, and other crops. Contains detailed master charts for reference and an excellent bibliography for general food-raising.

Jeavons, John; Griffin, J. Mogador; and Leler, Robin. 1983. The Backyard Homestead, Mini-Farm & Garden Log Book. Berkeley, CA: Ten Speed Press.

   A companion workbook to How To Grow More Vegetables... Especially useful for those wanting to begin collecting data. (See especially Chap. 3--Crop Testing.)

Knott, James Edward. 1941. Vegetable Growing. Philadelphia: Lea & Febiger.

   Tips on the production of seedlings. Good explanation on the culture of the individual crops.

Leonard, Warren H. and Martin, John H. 1963. Cereal Crops. N.Y.: MacMillan Publishing Co., Inc.

   Intended as a college text. Covers everything from botany to traditional techniques for corn, wheat, rye, barley, oats, rice, sorghum, and the millets.

Lorenz, Oscar A. and Maynard, Donald N. 1980. Knott's Handbook for Vegetable Growers. N.Y.: John Wiley & Sons.

   Update of Knott's 1957 edition of Handbook for Vegetable Growers. Useful crop-specific information in an easy to read, tabular form. Expensive. Used by professional growers. Some of the chemically-oriented sections may not apply.

Martin, John H. and Leonard, Warren H. 1949. Principles of Field Crop Production. N.Y.: Macmillan Company.

   Though tailored mostly to agriculture on a large scale, this book offers much useful quantitative crop-specific information for some of the more traditional "field crops."

Newcomb, Duane. 1982. Rx for Your Vegetable Garden. L.A.: J.P. Tarcher, Inc.

   A broad holistic approach to problems which plague the gardener. Covers environmental and cultural factors which interfere with plant growth as well as pests and diseases.

Organic Gardening magazine, Emmaus, PA: Rodale Press.

   A monthly periodical from Rodale containing articles whose nature varies from folk wisdom to the latest scientific updates. See the indices in December issues for reference to specific articles.

Reed, Clarence A. and Davidson, John. 1958. The Improved Nut Trees of North America and How To Grow Them. N.Y.: The Devin-Adair Company.

Has a commercial perspective which may provide important details for someone interested in serious food production.

Roberts, Hugh J., editor. 1982. Intensive Food Production on a Human Scale. Palo Alto, CA: Ecology Action of the Midpeninsula.

See especially: presentations on recent biointensive progress, by Jeavons; Strategies for Small Farmers, by Hugh L. Popenoe; Y.H. Yang on nutrition and intensive food production; and Liu Ying-Xiang on the fine-tuning of intensive Chinese wheat production.

Rodale, J.I., editor. 1973. How To Grow Vegetables & Fruits by the Organic Method. Emmaus, PA: Rodale Books, Inc.

Tips on the culture, storage, and harvest of many garden crops.

Root, Waverly. 1980. Food. N.Y.: Simon and Schuster.

Interesting historical information on individual crops and dishes.

Seymour, John. 1978. The Self-Sufficient Gardener. Garden City, NY: Doubleday & Company, Inc.

Contains many useful growing and storage tips, complete with illustrations. Treats the "deep bed" method, a variation of the biointensive method.

Villareal, Ruben L. and Griggs, T.D., editors. 1982. Sweet Potato: Proceedings of The First International Symposium. Shanhua, Tainan, Taiwan, China: Asian Vegetable Research and Development Center.

Covers many current research lines on the ever-important sweet potato plant. Useful for those who want to really explore sweet potato culture and nutrition.

Vilmorin-Andrieux, M.M. 1885, 1976. The Vegetable Garden. Berkeley, CA: Ten Speed Press.

Over 100 years old and now reprinted, this book is still one of the more comprehensive texts on vegetable growing. Of special interest to those wishing to find out about older varieties.

Walheim, Lance and Stebbins, Robert L. 1981. Western Fruit, Berries & Nuts: How To Select, Grow, & Enjoy. Tucson, Arizona: H.P. Books.

Detailed varietal and cultural information especially geared for gardeners in in the western U.S. Eastern Fruit, Berries & Nuts: How To Select, Grow & Enjoy is available for East coast gardeners.

# The Future

# ONE CIRCLE VILLAGE:
## a community yet to be

*by Gary Stoner*

*Welcome!*

*These are our mini-farms, where we work to raise a complete, nutritious diet on what little land we have. Please join us on a tour and we will show you what we've accomplished so far, and how we've done it.*

*Our collective program now includes 50 families, about 250 people. We are working together to meet our individual needs, to produce adequate food on limited resources, and to provide for the broader needs of the community, such as developing local industries and seeing that as many people as possible are provided with secure, meaningful employment. When we began the program ten years ago, we were faced with numerous problems. Our young adults were leaving the village to seek employment in the larger cities, result-ing in a loss of labor and energy that is vital in a community like ours. Also, many of the villagers were forced to take low-paying, seasonal jobs, and the majority of our income had to be used to purchase our food needs. We were dependent on an agricultural system that was not providing us with good quality, affordable staple foods. Poor agricul-tural practices were causing our prime farmland to be gradually lost to erosion and desertification. We had also lost control of many of the decisions that affected our lives and our futures, such as how our land was to be used and what type of crops would be grown.*

*There is still a great deal of work to do, but we are happy to be reaching the most important goals of providing for our essential dietary needs and determining how the land is to be used and preserved. This process has also had some unexpected benefits which we'll point out as we continue on the tour.*

*The most obvious part of our program is the use of raised beds here in the community gardens. There are still more of them around our homes where we grow a variety of vegetables, flowers, beans and grains. We never believed that so much nutritious food could be raised on this land until we began using the biointensive system. Notice how every square centimeter of space is being put to use; for even when a bed is not producing a food crop, we have the area filled with some type of cover crop to provide compost material, to avoid soil compaction, and to prevent erosion. We've found this method to be efficient and very enjoyable. Any hard labor we put into the manual techniques amply rewards us with good harvests most years.*

*Feel the soil here, and see how loose and moist it is in the growing beds. Smell it. Notice all the earthworms and see how they have helped give the soil a rich, crumbly texture. Before we initiated this method, the soil was parched and produced poorly. Our water supply was limited and the small amounts we could spare for food-raising seemed to evaporate before the crops could take it up. The amount of water available to us is still a concern, but we've learned to more fully use what we have, by building the organic matter content of the soil and minimizing evaporation by maintaining a dense canopy of plant cover.*

*Look! The plants are healthy and strong this year. See how vigorously our potatoes are growing. And the parsnips! Looks like our yields may be higher than last year. Our earlier problems with pests and diseases have decreased gradually as the health of the soil and our*

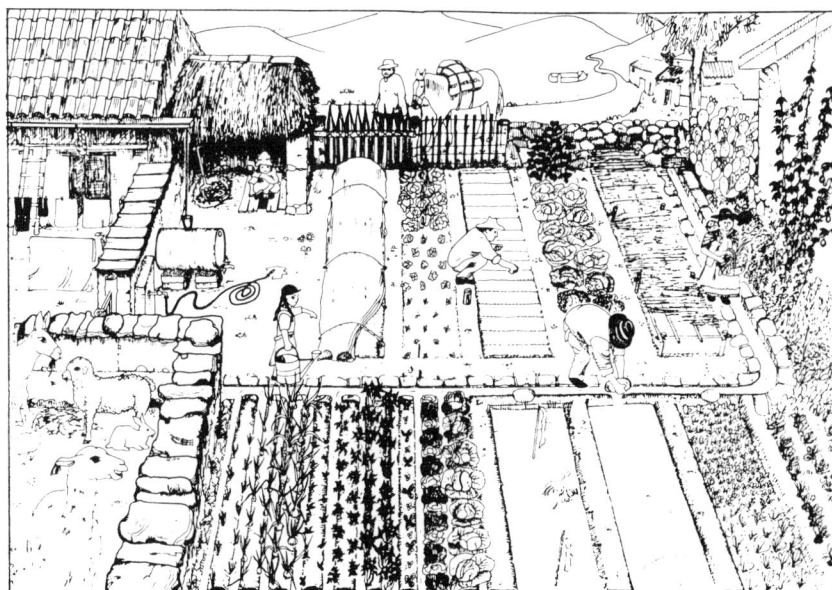

*Picture from <u>Cultivo de Hortalizas en la Huerta Familiar</u>, Hans Carlier, 1978, Instituto de Estudios Andinos, Apartado 289, Huancayo, Peru. Reviewed in <u>Appropriate Technology Sourcebook, volII.</u>, p 448.

131

awareness of its needs have developed. The use of man-made chemicals to overcome our food-raising problems is simply inappropriate, whether it be to fertilize the plants or to kill unwelcome soil and insect life. Such chemicals are expensive -- far beyond our means to pay for them season after season - and it takes a greater amount each year to achieve the same results.

More importantly, we have discovered that their use is an over-simplified response to problems more subtle and complex. By learning to recognize the causes of an agricultural problem - finding out _why_ an **insect or disease att**acks a crop - we can develop a response that reduces **or eliminates th**e problem, and prevents its recurrence. We are learning to tolerate a certain amount of unwelcome insects, so that other beneficial animals and insects that feed on them will continue to thrive. For instance, by introducing ladybugs back into our garden areas, we were able to bring an aphid infestation under control, a problem that plagued us for years. Now we need to keep enough aphids around to maintain a healthy ladybug population! Our crop losses average about ten percent, and most damage is cosmetic, and easier to live with than pesticides.

It has taken patience and careful observation, but the soil and the crops have responded to our efforts. These soybeans don't look as good as they might, but the first year we tried them we had to replant three times because of beetle infestations, and still lost the crop. Our soil-building together with practices like crop rotation, interplanting, better timing, selecting well-adapted varieties, and keeping only the seeds of the strongest plant has done more for us than what the use of chemicals could do.

The woman working to your left really loves the corn she is cultivating in the growing bed. While other villagers were changing to more nutritively productive crops like collards and turnips, she has been determined to save space every year for her beloved sweet corn. By using the biointensive techniques, testing for spacing, and through varietal development she has increased her yields significantly. Who knows, maybe in a few years she will be able to bring her production up to the levels of the crops considered more efficient.

We have found that the difficulty in establishing these more efficient crops is primarily a cultural one. Most of us did not consider ourselves capable of easily growing enough food to provide for the bulk of our needs. Also, many people shunned the idea of eating primarily from a selection of foods that seemed much narrower than those available in the stores. Yet upon closer scrutiny we discovered that our current diets were no more diverse - even less so in some cases. What continues to be a hurdle for some is an uneasiness with change - an unwillingness to depart from a diet that we are accustomed to. The common, less efficient crops were fine when there were fewer people to feed and we could use more extensive techniques. To eat these foods now, we have to import them from other places. By deepening our perception of complete balanced diets, and learning more about what "good food" is, we have begun to realize that we could produce all our food, and decrease our dependence on an imposed agricultural system that determined much of what we ate. The common practice of agriculture in this region has been to grow fewer staples, such as grains, plant more high value crops for export, and to concentrate production in a few centralized areas. This then requires a greater amount of processing and energy for shipment to increasingly distant markets. Combined with higher packaging and transportation costs, these practices have driven up prices and reduced the selection of food items available. Factors like colorful packaging contribute unnecessary costs, and none of us were comfortable with the growing use of chemicals to preserve, color, and enhance the taste of inferior foods.

This project was originally undertaken to see how a few of us (only five in the beginning) could grow some extra food to supplement our daily diet, using the land and resources we had available. The good yields and delicious vegetables encouraged others to join. We expanded both the number of people involved and the amount of land used, growing more food and a greater variety of crops including grains and beans. As our pool of labor and available land has increased, we have found that the key to making the program successful and sustainable is careful and thorough planning. This includes short-, medium-, and long-range planning. To make maximum use of the raised beds, we have to carefully time the planting of flats to keep us supplied with seedlings as we need them. This is especially important in succession planting, to provide seedlings to follow short season crops. We have found that a careful selection of early- and late-maturing crops can extend the growing season, which also requires advanced planning. Other factors must be considered too, such as a crop rotation scheme that will effectively discourage insect and weed build-up while systematically replacing nutrients that may have been depleted by a previous crop. We have realized that everything we do here affects the soil in some way, and we want to insure that the results of our efforts are worthy of being passed on to our children and those after them.

As the size of our program has increased, so too has the complexity of our research network. We are able to test many different varieties for each crop, like these potatoes, and the beds of onions here . Among the potato beds we are growing several red, blue and white varieties as well as testing some multi-colored ones that came to us from South America this year. The red torpedo-shaped onions on your right have proven to be prolific yielders, but we are also growing other types like these yellow and white ones, which we like for their taste and keeping qualities.

By having a larger number of people growing crops, many variables can be tested, such as plant spacing, different kinds and amounts of soil ammendments, and different interplanting combinations. This allows us to find just what the optimum growing conditions are for each plant and region. We can get the results much faster than we could on an individual scale, and pass them on to others. By growing different varieties of each crop, we are finding varieties that store longer. This has been essential to insure enough surplus so that no one here goes hungry.

Through careful observation we are able to select the seeds of the strongest and best-adapted plants. All of the plants you see here are open-pollinated varieties. We have found saving our seeds to be the best route to consistent crops, for with  careful selection, the plants adapt to our specific climate and soil type over time. Even though they might sometimes appear to be less prolific in yields than certain hybrids, they have proven to be more tolerant of seasonal variations in rainfall and the *average* yields are higher. And, of course, costs are greatly reduced when we do not need to pay for seeds and young plants every year.

Our planning still needs more work. We need to coordinate which crop follows another in a growing bed, to insure that there is enough compost for each bed when it's time to be re-dug. Because so many more people are involved in this process, individual differences in techniques and attitudes can make the fine-tuning of our program more difficult. We have divided into smaller groups of about ten families each, and try to meet monthly, rotating the decision-making and delegation of duties. Working in groups of this size can help us reach consensus on issues that have divided us in the past, such as the collection and mixing of compost materials, and how the finished compost is to be distributed to community beds or kitchen gardens. Finding a way to get people to work on one another's behalf as well as their own can be a slow and arduous process. We've had our setbacks, like disagreements between families over delegation of duties that have held us up when there is much work to be done, and early crop failures that caused some participants to lose faith in the program's viability. On the whole, though, we have made a great deal of progress in providing for our food needs.

By striving to include as many participants as possible in planning, we have seen our early efforts develop into a manifold process. For example, the simple act of asking certain community members to participate actively in the program, has given them an enthusiasm that seemed lacking in the past. It took two years to get anything to happen, but

*Picture from <u>Demystifying</u> <u>Evaluation</u>, Noreen Clark and James McCaffery, 1979, World Education, 1414 Sixth Avenue, New York, New York 10019.  Reviewed in Appropriate Technology Sourcebook, vol. II, p. 735.

*from some of the shared and recognizable successes and failures a stronger sense of commitment has developed to teach and share what we have learned. From this has emerged a leadership capability in some of the younger villagers, which has instilled pride in both the families of these people and the community as a whole. The young woman turning the compost pile under the tree over there has been asked to tour the research sites in some of the other villages, to share some of our new seeds and techniques.*

*We are learning to appreciate what food production really involves, so we seldom take anything for granted. The cycles of the seasons, the interactions of the plants and soil, the use of wastes and weeds as fertilizer, and the presence of an immense number of soil life forms all work together to form the most important circle, a cycle of life that is dynamic and indivisible.*

*Perhaps the most important aspect of our efforts has been learning to work together as a community. We share burdens like the hard work of digging beds, but we also share the fruits of our labor, like the rich compost we all contribute to. This pattern of give and take resembles that found in nature. We are learning to mesh the experience, insight and patience of older people with the energy, enthusiasm and creative instinct of youth. Thus we are learning to accept the variations in attitudes and needs that make us a diverse community and to respect one another.*

*Food links us together by the nature of common bonds. It is an individual need that is at the same time universal. We all need food to survive. It also points to the integral nature of our existence, as we cannot really possess the sustenance of food unless we discover the needs of the plant and the soil in which it grows, and provide for them in a way that will insure that its role in the cycle of life is permanently maintained. To do otherwise would mine the nutrients from the soil without returning them, and can only lead to eventual disruption in our gardens, in the form of disease, poor yields and crop failures. Unless we can recognize and provide for our needs as a people like good health, a secure future, and the freedom to benefit and suffer from our own choices, then we too face disruption, in the form of discontent, strife, and famine.*

136

If we take this idea of integral relationships seriously, and apply it earnestly, we will stand a better chance of producing not just bountiful gardens, but also a productive, healthy and peaceful society. The patience, careful observation, and respect for life we learn in the garden nurtures our community as well.

We come now to another aspect that is essential to our program. You see children involved here, especially in the planting and maintaining of trees. The trees provide us with a windbreak to prevent erosion of the area, and some of them produce fruit while others supply fuel. Some will one day provide building materials for the children and grandchildren of those planting the trees. We are learning that the trees play a larger role in the environment around us, affecting, for example, how moisture is retained in the soil and released into the atmosphere. They provide a habitat for other creatures, and besides, they are beautiful to look at! These trees being planted by the children are one of the most important measures we are taking to guarantee that what land we have for food and fuel production does not deteriorate or desertify, as has so much of the earth's surface.

One of the most positive trends emerging is that fewer of our young adults are choosing to leave our small village for the promises of the larger cities. As our food problems have decreased, employment has begun

to increase, and more people are finding that work in the community can be productive and meaningful. From the cooperative efforts of food-raising, some of us are finding ways to turn our particular skills into unique sources of income. Over here is a small pottery where locally dug clay is being used to produce a wide variety of items, from water containers and kitchen utensils to creative artwork. The couple who run the pottery are teaching children from the community. Other projects we hope to undertake are building a carpentry shop and the making and repairing of our tools.

This concludes the tour for today. Please feel free to walk back through any areas that have interested you, and to talk more with us. Thank you for coming to visit, and for showing your interest in what we are doing here.

We would like to leave you with a question as you go. Since our program has worked well for us and shown such potential for improvement, how do you suppose that we can best communicate our hopes to other individuals and villages who might benefit from a program similar to ours? It is only through such creative sharing that the earth can again be made productive. Please let us know your answer.

# CREATING OUR OWN PARADISE
### by David Duhon

When we consider our modern, urban culture, it is difficult to imagine that our future could be different because of a change in agriculture. Agriculture appears but one more industry supplying one of our many needs. Urban culture, however, co-evolved with extensive forms of agriculture. A shift to an intensive, small-scale, decentralized agriculture could mark the beginning of the evolution of a whole new culture with different kinds of individuals, small communities, towns, cities, and even a different order of world affairs.

In hunter/gatherer societies, it took about one square mile to provide the food for one person, so that only small groups of at most one hundred people were possible. In traditional societies based on extensive agriculture, houses were often clustered together into villages that included food storage but not food production. As a village grew, workers had to go further to reach the outlying fields. Eventually other villages sprang up that were more central to the distant fields.

An agriculture that takes ten acres to produce food for a family will produce smaller villages than one which takes only one acre. If a family needed only about a tenth of an acre to feed itself, then instead of housing being centralized and food production being spread around the periphery, the two could be integrated to create communities resembling large gardens dotted with houses. With intensive agriculture, larger populations need not increase the distance from house to fields, and larger, thriving agricultural communities would be possible that could provide a new synthesis of the best of urban and rural life. If each person's needs could be met in 4,000 square feet, a population density of over ten people per acre, or nearly 10,000 people per square mile would be possible. This is comparable to half the density of urban areas such as San Francisco county, California, or Queens county New York.

Our first towns, however, were not agricultural communities grown larger, but tranformed communities in which agriculture was increasingly replaced by non-agricultural occupations. Agricultural productivity had to increase to provide the needed surplus for urbanization. It may have been the case that forced payments of food as taxes to non-food producers in urban areas caused--out of necessity-- increases in total agricultural production through shifts to more extensive forms of agriculture that produced more per worker but less per area.

In order to feed the towns and cities, not only did there need to be a surplus, but it needed to be in a form that was concentrated in calories, easily transported, and easy to store--a form such as grains, oils, or herds of livestock. The specialized occupations of religion, government, commerce, industry, and the military produced no food and depended on--and could demand in the form of taxation--an agricultural surplus. Such complete divisions of labor might not be necessary in the future.

Shifts to a more intensive, efficient agriculture would not only free up land, but would also free up time for other pursuits. Small industries, the sciences, and the arts could all be maintained by people who also produce their own food, rather than by specialized occupations supported in great part by a wealthy urban elite. Art and sciences could receive more time rather than less; and the arts and sciences thus produced would flow from people's needs and values. With wealth accumulated more by individual households than by central urban governments, less people would be needed to protect and manage a society's wealth.

The values of rural life could be retained and integrated with many of the more favorable aspects of cities. High population densities with their accompanying urban stress need not be chosen. Just as a decrease in the area needed for agriculture allows for an integration of agriculture and housing, so will it allow the integration of human habitation and nature in the form of parks and wilderness areas. Many feel that it would be desirable for as much as fifty to seventy-five percent of the land to be left as wilderness. The choices available in the spectrum of city to country could be increased rather than decreased.

Large-scale military activities have historically made demands on agriculture similar to those of urbanization. What army could march off to conquer a neighboring state with their packs full of potatoes and onions! The creation of subject states or colonies serves to provide a country with the agricultural base needed for further growth of the already existing urban and military sectors. Both urbanization and military development require an agriculture that can produce large amounts of storable, transportable, and calorie-concentrated foods. It is not that a certain form of agriculture has created the urban-military state (which has developed into the military-industrial state), but rather that such nations have been able to manipulate their own agriculture and the agriculture of foreign lands that they influence or control to suit their needs.

What an improved agriculture with different goals could make possible is a true rural democracy. The benefits of such a society, which Thomas Jefferson recognized and advocated, can be possible for all. The values of a strong, agrarian democracy are part of the American tradition. These are the values upon which the notion of family farms are based.  These are the values that we have lost and need to return to.

Christianity tells us that we began in a highly productive garden and were forced out into the agriculture of fields and livestock due to the failings of humankind. A return to paradise may require that we abandon the agriculture whose origins are portrayed in the story of Eden and return to the garden.


*   *   *


Are such utopian dreams possible?  We have traveled our present paths for a period of centuries or even millenia.  Change will take time.  A more relevant question is how long can we continue on our present paths.  The life of luxury many Americans have come to take as their birthright is based largely on wealth, accumulated over time, which has been inequitably taken from other peoples and borrowed from our own descendants.  A dead-end of bankruptcy awaits that calls for a search for new paths.

Within various Eastern teachings is the concept of a multi-fold path; that there is some goal--enlightenment, nirvana, salvation--and a variety of paths which can be traveled down separately or all at once toward the same goal.  By taking a path such as "right livelihood" or "right thinking" to its greatest fulfillment, then the other paths are in effect traveled as well.

Changing society can be like that, although we can easily lose track of this fact in the pursuit of our own individual path.  Political activists tend to think that theirs is the only path, as might an artist, religious person, or couple raising a family.  Most people making the effort to improve society tend to see their own path as the only path to take.

How we sustain ourselves is an important path.  What could be a stronger poltical statement than developing a way of feeding and providing for ourselves that is in harmony with the needs of the planet?  Throughout the ages, the garden has been one of the few artistic pursuits attended to by nearly every class of society.  Your entire life can be a work of art.  The garden has also been central to people seeking lives of religious contemplation in the traditions of both East and West.  For centuries, Christian monks practiced self-sufficient food production--much of it using methods similar to modern biointensive techniques--in an effort to return to "the paradise of the garden of Eden."  Gardens might also replace television as the focal point of family life.

Many of us in this country are concerned with creating an improved agriculture as part of creating an improved society, and while some write about it, talk about it, and lobby for it, not enough of us choose to <u>practice</u> the sorts of agriculture that we advocate. Agriculture will not be changed by people advocating change. It can only be changed by people choosing to take direct responsibility for the care of the soil and the feeding of themselves and others. If we can show that people can take responsibility for producing their own food in less than a thousand square feet and in as little as an hour or two a day, then there can be few barriers to changing agriculture for those choosing to feed themselves in a just and responsible way. You do not have to wait until you move to the country, or until this or that change in the Department of Agriculture is made, or until you have gotten the perfect varieties for your locality, or the new miracle plants, or until you have figured out the final answer in companion planting. All you have to do is start. Your biggest barrier will always be yourself, but you can also be the source for a wealth of opportunities.

Take steps that you can live with--this year, next year, and the year after. The difficult part is to stay on a right path. Can I do this every year? Can my neighbor do this? What about starving people in another country? Can the technology I use to grow my food help create an equitable world food system, or am I using more than my share of the world's resources?

These are hard questions for Americans to ask because true equity is not a major part of our value system. Imagine a community of one hundred households, where twenty families, nearly all of whom are white, control the vast majority of the wealth of the community. Most of the other households contain darker skinned families and are very poor. In this poorer section, one entire household dies from starvation each year. Members of the poorer households earn less each day than members of the wealthy households earn in an hour. This is not South Africa. This is our own world community.

We have learned to accept that for one reason or another some people should get vastly more of the world's resources than others. Can we also accept the consequences of such inequalities? We would not allow such inequalities in our own neighborhood, nor do we approve of them in other communities around the world, such as those in South Africa. Why do we accept them within the world community?

Our planet is one circle. We cannot draw lines and claim that just this one little part is our world, and that on the other side of a river or ocean or imaginary line that the starvation and suffering is "their" problem. As we move closer to nuclear destruction we can realize the oneness of our destinies if war should start. If we choose instead to seek paradise, it must be for all. While the immediate problem is to feed people, true solutions will require changes in the values that control the world's resources. There can be no paradise when millions starve each year. A path can be found, and we are capable as individuals of taking first one step and then another.

Stephen Gaskin of The Farm in Tennessee said that what this country needs is for more people to become "voluntary peasants". To be a peasant does not imply to suffer or not to be able to enjoy life. It implies that you are responsible for the production of much of your own needs, and that you live for the most part outside of the money economy. To choose such a lifestyle is a choice to become a steward of the most precious resource we have--the earth. In the nurturing protection of the soil, water, crops and trees can be found the entire microcosm of artistic beauty, responsible intellect, and human wholeness which we all seek.

The right to vote is promoted as being an individual's access to influencing the government. Yet a citizen's vote will not stop one dollar from being spent on the build-up of military capabilities. Nor, in most cases does leafletting, writing letters, or taking part in political protests. Yet by lowering our income we can deny the defense department thousands and probably tens of thousands of tax dollars over the course of a lifetime.

Our free speech and the votes we make can be important for small changes, but our "dollar-votes" and our choices as to how we invest our time are the critical elements for making the larger changes that are needed. For those who do not approve of our growing military or other governmental policies, you can lower your income and legally withdraw your financial support. If it is a company that you do not approve of, then do not patronize it. You can if you wish lessen your dependence on the larger political-economic system, allowing you to withdraw your support from institutions you oppose, and invest your time and energy into more local systems such as your family, community, and garden.

When you produce food, or grow and harvest your own wood, or produce your own clothing you are producing wealth for yourself that is for the most part outside of the entangling web of our economic system. Most of your needs can be supplied from such wealth. Individuals may have little or no say in the control of our political-economic system, but they can control their own actions, and they can choose to help create different systems that are more responsible.

We are not islands, and it is important that we balance that which we withdraw from society with that which we choose to give in other ways. We can give food, time, money, and even compost to help feed others. We can do volunteer work within our community to help build the sort of world which we would like to have. We can attempt to become part of a community in some other, poorer part of the world and thus focus our efforts within our new community. We can give our time and good efforts to help in the problems of our own local governments. Most importantly, we can join in the community around us, no matter how different from us it may seem. The most powerful tool we all have in trying to make change is our own example. If we can live adequate, comfortable, and joyous lives that demonstrate to others that what we are advocating is both possible and rewarding, then we will have a strong and positive effect in our lifetime. If we are to return to the garden, we must create our own paradise, and we must begin in our own lives.

# TAKING ACTION NOW:
## you and Ecology Action

During the last 14 years Ecology Action has done many things to help others help themselves by trying to get the needed "tools" in place in time. Its techniques are now being used by an estimated one-half million people in over 100 countries, mostly informally and in some formal situations including the Peace Corps. Countries where it is being practiced include Australia, Canada, Botswana, the Peoples' Republic of China, Japan, Togo, Mexico, Tanzania, India, England, Zambia, Kenya, and the Philippines.

To keep people around the world current on new developments, Ecology Action maintains a newsletter and publishes practical research information in "how to" form. Included in these are <u>Intensive Food Production on a Human Scale</u>, a complete transcription of the 1981 Third International Conference on Small-Scale and Intensive Food-Raising attended by 100 individuals from fourteen countries, which Ecology Action co-sponsored. Ecology Action has also been helping people produce beautiful and bountiful gardens with seeds, tools, books, research advice, and supplies at its Palo Alto Educational Center and non-profit Organic Gardening Store, Common Ground. Many of these items are included in our Bountiful Gardens biointensive mail order service -- including Chase organically grown seeds.

As Ecology Action has released each of its new and pioneering findings, they have often been met initially with skepticism. For example, the reduced water application seemed overstated - but within five years this was accepted. Double-dug, raised growing beds were strange to many -- yet they have often become the norm.

In its ongoing quest to discover and document the smallest area on which one person can be self-reliant while maintaining soil health on a sustainable basis, Ecology Action has several long term objectives. We hope these objectives will begin to be fully developed within the next ten years -- and as an organization we intend to continue testing these methods over at least the next 50 to 100 years. This is especially important since the problems in agriculture often do not appear for 50 to 100 years.*

---

* No doubt this is why commercial chemical agriculture's dilemmas are just becoming apparent. Its techniques have only been used extensively for a relatively short period of time. Organically-based food-raising practices have been used for a much longer period of time throughout the world, though they are just beginning to be fully understood. It is commercial, chemical agriculture which represents the new and relatively untested path.

Some needed research and development objectives are:

1. <u>To grow a complete vegetarian diet in a sustainable way on 700 square feet (less than one circle).</u> This could probably eventually be done in under an hour a day (on the average) during an 8-month growing season -- a growing period experienced by most people in the Third World and many in the United States. In contrast, it takes approximately 4,800 square feet (about five circles) to grow a vegetarian diet in Japan using standard Japanese techniques, 10,000 square feet in the United States (ten circles), and 32,000 square feet (thirty-two circles) in India. A typical U.S. meat diet grown by standard U.S. techniques would require even more -- up to 45,000 to 85,000 square feet (forty-five to eighty-five circles). In contrast each person in the Third World may soon have as little as 2,100 square feet (about two circles) of agricultural land to use. More than 700 square feet would normally be required to grow a vegetarian diet, but the careful selection of crops using a detailed dietary knowledge makes the lower figure possible with yields generally only 2 times U.S. commercial averages. These yields are much less than the highest biointensive potential.

2. <u>To grow a complete diet for a goat or cow sustainably on a much smaller area than is required by current practices - probably in pasture and meadow lands.</u> In the United States about 20,000 square feet (twenty circles) are currently required to maintain one goat and 40,000 square feet (forty circles) for one cow. An even larger area is required to maintain these animals in most Third World situations. The area may be reduced to as little as 2,500 square feet (two and one-half circles) for one goat and 5,000 square feet (five circles) for one cow by using biointensive growing practices, Voisin harvesting techniques, weight- and area-efficient protein, calorie, and calcium concentrating plants, special feeding techniques.

3. <u>To annually grow 1,000 pounds of firewood, sustainably, on as little as 2,400 square feet (almost two and one-half circles) using biointensive and coppicing techniques.</u> This amount of fuel together with the use of specially prepared pieces of wood could provide all the fuel needs for one person in most climates. Currently, as much as 38,000 square feet (thirty-eight circles) and even more are probably used for this pur-

pose due to growing, processing, and burning inefficiencies. Growing firewood on such a small scale could mean that individuals could also be effective in our planet's reforestation. Trees grown by biointensive coppicing techniques could also produce some food in the form of nuts and fruit, and provide living fences for animals. These living fences could be used to help stop the current depletion of the Earth's surface through uncontained grazing.

4. To continue apprentice programs to train people to set up needed, fully-operating mini-farms for education, development, and research. Over the years, Ecology Action's program has taught more than 90 individuals. Thousands more have been reached through short classes, and hundreds of thousands through our publications. Only now, however, is the program beginning to teach teachers who may soon go out and set up sites capable of maintaining themselves both nutritionally through the use of One Circle-type diets, and financially on a low-income basis through the sale of a small percentage of the crops they grow. This food and financial self-reliance may be even easier in Third World countries. The cost of food makes up a higher portion of the average income (in comparison to the portion of income that food purchasing requires in the U.S.). Also, average income levels are much lower there than here. Therefore, a smaller growing area may bring in a good Third World income because food prices are relatively high and incomes are relatively low.

5. To develop a teaching model which will contain about 21 growing beds (a a little over two circles) -- seven beds for food, seven beds for cover crops, and seven beds for income. This is a good-sized learning unit. Eventually economic crops will need to be marketed from only about ten percent of one's growing beds, so that over time, the "exporting" of the soil's nutrients can be minimized.

6. To develop a full understanding of natural rainfall, arid cultivation, three-tiered agriculture, minimum tillage and other key modifications for biointensive food-raising. Much of the world's food is grown under natural rainfall, semi-arid and even arid conditions. Modifications to current biointensive practices may make much higher yields possible in these areas. Three-tiered agriculture in which a variety of plant forms

and sizes, such as trees, grapes, and vegetables or grains, are grown together to optimize space, light and soil nutrient consumption and to more closely mimic the natural environment, may also enhance bio-intensive techniques. Minimum tillage practices, such as those developed in <u>One Straw Revolution</u>, can produce high yields without chemical fertilizers and pesticides, and are especially attractive because they improve soil structure and fertility.

7. <u>To elevate farming to the status such an important, planet-nourishing profession deserves.</u> Instead of looking upon ourselves as "poor, dumb dirt farmers", who need to send our children to college so they can get out of farming and "improve their lot", we should strive to improve our agricultural self-image so that our youth might choose to learn biointensive mini-farming, tree culture and other sustainable practices at the highest levels of intelligence and sensitivity whether through college or some other route. Such intelligence and sensitivity is needed, so that our children can shape and create a sustainable, enjoyable world environment without hunger. We need to "return to the earth" literally and figuratively, so that our cities, civilizations and communities may be built upon a strong base.

8. <u>To continue and expand correspondence, outreach and publication programs, and to develop more staff with increased skills.</u> Ecology Action answers thousands of inquiries and hundreds of letters at its two locations. We also provide numerous "how to" classes, plus slide shows and talks on various food-raising topics and self-reliance skills as part of the educational process as we seek to enable others and ourselves to become better equipped with these skills in urban and rural areas.

We continue to run our non-profit retail and mail order "stores" and to gradually build our small teaching, demonstration, and research mini-farm. Growing beds are being developed, seedlings planted, compost made, successes and failures encountered and evaluated, students taught, and letters answered from around the world.

You can begin in this "growing" process, too, by taking action in your own life to make a positive difference. Then 50 to 100 years from now our children's children may be successful, skilled food-raisers in only a fraction of a day's time and the rest of the time may be spent pursuing other interests -- in business, science, and the arts.

Some possible activities for now might include:

- Beginning to grow all your food, clothing, fuel, and income in as little as 4,000 square feet (four circles).

- Growing all the seed for next year's crops at home in an area as small as 100 square feet (one-tenth of a circle).

- Supporting someone else to learn sustainable food-raising skills. For example, 20 people can each contribute $20 a month as an "Involvement Corps" for a person's living expenses. Another person can provide a room for her or him to live in. Others can provide meals. In this way, the learning process can begin now with support from local sources. This is one of the ways Ecology Action began in 1971.

- Starting a national contest to determine who can be the first to grow 52, one-pound loaves of bread in as little as 200 square feet in their own backyard.

- Teaching others food-raising skills.

- Planting a tree each year, month, or week.

- Setting up a tree nursery.

- While in school, selecting a report or thesis with long-term, sustainable implications which will result in practical, sophisticated, low-technology solutions to help each of us help ourselves to become more truly self-reliant and to ensure a healthy, abundant planet.

- Helping a neighborhood or community to become more self-reliant.

- Starting an urban or rural mini-farm and mini-ag station. Local, regional and national mini-farming sites, such as Ecology Action's, are needed as resource centers for gathering and sharing experience and information.


Over the years, Ecology Action has documented many of the biointensive mini-farming techniques and pioneered many mini-farming concepts and publications. Worldwide it is unique in this documentation process, in the scope and breadth of its detailed research and analysis, and in the tailoring of its work to the needs of the average person facing the world in the 1990 to 2000 period. Hopefully, by all working together, we can continue this process and provide a practical, personal base from which we all can thrive, in all of our diverse forms. With the soil's biological life as a base, humankind's wonderous potential can truly unfold.

# Solving The Diet

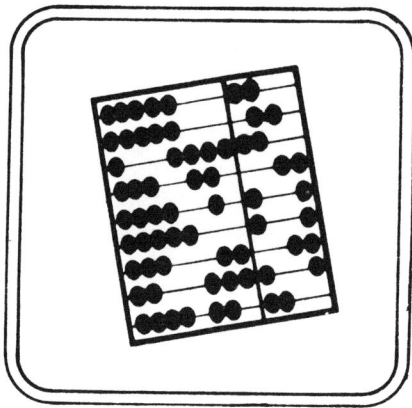

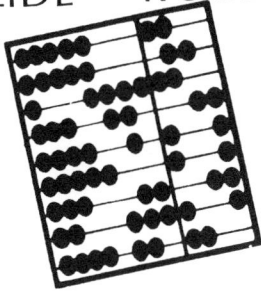

SLIDE RULES

The purpose of the fourteen crop slide rules is to enable you to make speedy estimations for each crop of the total annual yield (Y/yr), the average daily yield (Y/day = Y/yr ÷ 365), and the amounts of the various nutrients that are supplied daily when any one of these variables is known or assumed. For a given crop, if you set the appropriate number on the sliding log scale to annual yield, daily yield, area, or the amount for any single nutrient, you will then be able to read off the resulting numbers for all the other values. The following table shows the abbreviations used on the slide rules and the standard units that are assumed.

| | | |
|---|---|---|
| Cal = calories, kcal | Carb = carbohydrates, g | $B_6$ = vitamin $B_6$, mg |
| Pro = protein, g | Fat = fat, g | Pant = Pantothenic acid, mg |
| Iso = Isoleucine, mg | Lino = linoleic acid, g | I = Iodine, mcg |
| Leu = leucine, mg | A = vitamin A, RE | Zn = zinc, mg |
| C+M = cystine+methionine mg | $B_2$ = riboflavin, mg | Ca = calcium, mg |
| Tryp = tryptophan, mg | $B_3$ = niacin, mg | Fe = iron, mg |
| AREA = area, sq. ft. | Y/day = Y/yr ÷ 365, or the daily weight of food. | Y/yr = annual adjusted yields, pounds. |

kcal = calories of food energy
mg = milligrams, 1000 mg = 1 g
RE = Retinol equivalents, see the
    vitamin A section

g = grams, 454 grams = 1 pound
mcg = micrograms, 1000 mcg = 1 mg
sq. ft. = square feet, 100 square feet =
    9.29 square meters

Try it for yourself. Cut out all of the slide rules and log scales. Use a knife, single edged razor blade, or exacto knife to cut the dotted lines on either side of the slide rules. Insert the log scales as shown.

log scale

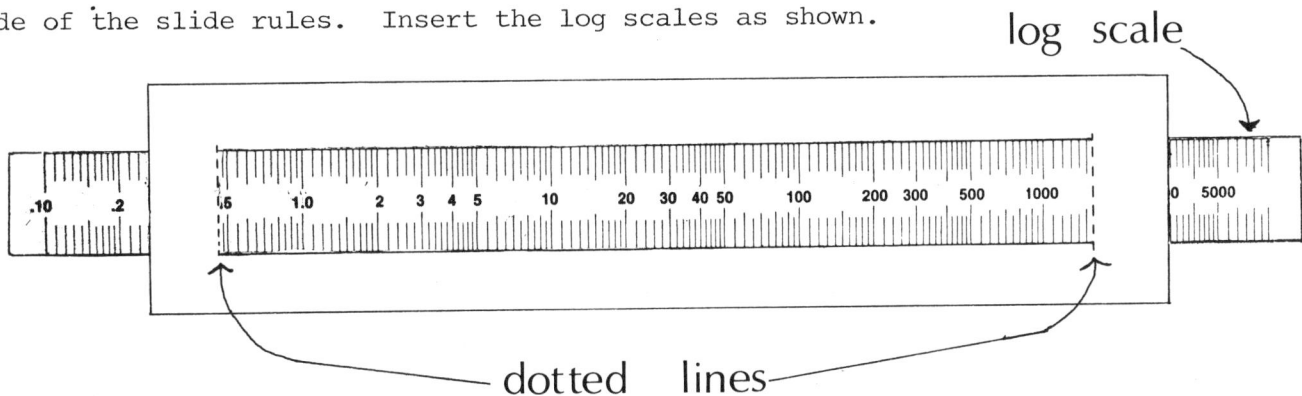

dotted lines

Now you are ready.

Take the slide rule for potatoes. Set 'AREA' at 100. Read off the annual adjusted yield, 'Y/yr', and the daily yield, 'Y/day'. See what some of the nutrient amounts that could be supplied are. Now set calories, 'Cal' at 2,000, and see what the daily amount (Y/day) would be to supply this amount of calories. Finally, set the daily potato consumption (Y/day) at 2.0--assume you will eat two pounds of baked potatoes per day. The area needed and nutrients provided can all be read. Try these calculations for other crops that are of special interest to you.

It is possible that in the process of designing a diet, one or more of the nutrient amounts, and possibly the weight per day (Y/day) will have a value below 0.1, and will therefore be off the scale, to the left of the lowest amount covered by the log scale. To correct for this problem, you can use a process called "factoring up". You will already have set the slide rule for a variable--area, weight, or a nutrient. You should reset this variable at a value that has been multiplied by a factor of ten or a hundred. All the other readings will now have to be correspondingly divided by a factor of ten or a hundred. This will allow you to get readings for values that were previously off the scale to the low end.

It is easy to change the yield figure for a crop to match yields that you have found in your garden. If, however, your yield data represents only one growing season, it might be good to balance this with the broader data base represented in the Good Yield figures from How to Grow More Vegetables.... This can be done by averaging the two yield figures; or with two years of data, you take a three way average of your two yields and the Good Yield figure. As you develop a larger data base--taking yield data over a number of years--it may be good to weight more heavily the last year or two's yields, as these may be better factors of prediction than your earlier yield data.

To "reset" your yield figures, use the following procedure:

1) Use a pencil and cross out 'AREA'.
2) Set 'Y/yr' at the correct adjusted yield.
3) Holding this setting, draw a line in pencil at the point corresponding to 100 on the log scale.
4) Label this line 'AREA'.

It is also possible to have more than one 'AREA' in order to deal with different assumptions as to yield. You could, for example, mark one 'AREA$_s$' to indicate a spring planted crop, and one 'AREA$_f$' for the fall planted crop. If this is confusing (that is, changing the 'AREA' marker when the yield is what is being changed), think of 'AREA' as reading "the area at the assumed yield".

Slide rules may easily be created for crops other than the fourteen dealt with in this edition of One Circle. Fourteen blank slide rules together with log scales have been included for this purpose. Take care in the selection of additional crops. It is easy to go to a lot of trouble researching a crop that is not that helpful in terms of reducing the area required for a complete diet. Be sure to see if the crop is efficient in at least some of the more problematic nutrients, such as calories, fat, linoleic acid, riboflavin, or iron for women. You may of course want to include a crop for other reasons, such as taste, storage qualities, or the fact that it may produce well during a season when none of your other crops do very well.

To set a blank slide rule once all the data has been collected and processed (see page 126), use the following procedure:

1) Find the nutrient that is lowest per pound in its standard unit. Mark and label this unit just to the right of the left-hand dotted line on the slide rule.

2) Move the log scale so that the correct value per pound for this nutrient is aligned with the mark. Keeping the log scale in this position, find 1.00, mark this spot, and label it 'Y/day' for yield per day.

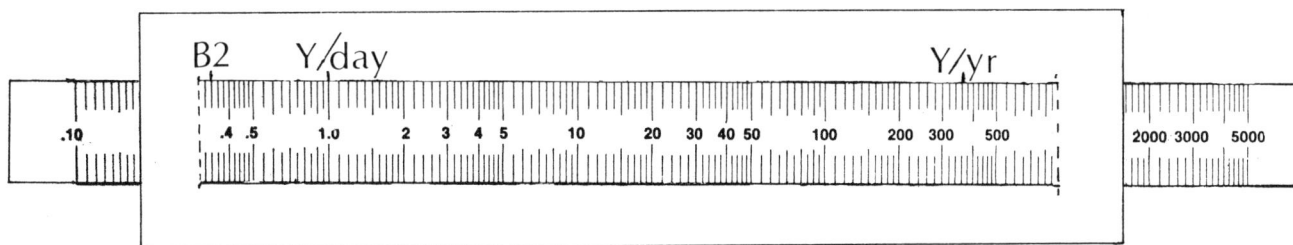

3) Keeping 'Y/day' at 1.00, mark and label all the other nutrients. Since some nutrients may have values close to each other, some planning is required to make a neat and easily readable slide rule. Remember that nutrients can be marked either above or below the log scale.

4) Still keeping 'Y/day' at 1.00, mark and label 'Y/yr' at the point corresponding to 365.

5) Move the log scale to align 'Y/yr' with the figure for adjusted annual yield.

6) Holding the slide rule in this position, mark the slide rule at the point corresponding to 100, and label this 'AREA'. Label the slide rule with the name of the crop in the upper right-hand corner.

In the process of solving for a diet, you have to do a large number of multiplication and division calculations. Two of the log scales can be used together as a simple slide rule for either division or multiplication. To find what percentage one number is of another, say, what percentage A is of B, you divide A by B and multiply by 100: A/B x 100. To give a more real example, lets say you have a mix of foods that can provide .86 mg of riboflavin, and your design target for riboflavin is 1.6 mg, and you need to determine what percentage of your design target you have--what percentage .86 mg is of 1.6 mg. To divide .86 by 1.6, you need to first arrange the two log scales, one above the other, so that their long edges are touching (see diagram). Line up .86 on the upper scale with 1.6 on the lower scale.

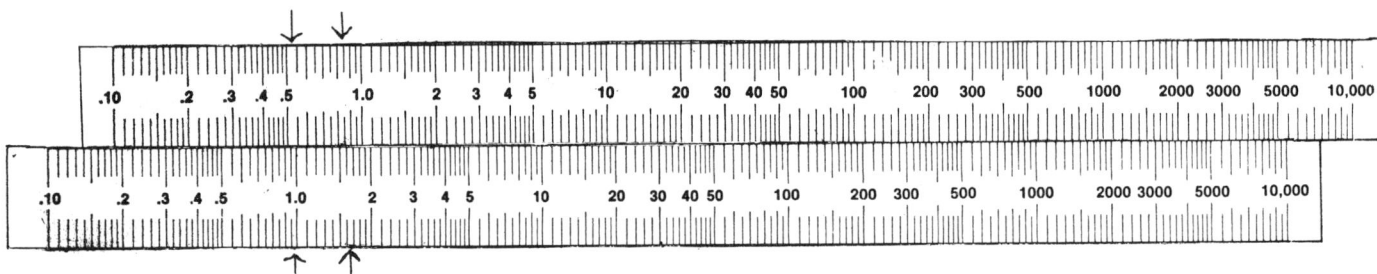

Now, without moving the scales, find 1.0 on the <u>lower</u> scale. The number corresponding to this on the <u>upper</u> scale is about .54, which is the answer, approximately, to .86 divided by 1.6. To multiply this by 100, simply move the digit over two places to the right, and you get the final answer of 54 percent.

To multiply two numbers, line up 1.0 on the <u>upper</u> scale with one of the numbers you want to multiply on the <u>lower</u> scale. Find the other number on the upper scale. The corresponding number on the <u>lower</u> scale is your solution. You may find it helpful in aligning the log scales to use some sort of straight edge.

## COLLARDS

B6  B2  Fat  B3  Pro  Carb  I  Cal  Y/yr  Leu
                                          Iso

Y/day  Pant  Fe        AREA  Tryp  C+M  Ca        A        © 1985

## FILBERTS

Y/day  B2  B3    Zn  Lino  Carb    Y/yr  Ca  C+M  AREA  Iso

        B6  Pant  I  Fe    A    Fat    Tryp  Cal  Leu        © 1985
                          Pro

## GARLIC

B2  Y/day  B3    Fe    Pro    Carb  AREA  Cal

    Fat        Zn  I        Ca  Y/yr        © 1985

## LEEKS

    Y/day  B3                AREA  Y/yr
B2      Fat    Fe  Pro    A        Cal    Iso  Leu

        B6  I                Carb    Ca    C+M        © 1985
          Zn

## ONIONS

        Y/day            AREA  Iso  Cal
Pant  B2    Fat    Zn    Pro    A  C+M  Ca    Y/yr

        B6      B3  Fe        Carb    Leu        © 1985
                                    Tryp

## PARSLEY

B6  B2  Fat  B3  Pro  Carb    Cal  Y/yr    Ca        A    PARSLEY

Y/day    Zn        Fe  C+M  Tryp  AREA        © 1985
    Pant

## PARSNIPS

B2  Y/day  Pant  Pro  I    AREA  Ca  Y/yr    PARSNIPS

    B6  B3  Fe    A    Carb    Cal        © 1985
      Fat

## PEANUTS

Carb    Y/yr                    Iso
B2    B6        Pant    Lino | Pro Fat |        Tryp  C+M |  Leu

Y/day            Fe  Zn        B3 |        Ca            Cal        © 1985

AREA

## POTATOES

B2   Fat Y/day  Zn        Pro        Ca | |  C+M  Y/yr |  Leu

Lino        B6 |  Fe  B3            Carb      Iso |        © 1985
Pant            Tryp    Cal

## SOYBEANS

B2   Y/day  B3  B6        Lino  Fat    Pro        Y/yr  Tryp  AREA  Iso

Zn    Pant  Fe  A  Carb        Ca  Cal    C+M      Leu  © 1985

## SUNFLOWER SEEDS

Y/day            B6        B3  A        Pro  Fat  Y/yr    C+M  Leu
Iso

B2                Fe  Carb |        Ca Tryp  Cal |  AREA  © 1985
Lino

## SWEET POTATOES

Zn        B6  Fat Pant  Pro        Tryp |  Carb Y/yr Cal

B2  Lino |        B3 |        Ca| Leu |            A  © 1985
Y/day    Fe            C+M  Iso    AREA

## TURNIPS

B2
Lino  B6 Y/day |    B3  Fe  Pro  Carb AREA Ca| | | Leu        C+M Y/yr

Pant        Fat            Zn            Tryp  Iso  Ca            A  © 1985

## WHEAT

Lino                    Y/yr  AREA  Leu
B2  Y/day    |  | Fat Fe      Pro    Ca Carb |        | C+M |

B6 | Zn  B3            Tryp  Cal | Iso    © 1985
Pant

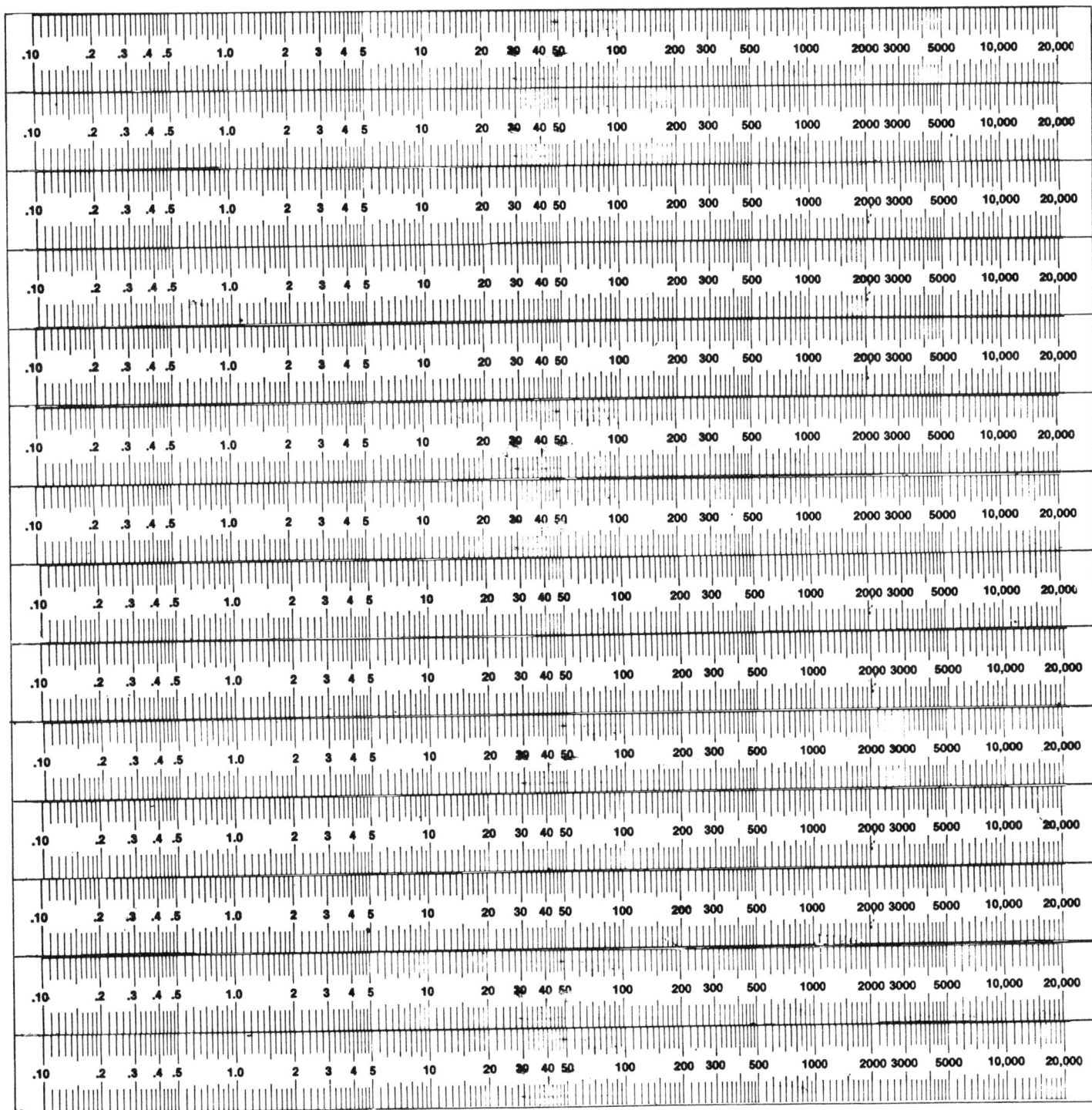

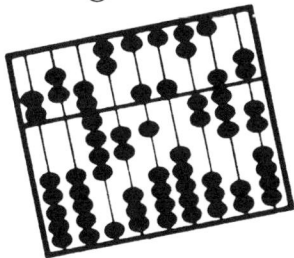

Solving

The Diet

There are undoubtedly excellent techniques that would allow a computer to quickly and accurately design a minimal area diet which would meet a set of specified assumptions. Such a design approach, however, can not easily and adequately meet the needs addressed in this book. Design techniques are needed that can deal with differing growing conditions, yield levels, food preferences, and other local variables. Periodic adjustments are also needed to account for improved techniques, changing yields, changing food preferences, and the introduction of new crops. A centralized, high-tech answer is not a good answer to development needs. It is important that as many people as possible understand and participate in the process of design, and that it be undertaken at a local level.

This chapter uses a number of techniques which may at first be difficult to understand. Patience and careful study of the examples should bring success to anyone who has progressed this far in the text. A person's interest and aptitude may, however, lead them to seek simpler approaches. While the diet plans listed in the next chapter are not being advocated, they may be used as a base, modified using the slide rules to meet your needs, and used as a good starting place. Even if you just shift your garden to include more efficient crops, particularly crops that are area efficient for calories, you can begin to produce more of your nutritional needs, monitor this progress, and respond to the results with shifts each year in your garden plan. This is an excellent design approach which takes a pragmatic rather than a theoretical approach.

The design approach that is presented in this book is not a final product, and while based on considerable research, it has not yet been fully tested. Improvements and further testing are needed, but so are answers that can begin to be applied immediately. The world food problem can not wait for answers that are completely neat and clean with all the bugs worked out. We must begin now, and all are invited to help.

The basic problem in the design of a minimal area diet is to supply adequate nutrition while keeping the weight of food within consumable limits and still keeping the area needed to produce the food as minimal as possible. The general process begins with minimizing the number of variables under consideration. This narrowing process has already been accomplished with the selection of the _Critical Nutrients_, and the fourteen efficient crops. The next step is to break the problem down into simpler components that are more easily solved. Once a tentative solution has been reached, all the nutrients must be checked, garden scheduling and cultivation practices must be worked out, and any needed readjustments made. The plan is then ready for testing--

first on the plate in front of you and then in the garden.

For the design process it is sometimes useful to be able to directly compare _Weight Efficiency Values_ and _Area Efficiency Values_. This is possible if these values are first converted into coefficients. An _Efficiency Coefficient_ shall be defined as the _Efficiency Value_ divided by the design target. Express the area design target in terms of the number of 100 square foot beds, so that 8.5 beds is equal to 850 square feet, and 5.5 beds is equal to 550 square feet. A food is efficient for a given nutrient if the appropriate _Efficiency Coefficient_ is 1.00 or less.

These coefficients give a useful basis for understanding and comparing efficiency values, even if one is for area and the other for weight. If the _Weight Efficiency Coefficient_ for a food for a nutrient is .86, then that food can produce all of the need for that nutrient in 86 percent of the design target for weight. If the _Area Efficiency Coefficient_ for another food and another nutrient is .66. then this second food can be said to be more efficient in meeting the area design target for the nutrient under consideration than was the first food in meeting the weight design target for its nutrient since it meets the nutrient need in only 66% of the weight target.

The tables on the next two pages give _Efficiency Coefficients_ for all the foods and nutrient combinations for which the needed data has been found for the fourteen crops. These are given for both men and women. These charts will still be useful for comparing crops if you use different area targets. You may find it useful later to cut out this sheet rather than to constantly be flipping back to this section.

A lengthy and careful examination of these numbers will help bring about an understanding of the relationship between crop characteristics and diet design. Such a general understanding can be of great help. You should also refer to these charts frequently during the design process.

Get pencil and paper and use the charts to answer the following questions:

1. _Which nutrients will be easy to provide within the weight and area constraints?_

2. _Which nutrients will prove the most difficult to provide?_

3. _Which foods can act as supplements for certain nutrients by providing much of the needs for that nutrient in a very small area and weight? Try defining supplements as foods whose Weight and Area Coefficients are both 0.25 or less for a given nutrient._

4. _Which foods are especially good overall performers for a variety of nutrients for both weight and area?_

5. _For those foods that are neither supplements nor good overall performers, why are they included--what problem nutrient are they especially efficient for relative to weight or area._

| WEIGHT EFFICIENCY COEFFICIENTS Nutrient | | Collards | Filberts | Garlic | Leeks | Onions | Parsley | Parsnips | Peanuts | Potatoes | Soybeans | Sunflower Seeds | Sweet Potatoes | Turnips | Wheat |
|---|---|---|---|---|---|---|---|---|---|---|---|---|---|---|---|
| Calories | M | 2.47 | .16 | .72 | 1.91 | 2.60 | 2.27 | 1.32 | .17 | 1.07 | .84 | .18 | .70 | 3.48 | .41 |
| | F | 2.00 | .13 | .58 | 1.54 | 2.10 | 1.84 | 1.07 | .14 | .86 | .68 | .14 | .57 | 2.81 | .33 |
| Protein | M | .57 | .16 | .33 | .93 | 1.37 | .57 | 1.21 | .08 | .79 | .21 | .09 | .98 | .83 | .21 |
| | F | .51 | .15 | .30 | .84 | 1.23 | .51 | 1.09 | .07 | .71 | .19 | .08 | .88 | .74 | .19 |
| Isoleucine | M | .41 | .03 | -- | .26 | 2.31 | -- | -- | .05 | .61 | .07 | .07 | .96 | .55 | .15 |
| | F | .37 | .03 | -- | .24 | 2.09 | -- | -- | .04 | .55 | .07 | .07 | .87 | .50 | .14 |
| Leucine | M | .31 | .04 | -- | .21 | 1.67 | -- | -- | .03 | .51 | .06 | .06 | .87 | .37 | .10 |
| | F | .28 | .04 | -- | .19 | 1.51 | -- | -- | .03 | .46 | .05 | .06 | .79 | .34 | .09 |
| Cystine + Methionine | M | .37 | .13 | -- | .19 | 2.40 | 2.13 | -- | .05 | 1.01 | .11 | .08 | 1.07 | .85 | .10 |
| | F | .33 | .12 | -- | .18 | 2.18 | 1.94 | -- | .05 | .92 | .10 | .07 | .98 | .78 | .09 |
| Tryptophan | M | .23 | .04 | -- | -- | .58 | .16 | -- | .04 | .35 | .07 | .06 | .53 | .33 | .12 |
| | F | .21 | .04 | -- | -- | .52 | .14 | -- | .03 | .32 | .06 | .05 | .47 | .29 | .10 |
| Carbohydrate | M | 2.06 | .89 | .48 | 1.33 | 1.71 | 1.75 | .85 | .84 | .70 | 1.47 | .75 | .45 | 2.74 | .29 |
| | F | 1.67 | .72 | .39 | 1.07 | 1.38 | 1.41 | .69 | .68 | .57 | 1.19 | .60 | .37 | 2.22 | .23 |
| Fat | M | 1.56 | .02 | 5.56 | 3.57 | 10.0 | 1.85 | 2.17 | .02 | 10.0 | .22 | .02 | 2.17 | 4.03 | .76 |
| | F | 1.25 | .01 | 4.44 | 2.86 | 8.00 | 1.48 | 1.74 | .02 | 8.00 | .17 | .02 | 1.74 | 3.23 | .61 |
| Linoleic Acid | M | -- | .02 | -- | -- | -- | -- | -- | .01 | 2.88 | .06 | .004 | .97 | 4.42 | .34 |
| | F | -- | .01 | -- | -- | -- | -- | -- | .01 | 2.31 | .04 | .004 | .78 | 3.53 | .27 |
| Vitamin A | M | .03 | 2.06 | -- | 5.56 | 5.56 | .03 | 7.25 | -- | -- | 7.34 | 4.39 | .03 | .04 | -- |
| | F | .03 | 1.80 | -- | 4.85 | 4.85 | .02 | 6.32 | -- | -- | 6.41 | 3.83 | .02 | .03 | -- |
| Riboflavin | M | .19 | .11 | .74 | .99 | 1.48 | .23 | .65 | .45 | 1.48 | .65 | .26 | .83 | .19 | .68 |
| | F | .15 | .09 | .61 | .81 | 1.21 | .18 | .53 | .37 | 1.21 | .53 | .21 | .68 | .16 | .56 |
| Niacin | M | .39 | .73 | 1.32 | 1.30 | 3.37 | .55 | 3.33 | .04 | .39 | 1.11 | .12 | .94 | .88 | .21 |
| | F | .31 | .58 | 1.04 | 1.03 | 2.63 | .43 | 2.63 | .03 | .31 | .88 | .10 | .74 | .70 | .17 |
| Vitamin $B_6$ | M | .37 | .13 | -- | .37 | 1.15 | .46 | .81 | .25 | .31 | .11 | .06 | .34 | .78 | .11 |
| | F | .41 | .14 | -- | .40 | 1.25 | .50 | .91 | .28 | .34 | .12 | .06 | .37 | .85 | .12 |
| Pantothenic Acid | M | .42 | .16 | -- | -- | 10.4 | .60 | .31 | .08 | .51 | .11 | -- | .22 | 1.77 | .23 |
| | F | .45 | .18 | -- | -- | 11.4 | .66 | .33 | .08 | .55 | .12 | -- | .24 | 1.93 | .26 |
| Iodine | M | .28 | 2.41 | 1.76 | -- | .34 | -- | 1.33 | .24 | .32 | -- | -- | .43 | .08 | 6.61 |
| | F | .24 | 2.02 | 1.48 | -- | .28 | -- | 1.22 | .20 | .27 | -- | -- | .36 | .07 | 5.54 |
| Zinc | M | -- | .12 | .28 | 1.18 | 1.04 | .41 | -- | .11 | .61 | .55 | -- | 4.76 | .14 | .21 |
| | F | -- | .13 | .30 | 1.29 | 1.14 | .44 | -- | .12 | .67 | .66 | -- | 5.20 | .15 | .23 |
| Calcium | M | .09 | .09 | .63 | .35 | .68 | .09 | .37 | .31 | 2.03 | .25 | .15 | .46 | .10 | .62 |
| | F | .10 | .10 | .69 | .39 | .74 | .10 | .40 | .34 | 2.22 | .27 | .17 | .50 | .10 | .68 |
| Iron | M | .37 | .11 | .25 | .33 | .72 | .06 | .52 | .18 | .52 | .14 | .05 | .41 | .25 | .15 |
| | F | .73 | .21 | .48 | .66 | 1.42 | .12 | 1.02 | .36 | 1.02 | .27 | .10 | .80 | .49 | .30 |

| AREA EFFICIENCY COEFFICIENTS / Nutrient | | Collards | Filberts | Garlic | Leeks | Onions | Parsley | Parsnips | Peanuts | Potatoes | Soybeans | Sunflower Seeds | Sweet Potatoes | Turnips | Wheat |
|---|---|---|---|---|---|---|---|---|---|---|---|---|---|---|---|
| Calories | M | 2.12 | 3.25 | 1.55 | 2.05 | .84 | 8.34 | .71 | 4.51 | .73 | 9.02 | 4.55 | 2.66 | 1.66 | 3.83 |
|  | F | 2.53 | 3.69 | 1.78 | 2.34 | .96 | 9.58 | .82 | 5.18 | .84 | 10.3 | 5.24 | 3.05 | 1.90 | 4.39 |
| Protein | M | .49 | 3.39 | .71 | 1.00 | .44 | 2.11 | .66 | 2.02 | .54 | 2.25 | 2.19 | 3.72 | .40 | 1.99 |
|  | F | .62 | 4.27 | .91 | 1.27 | .56 | 2.67 | .83 | 2.59 | .69 | 2.85 | 2.79 | 4.72 | .50 | 2.54 |
| Isoleucine | M | .36 | .66 | -- | .28 | .74 | -- | -- | 1.20 | .42 | .79 | 1.89 | 3.65 | .26 | 1.40 |
|  | F | .46 | .85 | -- | .36 | .95 | -- | -- | 1.53 | .53 | 1.02 | 2.39 | 4.67 | .34 | 1.80 |
| Leucine | M | .26 | .86 | -- | .22 | .54 | -- | -- | .86 | .35 | .61 | 1.67 | 3.30 | .18 | .92 |
|  | F | .34 | 1.12 | -- | .28 | .69 | -- | -- | 1.06 | .45 | .77 | 2.12 | 4.22 | .23 | 1.18 |
| Cystine + Methionine | M | .31 | 2.77 | -- | .21 | .77 | 7.85 | -- | 1.42 | .69 | 1.15 | 1.98 | 4.07 | .41 | .95 |
|  | F | .41 | 3.58 | -- | .27 | 1.00 | 10.1 | -- | 1.79 | .89 | 1.49 | 2.52 | 5.24 | .53 | 1.22 |
| Tryptophan | M | .20 | .90 | -- | -- | ..19 | .58 | -- | .99 | .24 | .70 | 1.46 | 1.99 | .16 | 1.07 |
|  | F | .25 | 1.18 | -- | -- | .24 | .74 | -- | 1.26 | .31 | .88 | 1.86 | 2.55 | .20 | 1.37 |
| Carbohydrate | M | 1.77 | 18.5 | 1.04 | 1.43 | .55 | 6.44 | .46 | 21.8 | .48 | 15.8 | 19.3 | 1.72 | 1.31 | 2.70 |
|  | F | 2.03 | 21.2 | 1.19 | 1.63 | .63 | 7.73 | .52 | 24.9 | .55 | 18.1 | 22.0 | 1.97 | 1.50 | 3.09 |
| Fat | M | 1.34 | .38 | 11.9 | 3.83 | 3.22 | 6.82 | 1.18 | .60 | 6.84 | 2.31 | .60 | 8.21 | 1.93 | 7.09 |
|  | F | 1.52 | .43 | 13.5 | 4.34 | 3.65 | 7.73 | 1.33 | .66 | 7.76 | 2.63 | .66 | 9.34 | 2.18 | 8.03 |
| Linoleic Acid | M | -- | .35 | -- | -- | -- | -- | -- | .30 | 1.97 | .59 | .13 | 3.69 | 2.11 | 3.18 |
|  | F | -- | .37 | -- | -- | -- | -- | -- | .33 | 2.24 | .66 | .16 | 4.19 | 2.38 | 3.62 |
| Vitamin A | M | .03 | 42.7 | -- | 5.96 | 1.79 | .10 | 3.92 | -- | -- | 78.8 | 113 | .10 | .02 | -- |
|  | F | .03 | 52.8 | -- | 7.38 | 2.21 | .11 | 4.85 | -- | -- | 97.4 | 140 | .13 | .02 | -- |
| Riboflavin | M | .16 | 2.28 | 1.59 | 1.06 | .48 | .83 | .35 | 11.6 | 1.01 | 6.98 | 6.61 | 3.16 | .09 | 6.36 |
|  | F | .19 | 2.67 | 1.84 | 1.23 | .55 | .97 | .41 | 13.5 | 1.18 | 8.10 | 7.63 | 3.66 | .11 | 7.39 |
| Niacin | M | .33 | 15.2 | 2.84 | 1.40 | 1.07 | 2.02 | 1.80 | 1.07 | .27 | 11.9 | 3.13 | 3.55 | .42 | 1.99 |
|  | F | .37 | 16.9 | 2.05 | 1.56 | 1.20 | 2.27 | 2.01 | 1.19 | .30 | 13.3 | 3.52 | 3.96 | .47 | 2.21 |
| Vitamin $B_6$ | M | .32 | 2.66 | -- | .39 | .37 | 1.68 | .44 | 6.53 | .22 | 1.23 | 1.50 | 1.28 | .38 | 1.01 |
|  | F | .50 | 4.11 | -- | .61 | .57 | 2.60 | .68 | 10.1 | .33 | 1.91 | 2.33 | 1.97 | .57 | 1.56 |
| Pantothenic Acid | M | .36 | 3.35 | -- | -- | 3.35 | 2.22 | .17 | 1.98 | .35 | 1.17 | -- | .85 | .85 | 2.19 |
|  | F | .55 | 5.18 | -- | -- | 5.18 | 3.44 | .26 | 3.05 | .53 | 1.81 | -- | 1.31 | 1.31 | 3.38 |
| Iodine | M | .24 | 49.8 | 3.79 | -- | .11 | -- | .72 | 6.14 | .22 | -- | -- | 1.64 | .04 | 61.4 |
|  | F | .29 | 59.4 | 4.49 | -- | .13 | -- | .93 | 7.30 | .26 | -- | -- | 1.95 | .05 | 73.1 |
| Zinc | M | -- | 2.49 | .59 | 1.27 | .34 | 1.50 | -- | 2.83 | .42 | 5.90 | -- | 18.1 | .07 | 1.96 |
|  | F | -- | 3.85 | .91 | 1.96 | .52 | 2.31 | -- | 4.38 | .65 | 9.13 | -- | 27.9 | .10 | 3.02 |
| Calcium | M | .08 | 1.83 | 1.36 | .38 | .22 | .33 | .20 | 8.03 | 1.39 | 2.70 | 3.95 | 1.74 | .05 | 5.77 |
|  | F | .12 | 2.83 | 2.11 | .59 | .34 | .51 | .31 | 12.4 | 2.15 | 4.17 | 6.11 | 2.68 | .07 | 8.93 |
| Iron | M | .32 | 2.24 | .53 | .36 | .23 | .22 | .28 | 4.72 | .36 | 1.45 | 1.33 | 1.54 | .12 | 1.43 |
|  | F | .88 | 6.25 | 1.46 | 1.00 | .65 | .61 | .78 | 13.1 | .99 | 4.04 | 3.72 | 4.28 | .33 | 3.98 |

Keep these lists, for they may be of help to you in the design of your diet plan. The following chart gives the crops that are the most efficient for each nutrient for weight and area:

| | AREA EFFICIENCY | | | WEIGHT EFFICIENCY | | |
|---|---|---|---|---|---|---|
| | Most Efficient | Coefficient | | Most Efficient | Coefficient | |
| Nutrient | Crop | Men | Women | Crop | Men | Women |
| Calories | Parsnips | .71 | .82 | Filberts | .16 | .13 |
| Protein | Turnips | .40 | .50 | Peanuts | .08 | .07 |
| Isoleucine | Turnips | .26 | .34 | Filberts | .03 | .03 |
| Leucine | Turnips | .18 | .23 | Peanuts | .04 | .04 |
| Cystine + Methionine | Leeks | .21 | .27 | Peanuts | .05 | .05 |
| Tryptophan | Turnips | .16 | .20 | Peanuts | .04 | .03 |
| Carbohydrates | Parsnips | .46 | .52 | Wheat | .29 | .23 |
| Fat | Filberts | .38 | .43 | Filberts | .02 | .01 |
| Linoleic Acid | Sunflower seeds | .13 | .16 | Peanuts | .01 | .01 |
| Vitamin A | Turnips | .02 | .02 | Parsley | .03 | .02 |
| Riboflavin | Turnips | .09 | .11 | Filberts | .11 | .09 |
| Niacin | Potatoes | .27 | .30 | Peanuts | .04 | .03 |
| Vitamin B$_6$ | Potatoes | .22 | .33 | Sunflower seeds | .06 | .06 |
| Pantothenic Acid | Parsnips | .17 | .26 | Peanuts | .08 | .08 |
| Iodine | Turnips | .04 | .05 | Turnips | .05 | .05 |
| Zinc | Turnips | .07 | .10 | Turnips | .16 | .11 |
| Calcium | Turnips | .05 | .07 | Collards | .09 | .10 |
| Iron | Turnips | .12 | .33 | Sunflower seeds | .05 | .10 |

Remember to be realistic in your design process. If you are really out to break all records and attempt to live within the smallest possible area, then at least try eating the diet that you are proposing before trying to grow it--buy and/or harvest the mix of foods that you are considering and try living on them for a month. You may discover that a daily intake of five pounds of potatoes or eight ounces of garlic is really much more than you can handle for these particular foods. You may also desire more diversity, or more foods that you are accustomed to eating such as grains and beans. You may find it difficult to quickly adjust to a diet that is especially low in fat. The wise course is to proceed a step at a time.

Rapid and drastic changes in diet can be unhealthy in themselves--it takes the body a while to adjust and to be able to make the best use of the new mix of foods. It may be helpful to start with an area that--given a maximally efficient design-- could provide all of your diet needs, feeding you a full seven days a week; but to actually _plant_ a first year garden plan that is closer to the diet you are used to--more diverse and (therefore) less efficient. For a woman, a minimal area might be 550 square feet, and for a man it might be 850 square feet. A relatively normal vegetarian diet (but lower in fats and sugars than might be typical) could be produced in three to four times these areas, so that a scaled down version of this more normal and diverse diet, if limited to 550 square feet for women and 850 square feet for men, would provide only only about two days per week of full nutrition at good yields.* Staying with this same initial area, though, as your body and your garden become more finely tuned, you can change your plan each year, and gradually increase the percentage of your total weekly diet that you produce from the same original area, until you are able to feed yourself a full seven days a week from a truly minimal area diet.

Similarly, in a development project, if the people in the first year are willing to switch from their traditional methods and mixes of foods for a small amount of their land and labor time to produce the meals for perhaps one or two days a week, they may decide to make changes each year if the new approach proves itself. The benefit of these changes may also be shown by a development worker who acts as a model and lets the people see what the results could be.

The slide rules make it possible to rapidly check the nutrients that can be provided by a given area or weight of a crop. They can also be used to obtain the area, weight, and nutrient amounts if one of the nutrients for a crop is set at a specified level--say if you wanted to get 1500 calories a day from potatoes.

The general procedure for solving for the diet is a sophisticated form of trial and error. The slide rules allow you to quickly check the results of adding some given amount of a crop to the plan. The charts of _Efficiency Coefficients_ will help in selecting crops. You begin with a clean slate--none of the weight, area, or nutrients are accounted for yet. You add some of this crop and some of that, and sometimes subtract some of a crop that was previously added. At each stage you will try to determine the nutrient or nutrients that appear to be the most problematic, and then find the most efficient crop or crops for dealing with the nutrient.

*If you only achieve beginning yields, you might produce only one day a week of full nutrition. These area figures also assume a growing season of eight months, or one that can be extended (with mini-greenhouses) to eight months. Also assumed is the ability to irrigate. A four month growing season might double the area requirements, as might the inability to irrigate, or an especially poor soil.

Using the charts of _Efficiency Coefficients,_ it is easy to see that calories is a good place to start. Since no single crop is especially efficient for both weight and area for calories, it is probably a good idea to choose a mix of crops. Those crops supplying most of the calories may be called the staples of the diet. A diet might be designed using a single food such as potatoes, sweet potatoes, or wheat as a staple, but a better design would probably use a mixture of staples.

It is tempting to derive a large amount of the needed calories from potatoes, due to its efficiency for not just calories, but most of the other nutrients. Americans generally eat less than a pound of potatoes a day on the average, but could probably get used to eating between one and three pounds a day. A diet pushing the limit of the smallest area might have an even higher level of potato consumption.

Wheat (assumed in this analysis to be eaten as bread) is tempting as a staple because it is a food we are used to--_our daily bread._ Many may also imagine a serving of wheat bread with cooked beans as a major component of a minimal area diet. While using grains and beans as staples is a major improvement over the typical American diet, it is not the best way to minimize area, as can be seen by working with the slide rules for soybeans and wheat, or by examining the _Area Coefficients_ for these two crops.

The _initial mix_ of staple crops should provide between about _one third and two thirds of total calorie needs_--this will be enough to give you a good start. _If the foods chosen are especially efficient, it may be good to set their initial amounts near the upper limit that you would want to consume_ of these foods. For example, perhaps three or four pounds of potatoes and an ounce or two of garlic is as much as you would want to consume daily of these calorie efficient foods. These amounts can be used to set the slide rules and thus determine the area and nutrient amounts. _If, instead, the staples chosen include foods_ such as wheat and soybeans _that are not particularly efficient for calories,_ it may be good to _set these according to the amount that you would_ minimally _want to consume each day of these foods._

With experience, more of these trade-offs and broad principles can be included in what will at first be a mostly trial-and-error process. There are other techniques which can be developed and added, but these are presently too difficult and poorly understood to easily explain or teach. Such refinements, however, are generally nuances used only in fine tuning. They are useful in eliminating the last five or ten percent of the area, but are not essential to creating a good design. With practice you will develop your own design style and special techniques.

While it depends on the staples that you select, fat and linoleic acid should probably be the next consideration after calories. It is unlikely that other foods that might be selected for their efficiency in some other nutrient will contribute much in the way of either fat or linoleic acid. *It is wise, then, to provide between 70 and 100 percent of your targets for these nutrients at this early stage.* If this later proves to be too much or too little, the appropriate adjustment can then be made. In the prototype diets, linoleic acid is provided for, but not necessarily fat. While there is no actual requirement for fat as a nutrient, an extremely low fat diet may cause physical and psychological adjustment problems. A person accustomed to a low fat diet, which for the U.S. might be one that derives 30 percent of its calories from fat, might choose to try a diet in which fat makes up only about ten percent of the calories. A good approach is to make diet changes slowly, possible changing over to a new diet one additional day per week each year, so that a full change in diet would take seven years. This would allow you the time needed for learning more about your body and your garden, so that you could adjust your plans accordingly. Most people in poorer countries get much less fat, and probably fall short of their needs for some nutrients, which should make for an easier and faster transition to a minimal area diet.

The next nutrient to be considered is determined by examining the cumulative totals for weight, area, and the nutrients for the crops thus far included. First express each total as a percentage of the target amount. If your target for weight is six pounds and your cumulative total for weight is up to three pounds, then you are at 50 percent of target. If your area target is 850 square feet and you are at 510 square feet, then you are at 60 percent for area. If the nutrient that was lowest on a percentage basis was vitamin A at 20 percent, with only 200 RE of a target of 1,000 RE being provided, then vitamin A would be a likely choice for the next nutrient to be considered. In this example, since a higher percentage of area than weight has been accounted for, area should be viewed as the limiting constraint, and a food that is *Area Efficient* for vitamin A would be a good choice for the next crop to be added.

The basic procedure for adding crops can be summarized as follows:

1. Make incremental changes in crops and determine the new cumulative totals for weight, area, and nutrients.

2. Convert the cumulative totals for weight, area, and each nutrient to percentages of their design target. It is at this point that you check to see if you have a potential solution for weight and possibly area.

3. Determine which nutrient is most lacking on a percentage basis and whether area or weight is the more limiting constraint.

4. Choose the crop or crops that is most efficient for the limiting nutrient(s) for the limiting constraint (weight or area).

5. Determine the amount of the crop or crops that should be added.

6. Read and enter the amounts from the slide rule for area, weight, and all the nutrients for each crop. This returns you to the first step.

A more detailed explanation of these steps follows:

1) <u>Make incremental changes in crops and determine the new cumulative totals for weight, area, and the nutrients</u> - One way to start is to simply make guesses at approximate amounts and use the slide rules to refine these guesses. It may also help to keep crop additions in increments of either 25 square foot or 2 ounce (0.125 pound) multiples. These guesses are improved with experience in the procedure and are affected by various factors.

For example, when designing a minimal area diet for the Ecology Action research site in Northern California, I know I will probably need mini-greenhouses for either peanuts or sweet potatoes. This suggests increments of 50 square feet, the size of most of our mini-greenhouses; but the crops can also be mixed to make a total of 50 square feet. I will also try to use at most one or two mini-greenhouses per individual diet, as they are somewhat expensive and a limited resource. For filberts, I know that one tree takes about 240 square feet, so I try to either allot this area to an individual diet or to divide a tree's output between two or more diets.

2) <u>Convert the cumulative totals for weight, area, and each nutrient to percentages of their design target</u> - If all the percentages for the nutrients are equal to or less than the percentage for weight, then a <u>satisfactory</u> solution meeting the weight constraint and all the nutrient targets can be had by multiplying all the amounts by $100 \div x$, where $x$ is the percent of target for the nutrient whose percentage was lowest. If all the percentages for the nutrients are at least equal to the percentages for <u>*both weight and area*</u>, then an <u>excellent</u> solution can be found using the same method. This solution will meet both the weight and area constraints.

3) <u>Determine which nutrient is most lacking on a percentage basis and whether area or weight is the more limiting constraint</u> - Just as in chess, it is good to think a few moves ahead. Several nutrients may be similarly lacking, even though one may be lower on a percentage basis. If this is recognized at this step, a crop or crops may be chosen in the next step that are effective for the mix of limiting nutrients and that may be more efficient than if these nutrients were dealt with one at a time.

4) <u>Choose the crop or crops that is most efficient in the limiting nutrient(s) for the limiting constraint (weight or area)</u> - Other problem nutrients, whether previously dealt with or foreseen, should also be considered. If the most efficient crops for the nutrient being considered are similar in efficiency, then the more efficient one for calories or another problem nutrient might be given priority. Personal taste may enter into the choice as well.

5) <u>Determine the amount of the crop or crops that should be added</u> - You should add enough of a crop to bring the nutrient being considered up to a level somewhere between the percentage for whichever is the more limiting constraint (weight or area) and 100 percent. For example, if the weight is 50 percent of its target, and the area 60 percent of its target, then area is more limiting. If the limiting nutrient is vitamin A at 20 percent--perhaps 200 RE with a target of 1000 RE--then you'd want to add enough of a crop that is area efficient for vitamin A to bring the vitamin A level up to between 60 percent (the percent of target for the more limiting constraint, area) and 100 percent. The percentage selected within this range will at first be mostly a guess, but will have more basis with practice. In this case, let's assume that you decide to aim for 80 percent--you are guessing that the other 20 percent may be contained in other crops yet to be added (crops that will be added because of their efficiency for other nutrients). If the guess is wrong, an adjustment can always be made later in the fine-tuning stage by either adding or subtracting some of this crop. Since the target is 1,000 RE, then 80 percent of this would be 800 RE. Your cumulative total is already at 200 RE, so you need 600 RE more. Take the slide rule out for the _Area_ _Efficient_ crop you have chosen for vitamin A and set vitamin A at 600 RE. This will determine the weight and area of the crop that should be added.

6) <u>Read and enter the amounts from the slide rule for the weight, area, and all the nutrients</u> - It is important to remember that this is only a slide rule approximation, and also a step that is quite vulnerable to error. It is good to recheck cumulative totals every five or ten entries (whether "in-your-head" or using a calculator). It is also a good idea to give all the numbers a check independent of the slide rules as you get close to what appears to be a solution. You can waste a lot of time trying to fine-tune what appears to be nearly a solution when hidden errors mean that you are still a long ways off. To do this check, first combine any multiple entries for a crop--say, if you had first added 25 square feet of a crop, and then later subtracted ten square feet of the same crop.* Next make sure that all the weight and area numbers match. Then, for each crop, multiply the weight of food consumed each day by the nutrient amount per pound for that crop to come up with the amounts of each nutrient contributed by each crop. Finally, check the column totals for weight, area, and the nutrients, and convert these into percentages of their respective targets.

* Be careful never to subtract more of a crop than you have previously added. The most _Area_ _Efficient_ diet I ever came up with contained a negative 200 square feet of wheat!

The entry of the amounts for all the nutrients and the weight and area for the selected crops completes this cycle, and returns you to step one. This stage of the solution is complete when you find at step two that you either have a <u>satisfactory solution</u> or an <u>excellent solution</u> depending on whether you have satisfied just the weight or both the weight and area constraints.

Now to review the overall process. You first need to establish design targets for the weight of food you think you can consume each day, the area of land that you are going to attempt to produce the food in, and the amount of each nutrient that you believe you need to consume each day. You will also need information on your expected crop yields, your growing season, the time to maturity for each crop, nutrient amounts for each crop, and a factor that can convert the weight of a crop in the form that it is harvested to its weight in the form as it is consumed (e.g. one pound of beans as harvested may convert to three pounds of beans as consumed). This is the <u>basic data</u> that you will need.

From the design targets and the nutrient information for the foods, you derive the weight of each food that it would take to fulfill your nutrient targets. This amount is called the *Weight Efficiency Value*. From the growing information for the crops, you calculate the annual yield potential for each crop expressed in terms of the weight as consumed--how many pounds of cooked beans might a 100 square foot area produce in a year. Using this amount and the *Weight Efficiency Value*, you calculate the area, in terms of the number of one hundred square foot beds, that it would take for each food to produce all of the needed amount for each nutrient. These figures are called the *Area Efficiency Values*.

The *Area Efficiency Values* and the *Weight Efficiency Values* are used to develop a list of the nutrients that are more difficult to provide within the constraints of weight and area. These are referred to as the *Critical Nutrients*. Potential crops are surveyed and a list of crops especially efficient in the *Critical Nutrients* is assembled. In <u>One Circle</u>, the fourteen crops used include at least three crops that are *Weight Efficient* and at least three crops that are *Area Efficient* for each nutrient. The material thus far in this review is covered in the first chapter, 'Nutrition Reconsidered'. You could change the <u>basic data</u>--the assumptions as to your needs, your crops, and your growing conditions--and use the same process to come up with different *Critical Nutrients* and a different list of crops. This narrowing process is important in simplifying the process of solving for a diet, and also narrows considerably the range of possible solutions.

The solution process is given in this chapter. First, one more tool has been added, the *Efficiency Coefficients*, which are derived by dividing the *Efficiency Values*

by the appropriate design target, either for weight or for area. _Efficiency Coeffi-_
_cients_ make it easier to consider as a whole the choices of food relative to nutrients--
to look and compare more easily.

The initial phase in the solution process is a matter of establishing the staple
crops--the foods that provide most of your calories, take up most of the area in the
garden plan, and take up most of the weight in the daily diet. The bulk of not just
calories, but the problem calorie-nutrients, fat and linoleic acid, should be dealt with
in the process of choosing staples. These choices are influenced not just by the
efficiency of each crop, but also by the preferences of each person who designs a diet.
For the more efficient staples, such as potatoes and garlic, the question is what is
the largest amount of these foods that you are willing to eat. For the less efficient
staple crops, such as wheat and soybeans, the question is, what is the least amount
of these that you feel you need in your regular diet. Within a narrowed list of crops,
such personal taste choices can go a long ways toward determining the bulk of a diet.

After establishing the staples, the nutrients other than calories are dealt with
one at a time, starting with whichever seems the most problematic, adding a food that
seems most effective for this problem nutrient, and recalculating to determine the new
nutrient that seems most problematic after this addition. Foods are added in this
manner until the percentage accounted for, for each of the nutrients, is equal to or
greater than the percentage for weight. At this point you can derive a solution that
satisfies the weight constraint. If the percentages for all the nutrients are equal
to or greater than the percentage for area as well, then you have also solved for the
area constraint. To get a solution in either case, multiply the amounts for all the
crops by 100 divided by the percentage for the crop whose percentage of target is
lowest.

You should go over this review of the entire process, going back into the main
text for anything that is confusing to you, until it begins to make sense as a whole.
A real understanding takes time. The example solution that follows should help, as
will a study of the example diets in the next chapter. Trying to design plans on your
own will teach you a lot. Go slow, and try to understand what you are doing at each
step.

It is important to keep in mind that this is an incomplete process with regards
to the objective of sustaining soil fertility. This process is however, both a good
first step, and also a training process that you must master before further steps or
integrations are possible. Sustainability cannot be reached in a single step, and
the understanding for each additional step will probably require that you first take
the previous step and integrate it into your overall life.

166

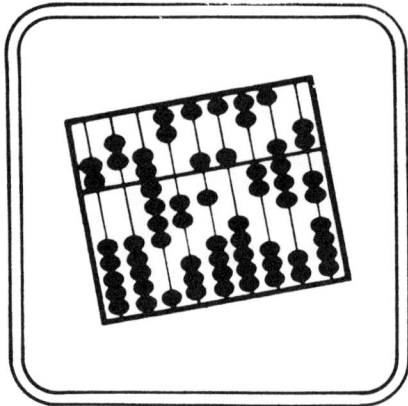

# A SAMPLE
# SOLUTION

## Some Assumptions

It is necessary to use specific numbers to explain a process such as this, but this should not be taken as these specific figures being advocated as being the <u>right</u> ones. These are the ones that I personally feel good about for myself, and that is all. They are used as an example to show what you can do using the numbers that feel most accurate to you.

The climate is assumed temperate with cool summer nights, wet winters, and dry summers. The diet is for a man who can comfortably consume six pounds of food daily, and whose nutrient needs are the same as the design targets (p.69)

The target for area is guessed to be about 1400 square feet. An examination of the three pairs of example diets will help you get a feel for the effects on area of your consumption and nutrient targets and your food preferences. Changing some nutrient targets (such as calories) only a little can cause significant change in the area requirements. Other nutrient targets (such as vitamin A) could be increased significantly without greatly adding to the area requirements. Using the fourteen efficient crops, it would be difficult to exceed a 2800 square foot diet, suggesting a spectrum from about 700 square feet to about 2800 square feet for the average adult. For women, the range is about 550 to 2200 square feet, and for men, about 850 to 3400 square feet. A shorter growing season, not being able to irrigate, poorer soil, or other factors affecting yield might significantly increase these ranges.

The initial crop amounts should be considered flexible and will not be held to firmly in the design process. Staying within fixed limits requires a more complex procedure. In this easier approach, once the percentage of target for all the nutrients is equal to or greater than the percentage of target for weight (and possibly area), everything is proportionally increased to bring the amount for the most limiting nutrient up to 100 percent. To stay within the original limits, all the nutrients would have to be brought up incrementally all the way to 100 percent. This solution using the easier method is a compromise between a $\underline{good}$ $\underline{process}$ that is easy to understand and a $\underline{good}$ $\underline{final}$ $\underline{product}$ that you would want to use for a plan. It might be a usable, but not optimal plan.

Potato consumption is initially set at around three pounds per day and garlic at 0.125 pounds (2 ounces). Enough soybeans have been included to produce .25 pounds of cooked beans. Instead, enough tempeh could be produced to supply your $B_{12}$ needs.* Two ounces of wheat used as bread is included, enough for a small loaf each week.

Parsnips have been limited initially to 0.25 pounds per day, as most people are probably unfamiliar with either how to grow them or how to cook them. There are also concerns that too much parsnips could be a health hazard (see parsnips section). Filberts are excluded due to their slow start-up time and limited range. Other crop or food preferences are judged according to how much extra area or weight they require. Choosing a less than optimally efficient crop may not affect weight or area very much and might make your diet much more enjoyable to you. These initial assumptions have been included with the goal of producing a diet design that is easy to grow, pleasant to consume, and nutritionally adequate.

* See The Book of Tempeh, by William Shurtleff and Akiko Aoyagi (Harper and Row, 1979) for information on the nutrition and preparation of tempeh.

| CROP | AREA 1400 | Y/day 6.0 | Cal 2700 | Pro 56 | Iso 1260 | Leu 1680 | C+M 1050 | Tryp 315 | Carb 405 | Fat 30 | Lino 4.5 | A 1000 | B2 1.6 | B3 18 | B6 2.0 | Pant 5 | I 130 | Zn 10 | Ca 500 | Fe 10 (5)(6) |
|---|---|---|---|---|---|---|---|---|---|---|---|---|---|---|---|---|---|---|---|---|
| Garlic | 38 | .125 | 77 | 3.5 | — | — | — | — | 17 | .1 | — | — | .04 | .18 | — | — | 1.5 | .8 | 16 | .8 |
| Parsnips | 19 | .25 | 86 | 1.9 | — | — | — | — | 19 | .6 | — | — | .10 | .22 | .10 | .66 | 4.1 | — | 57 | .8 |
| Potatoes | 290 | 3.00 | 1250 | 35.0 | 1050 | 1610 | 520 | 450 | 290 | 1.5 | .76 | — | .55 | 23 | 3.2 | 4.9 | 200 | 8.0 | 125 | 9.5 (1) |
| Soybeans | 380 | .25 | 132 | 11 | 730 | 1220 | 420 | 200 | 11 | 5.8 | 3.45 | 6 | .10 | .68 | .72 | 1.9 | — | .8 | 84 | 3.1 |
| Wheat | 170 | .125 | 135 | 5.5 | 175 | 355 | 220 | 57 | 29 | .8 | .27 | — | .05 | 1.7 | .36 | .41 | .4 | 1.0 | 17 | 1.3 |
| Cum. Total | 897 | 3.75 | 1680 | 56.9 | 1955 | 3185 | 1160 | 707 | 366 | 8.8 | 4.48 | 12 | .84 | 25.9 | 4.38 | 7.87 | 206 | 10.6 | 299 | 15.5 (3) |
| % of Target | 64 | 63 | 62 (16) | 102 | 155 | 190 | 110 | 224 | 90 | 29 (8) | 100 (10) | 1 (7) | 53 (2) | 144 | 219 | 157 | 158 | 106 | 60 | 155 (4) |
| Peanuts | 50 | .01 | 35 | 1.6 | 62 | 120 | 37 | 19 | 1 | 3.0 | .87 | — | .01 | 1.0 | .02 | .15 | 1.2 | .2 | 4 | 1 (9) |
| Sunflowers | 300 | .08 | 200 | 8.6 | 230 | 350 | 180 | 73 | 7 | 17 | 10.9 | 3 | .08 | 1.9 | .45 | — | — | — | 43 | 2.6 (12) |
| Cum. Total | 1247 | 3.84 | 1915 | 67.1 | 2247 | 3655 | 1377 | 799 | 374 | 28.8 | 16.3 | 15 | .93 | 28.8 | 4.85 | 8.02 | 207 | 10.8 | 346 | 17.9 |
| % of Target | 89 (19) | 64 | 71 | 120 | 178 | 218 | 131 | 254 | 92 | 96 (11) | 361 | 2 (13) | 58 (14) | 160 | 243 | 160 | 159 | 108 | 69 | 179 |
| Collards | 22 | .18 | 33 | 3.0 | 93 | 165 | 85 | 42 | 6 | .6 | — | 880 | .25 | 1.4 | .16 | .36 | .4 | — (15) | 162 | .8 (17) |
| Cum. Total | 1269 (21) | 4.02 | 1948 | 70.1 | 2340 | 3820 | 1462 | 840 | 380 | 29.4 | 16.3 | 895 (18) | 1.18 | 30.2 | 5.21 | 8.38 | 221 | 10.8 | 508 | 18.7 (20) |
| % of Target | 91 (22) | 67 | 72 | 125 | 186 | 227 | 139 | 267 | 94 | 98 | 361 | 90 | 74 | 168 | 261 | 168 | 170 | 108 | 102 | 187 |

*Use the numbers in parentheses as a guide in the text below.*

*See pages 69–71 for standard units and an explanation of the targets.*

# The Basic Solution

Using these assumptions as to crop amounts forms the skeleton of the diet. The daily weights of these foods are given above, together with their area and nutrient amounts (1). Check these with your slide rules to get some practice. Note that when the garlic slide rule is set at .125 pounds, $B_2$ is "off the scale" to the left. Set Y/day up a factor of ten to 1.25, and read the amount for vitamin $B_2$—about 0.44. Divide this by ten to get 0.04 as the $B_2$ value for garlic (2). The next line after wheat gives the cumulative totals (3). The next line (4) gives the amount that each total is of its target. Targets (5) and column labels (6) are at the top.

While vitamin A's percent of target (7) is lower than fat's (8), deal with fat first because it's a calorie nutrient. In the *Efficiency Coefficient* charts, several foods are weight efficient for fat (coefficients =1.00), but only filberts, peanuts, and sunflower seeds are also area efficient. Filberts have been excluded. Peanuts in the assumed climate will need a mini-greenhouse. This suggests an increment of 50 square feet (9), which would produce 3.0 g of fat (10). Use this amount of peanuts to bring fat up to about 11.8 grams. Rather than use more mini-greenhouses for peanuts, it is probably best to use sunflowers for most of the rest of the fat. If 17 grams of fat came from sunflower seeds, the cumulative fat total would be up to 28.8 grams (11), close to the target. Use this amount of sunflower seeds (12). Small amounts of fat will come from other foods, and the amount of sunflowers can be adjusted later in the fine-tuning stage.

At this point, the low nutrients on a percentage basis are vitamin A at 2% (13), vitamin $B_2$ at 58% (14), calcium at 69% (15), and calories at 71% (16). Area at 89% (19) is a more limiting constraint than weight. What is needed is a crop that is area efficient for vitamin A and also does well at $B_2$, calcium and calories. Both turnips and collards do well in these nutrients. Adding either 14 square feet of turnips or 22 square feet of collards (17) will bring the vitamin A up to about 90% of target (18), which is between the percent of target for the more limiting constraint (19) and 100 percent. Collards are chosen for taste preferences. They can also more easily provide a more continuous supply of greens.

Examine the new percent of target numbers (20). All of the nutrient percentages are now greater than the weight percentage. A satisfactory solution could be had by multiplying all the amounts by $100 \div x$, where x is the percent for the nutrient whose percent is lowest, calories at 72%. Multiplying 1,269 square feet by $100 \div 72$ gives a tentative area total of 1,763 square feet.

| CROP | 1400 AREA | 6.0 Y/day | 2700 Cal | 56 Pro | 1260 Iso | 1680 Leu | 1050 C+M | 315 Tryp | 405 Carb | 30 Fat | 4.5 Lino | 1000 A | 1.6 B2 | 18 B3 | 2.0 B6 | 5 Pant | 130 I | 10 Zn | 500 Ca | 10 Fe |
|---|---|---|---|---|---|---|---|---|---|---|---|---|---|---|---|---|---|---|---|---|---|
| Garlic | 38 | .125 | 78 | 3.5 | -- | -- | -- | -- | 18 | .1 | -- | -- | .05 | .28 | -- | -- | 1.5 | .8 | 17 | .9 |
| Parsnips | 19 | .247 | 84 | 1.9 | -- | -- | -- | -- | 20 | .6 | .10 | .22 | .10 | .22 | .10 | .67 | 4.0 | -- | 56 | .8 |
| Potatoes | 290 | 2.99 | 1261 | 35.2 | 1031 | 1640 | 517 | 448 | 286 | 1.5 | .78 | -- | .54 | 23.0 | 3.17 | 4.93 | 203 | 8.12 | 122 | 9.6 |
| Soybeans | 380 | .25 | 134 | 11.2 | 717 | 1227 | 409 | 202 | 12 | 5.8 | 3.41 | 6 | .10 | .68 | .73 | 1.91 | -- | .8 | 83 | 3.1 |
| Wheat | 170 | .129 | 141 | 5.6 | 181 | 369 | 224 | 59 | 30 | .8 | .28 | -- | .05 | 1.82 | .40 | .46 | .4 | 1.0 | 17 | 1.4 |
| Peanuts | 50 | .013 | 35 | 1.6 | 61 | 115 | 43 | 19 | 1 | 3.0 | .6 | -- | .01 | .97 | .02 | .15 | 1.2 | .2 | 4 | .1 |
| Sunflowers | 300 | .081 | 206 | 8.8 | 234 | 351 | 185 | 74 | 7 | 17.4 | 10.9 | 3 | .08 | 1.98 | .46 | .62 | -- | -- | 44 | 2.6 |
| Collards | 22 | .181 | 33 | 2.9 | 92 | 166 | 86 | 41 | 6 | .6 | -- | 889 | .25 | 1.39 | .16 | .36 | 13.9 | -- | 167 | .8 |
| Cum. Total | 1269 | 4.016 | 1972 | 70.7 | 2316 | 3868 | 1464 | 843 | 380 | 29.8 | 16.2 | 904 | 1.18 | 30.3 | 5.04 | 8.48 | 224 | 10.9 | 102 | 193 |
| % of target | 91 | 67 (23) | 73 | 126 | 184 | 230 | 139 | 268 | 94 | 99 | 360 | 90 | 74 | 169 | 252 | 170 | 172 | 109 | 102 | 193 |
| Onions | 27 | .6 | 104 | 4.1 | 55 | 101 | 44 | 55 | 24 | .3 | -- | 16 | .10 | .54 | .17 | .05 | 39 | .9 | 74 | 1.4 (24) |
| Cum. Total | 1296 | 4.616 | 2076 | 74.8 | 2371 | 3969 | 1510 | 896 | 404 | 30.1 | 16.2 | 920 | 1.28 | 30.8 | 5.21 | 8.53 | 243 | 11.8 | 584 | 20.7 |
| % of target | 93 | 77 (26) | 77 | 134 | 188 | 236 | 144 | 285 | 100 | 100 | 360 | 92 | 80 | 171 | 261 | 171 | 187 | 118 | 117 | 207 |
| -Sunflowers | 115 | .032 | 81 | 3.4 | 91 | 136 | 72 | 29 | 3 | 6.9 | 4.3 | 1 | .03 | .78 | .18 | -- | -- | -- | 17 | 1.0 |
| Cum. Total | 1181 | 4.584 | 1995 | 71.2 | 2280 | 3833 | 1438 | 869 | 401 | 23.2 | 11.9 | 919 | 1.25 | 30.1 | 5.03 | 8.53 | 243 | 11.8 | 567 | 19.7 |
| % of target | .84 | 76.4 | 73.9 | 127 | 181 | 228 | 137 | 276 | 99 | 77.3 (25) | 264 | 92 | 78 | 167 | 252 | 171 | 187 | 118 | 113 | 197 |
| -Collards | 3 | .025 | 4 | .4 | 12 | 23 | 11 | 6 | 1 | .1 | -- | 121 | .04 | .19 | .02 | .05 | 2 | -- | 23 | .1 (29) |
| -Onions | 10 | .22 | 38 | 1.5 | 20 | 36 | 16 | 20 | 9 | .1 | -- | 7 | .04 | .20 | .07 | .02 | -- | .04 | 27 | .5 |
| Cum. Total | 1168 | 4.339 | 1953 | 69.3 | 2248 | 3774 | 1411 | 843 | 391 | 23.0 | 11.9 | 791 | 1.17 (28) | 29.7 | 4.94 | 8.46 | 241 | 11.8 | 517 | 19.1 |
| % of target | 83 | 72.3 (27) | 72.3 | 124 | 178 | 225 | 134 | 268 | 97 | 76.7 | 264 | 79.1 | 73.1 | 165 | 247 | 169 | 185 | 118 | 103 | 191 |

172

## FINE-TUNING

Fine-tuning is part art and part science. This "map" of the process lacks in fine detail. Fine-tuning is also a little more complicated. These figures have all been re-checked independently of the slide rules--note that some do differ slightly.

What is needed to help reduce area is a crop that is area efficient for calories. The only such crop besides potatoes and parsnips is onions (see the _Area Efficiency Coefficients_ chart). Onions, however, are not weight efficient for calories. What this means is that as more onions are added, the area efficiency of the diet will improve (given that calories is the limiting nutrient and area the limiting constraint), but at a certain point, as more onions are added, the percent of target for weight will surpass that for calories, and there will no longer be a satisfactory solution. The amount of onions to add, then, is that which would set the percentage of target for weight equal to the percentage of target for calories. The onion slide rule can generate a chart as is given below--note that each 0.1# onions adds 17.3 calories.

(23)

| | Y/day | Y/day% | cal. | cal% |
|---|---|---|---|---|
| Cumulative total: | 4.016 | 67 | 1972 | 73 |
| Cum. total + .1# onion | 4.116 | 69 | 1989 | 74 |
| Cum. total + .3# onion | 4.316 | 72 | 2024 | 75 |
| Cum. total + .5# onion | 4.516 | 75 | 2059 | 76 |
| Cum. total + .6# onion | 4.616 | 77 | 2076 | 77 |

These numbers suggest adding 0.9 pounds of onions, the amount that would make the percentage of target for both weight and calories (24). Now it would be possible to derive a satisfactory solution by multiplying all the amounts by 100÷77. This would give an area figure of 1683 square feet, down 80 sq. ft. from the 1763 sq. ft. estimate from before the onions.

Since the percentage of target for fats is at 100% (25), well above 77%, area savings are possible through a reduction in the area of sunflowers. 77% of the target of 30 g of fat would be 23 g. Fat is presently at 30 g, suggesting that 7.0 g of fat be taken away in the form of sunflowers. This corresponds to 115 sq. ft., or .032 pounds. Subtract this amount (26).

Calories has now been dropped below weight per day on a percentage basis (27). Vitamins A and $B_2$ (28) are both above minimum--their percentages of target are more than the 76% for weight. Remember that collards--a crop _not_ weight efficient for calories--was added to provide for vitamins A and $B_2$, so perhaps collards should be decreased a little. Decreasing onions also helps in the balance between calories and weight. Collards can be decreased by 0.025 pounds or 3 sq. ft (29) without Vitamins A or $B_2$ being brought too low. This, together with a reduction of onions by 10 sq. ft. or 0.22 pounds brings calories and weight into balance (30). A new satisfactory solution can now be reached by multiplying all the figures by 100÷72.3 percent.

| Nutritional Analysis of the Sample Solution of A Man's Diet. | Standard Units | Garlic | Parsnips | Potatoes | Soybeans | Wheat | Peanuts | Sunflowers | Collards | Onions | Total | Design Target | Percent of Target |
|---|---|---|---|---|---|---|---|---|---|---|---|---|---|
| Food weight/day | lbs. | .173 | .342 | 4.14 | .346 | .178 | .018 | .069 | .221 | .512 | 6.00 | 6.00 | 100 |
| Calories | kcal | 108 | 117 | 1747 | 185 | 194 | 46 | 175 | 40 | 89 | 2701 | 2700 | 100 |
| Protein | g | 4.9 | 2.6 | 48.9 | 15.4 | 7.8 | 2.1 | 7.5 | 3.6 | 3.5 | 96.3 | 56 | 172 |
| Isoleucine | mg | -- | -- | 1428 | 989 | 249 | 80 | 199 | 112 | 47 | 3104 | 1260 | 246 |
| Leucine | mg | -- | -- | 2273 | 1692 | 509 | 153 | 299 | 203 | 86 | 5215 | 1680 | 310 |
| Lysine | mg | -- | -- | 1805 | 1389 | 218 | 85 | 168 | 188 | 146 | 3999 | 1260 | 317 |
| Cystine+Methionine | mg | -- | -- | 716 | 564 | 308 | 58 | 158 | 105 | 37 | 1946 | 1050 | 185 |
| Tyrosine+Phenylalanine | mg | -- | -- | 2538 | 1758 | 572 | 213 | 295 | 276 | 89 | 5741 | 1680 | 342 |
| Tryptophan | mg | -- | -- | 621 | 279 | 81 | 25 | 63 | 50 | 47 | 1166 | 315 | 370 |
| Threonine | mg | -- | -- | 1486 | 2362 | 310 | 68 | 285 | 114 | 47 | 4672 | 840 | 556 |
| Valine | mg | -- | -- | 1747 | 1045 | 337 | 100 | 236 | 181 | 70 | 3716 | 1470 | 253 |
| Histidine | mg | -- | -- | 546 | 1431 | 219 | 61 | 184 | 87 | 33 | 2561 | -- | -- |
| Carbohydrates | g | 24 | 27 | 397 | 16 | 41 | 1 | 6 | 7 | 20 | 539 | 405 | 133 |
| Fat | g | .2 | .8 | 2.1 | 8.0 | 1.2 | 4.0 | 14.8 | .7 | .3 | 32.1 | 30 | 107 |
| Linoleic Acid | mg | -- | -- | 1.08 | 4.71 | .39 | 1.14 | 9.3 | -- | -- | 16.6 | 4.5 | 369 |
| Vitamin A | RE | -- | 8 | -- | 8 | -- | -- | 3 | 1087 | 15 | 1121 | 1000 | 112 |
| Thiamin | mg | .20 | .12 | 1.86 | .49 | .33 | .08 | .61 | .20 | .07 | 3.96 | 1.4 | 283 |
| Riboflavin | mg | .06 | .14 | .75 | .14 | .07 | .01 | .07 | .31 | .09 | 1.64 | 1.6 | 103 |
| Niacin | mg | .39 | .31 | 31.9 | .93 | 2.51 | 1.29 | 1.69 | 1.70 | .46 | 41.2 | 18 | 229 |
| Vitamin B6 | mg | -- | .14 | 4.39 | 1.01 | .54 | .02 | .39 | .20 | .15 | 6.84 | 2.0 | 342 |
| Folic Acid | mg | .79 | .04 | .29 | .35 | .03 | -- | -- | .10 | .16 | 1.76 | .4 | 440 |
| Pantothenic Acid | mg | -- | .93 | 6.83 | 2.64 | .63 | .20 | -- | .44 | .04 | 11.7 | 5 | 234 |
| Vitamin C | mg | 12 | 25 | 377 | 27 | -- | -- | -- | 92 | 23 | 556 | 45 | 124 |
| Vitamin E | IU | -- | 2.3 | .8 | 11.8 | 1.5 | .9 | -- | 3.0 | .7 | 21.0 | 6 | 350 |
| Iodine | mcg | 2 | 6 | 282 | -- | 1 | 2 | -- | 17 | 33 | 343 | 130 | 264 |
| Zinc | mg | 1.0 | -- | 11.3 | 1.1 | 1.4 | .3 | -- | -- | .8 | 15.9 | 10 | 159 |
| Calcium | mg | 23 | 78 | 170 | 115 | 24 | 5 | 38 | 204 | 63 | 720 | 500 | 144 |
| Iron | mg | 1.2 | 1.1 | 13.2 | 4.3 | 1.9 | .2 | 2.2 | 1.0 | 1.2 | 26.3 | 10 | 263 |
| Phosphorous | mg | 159 | 120 | 1221 | 300 | 224 | 33 | 26 | 63 | 83 | 2229 | 800 | 279 |
| Potassium | mg | 416 | 840 | 9546 | -- | 216 | 55 | 288 | 402 | 365 | 12038 | 2500 | 482 |
| Magnesium | mg | 28 | 50 | 638 | 208 | 91 | 17 | 12 | 57 | 28 | 1129 | 350 | 323 |
| Copper | mg | -- | -- | 3.4 | 1.8 | 0.4 | .1 | .6 | -- | -- | 6.3 | 2 | 315 |

174

The table to the left gives the weight and nutrients contributed daily by each crop using the final amounts which have been calculated by multiplying the solution results from the previous table by 100÷74.6. The totals express the daily totals for each nutrient and for the weight of the food as consumed. The percentage of target figures give the percent that each figure is of its design target. Note that all the nutrient design targets, not just those for the _Critical Nutrients_ have been checked.

The table below gives the area amounts when multiplied by 100÷74.6, the number of plantings assumed for each crop, the yield level per planting for each crop, and the estimated annual yield for each crop in the form in which it is harvested. The final column gives daily amounts in their form as harvested. In the case of foods that are cooked, these are different from the amounts of foods in the form as consumed, which are given in the table to the left.

| CROP | Total Area | | Number of Plantings | | Yield per Planting | | Estimated Annual Yield | | Daily Amounts (as harvested) |
|---|---|---|---|---|---|---|---|---|---|
| | # 100 square foot beds | | | | pounds per 100 square feet | | pounds | | pounds |
| | A | x | B | x | C | = | D | ÷ 365 = | E |
| Garlic | .53 | | 1 | | 120 | | 63.6 | | .17 |
| Parsnips | .26 | | 2 | | 238 | | 123.8 | | .34 |
| Potatoes | 4.01 | | 2 | | 200 | | 1604 | | 4.39 |
| Soybeans | 5.26 | | 1 | | 8 | | 42.1 | | .12 |
| Wheat | 2.35 | | 2 | | 10 | | 47 | | .13 |
| Peanuts | .69 | | 1 | | 10 | | 6.9 | | .02 |
| Sunflowers | 2.56 | | 2 | | 5 | | 25.6 | | .07 |
| Collards | .26 | | 1 | | 300 | | 78 | | .21 |
| Onions | .24 | | 2 | | 400 | | 192 | | .53 |

The next step is to use this last column--the daily amounts in the form as harvested as a guide to testing whether this is a diet you could live with for one or two days a week.  Use home-grown and any necessary purchased foods and try eating from your proposed diet.  Do this for three weeks at one or two days a week, and then follow this with a week of eating for all seven days only from your proposed plan.  If you wish, use small amount of herbs from your garden, but it is probably better not to use anything else not in the plan--particularly any oils or sugars.  It can also be enlightening to eat food without added salt or salt products such as soy sauce.  It is good to discover what foods really taste like.  This is also a good time to examine your regular diet as well.  You might consider limiting your regular diet to 28 foods, the 14 from One Circle, and 14 additional ones that you could put on the back of the original slide rules.

Take notes on ideas for these four weeks.  At the same time, you should study and consider any nutrients that your diet might be marginal in, or any imbalances between the nutrients.  Study the crops that you have chosen, particularly the ones that you are planning on growing a lot of.  Study the timing of the availability of any of your chosen crops that do not store well.  Find out if anyone in your area grows fall potatoes and how they do it, what planting and harvesting dates might be right locally for winter and spring wheat, whether you'll need mini-greenhouses for peanuts and sweet potatoes, and whether parsnips and filberts do well in your area.  Immerse yourself in the diet as much as you can, especially on those days that you are eating from it.  Collect, sort, and begin to analyze as much relevant information as you feel that you need to, but try to hold off as long as you can on making changes in your plans.  Try as hard as you can to figure out how to make the diet work for you using the smallest possible area.  Give all of your senses a chance to work on the problem.  After four weeks attempt to decide on your diet and garden plan.  Know that it won't be perfect, but know that you can learn more and do better each year.

You need to figure out how to get the equivalent of two crops per year from any crops that you have calculated to be half-season crops for your growing season.  This is both a tricky and a site-specific question.  There are a variety of strategies available for this problem.  It is possible to harvest a spring planted crop and follow it with a late summer of fall planted crop.  If you need 100 square feet of each of two half-season crops , you can first grow 200 square feet of one and then 200 square feet of the other, and work out the proper timing of the two.  A quick maturing crop such as turnips can be snuck in fairly easily in the spring before a warm season crop such as soybeans, sweet potatoes, or peanuts.  Some of the strategies may require the use of season extenders such as shade netting or mini-greenhouses.

What is really needed are locally specific rotations that provide for both staples to feed us, and sufficient organic matter and minerals to feed the topsoil. These are the sorts of things that will evolve on their own over time if you can let the garden be a lens for you to bring into focus the workings of nature within the garden ecosystem. You can not sit down with a stack of books, a slide rule, and pencil and paper, or even a well-fed computer, and design a sustainable food system for yourself. *Learning to feed yourself, the soil, and the planet is a slow process with many steps. Do not be frustrated because the first steps represent an incomplete answer.*

Many people relate to nutrition on a concentration of nutrients basis--you get concentrated calories from this source, concentrated protein from these foods, and vitamins and minerals from various foods which your mind identifies as being rich in calcium or vitamin A. At this integration, a "nutritious" diet is one that contains "nutritious" foods, and nutritious foods are those that are concentrated in certain nutrients which we have come to believe are problems. A higher level of integration matches an amount of food to a level of nutrition--this amount of beans and rice provides all my protein needs; this amount of collards all my calcium and Vitamin A.

The level of integration that Diet for a Small Planet introduced many of us to examines the effects of combining mixes of foods to meet mixes of nutrient needs--the way grains combine with beans to provide a better mix of amino acids. This same principle can be applied to all nutrients and foods, but is most useful when applied to nutrients that are the most difficult to supply--the limiting nutritional factors in your diet--together with the foods that are the most effective in providing these nutrients.

The level of integration undertaken in One Circle combines nutritional analysis with an examination of crop yield potentials. This adds area as a new variable in the analysis. Yet the area of land available is only one factor in sustainable food production.

A good path to understanding will integrate first one factor and then another. Sustainable agriculture is like a multi-dimensional game or puzzle. At one level, the variables are so many and complex that we cannot even conceive of, or "chart out" a "playing board" or "map" for sustainability. This lack of understanding is not a problem in itself. As long as we keep getting closer to being sustainable, we can succeed--perhaps even in as little as seven years. *Real solutions to such a worldwide problem develop in small increments--one person at a time, one step at a time.*

The level of complexity required to truly integrate the world food problem is probably beyond the scope of current understanding, yet it is possible right now for millions of people to advance their level of integration: to begin to get better nutrition, to take better care of the soil, to consider diet is good both relative to our personal nutrition and the nutrition of the soil and planet, to question what area is required, and how this area of soil can be brought to a higher, yet sustainable level of fertility. Each step that each person takes is useful and important.

Any answer produced using only the design methods outlined in <u>One Circle</u> will be an incomplete one. Even if you recycle all your nutrients back into your garden, grow all your food in 350 square feet using excellent biointensive techniques, and can think of nothing tastier than a dish of potatoes with a little parsley and toasted grashopper, most likely you will still not be practicing a truly sustainable agriculture. Most likely, your system will lose more carbon and nitrogen back to the atmosphere than its life forms will be able to remove from the atmosphere. Minerals will be leached from your soil. Your region may even be losing water and undergoing desertification due to matters beyond your control. Each such factor requires that our integration include additional variables.

We must find out how much of various legumes we must grow each year to help balance our nitrogen cycle. This combines closely with the question of how to maintain organic matter at an appropriate level within our soil. Perhaps we will need to use crops especially efficient in producing organic matter, such as radishes grown till they become almost woody, or perhaps we will need to switch our food plants to crops whose by-products include large amounts of organic matter, such as the straw in a wheat crop, particularly the straw from a tall-stalk variety. Grains and beans could prove to be the most efficient diet, not for our nutrition, but for the nutrition of the soil. Certain deep rooted or accumulator plants such as rye and comfrey may be important in not only catching leached nutrients, but also in tapping into the vast reservoirs that exist in many clay subsoils, but which are not readily usable by most of our shallow rooted annual food crops. Tree crops may be important not only in helping to complete our circle of recycled soil minerals, but also in correcting some of the planetary imbalances such as the loss of our forests, the growth of our deserts, and the rising carbon dioxide levels in the atmosphere.

*While there may not be a complete and perfect answer available to you in the instant, there is an answer that can be grown into, and you are capable of taking the first step.* After four weeks of eating a set of foods, studying their nutrition, researching the agronomic properties of the crops, sketching out garden plans, contemplating traditional or future cultures based around your diet...and all the rest--stop--figure out what is important to you, how important it is, and how to go about attaining your goals. Come up with a plan. It will represent a set of complex compromises between diverse variables. Keep the plan simple, and make changes at a rate appropriate to you. Each year the changes that you will need to make will be more obvious and can be undertaken with more certainty. Do not get hung up in trying to create the perfect system your first year. You will likely feel mired in uncertainty and frustration. Do not let such confusion become a barrier to your effort. Probably the worst thing that could happen would be to fool yourself into thinking that you had the answer. Choose a simple path and move down it and learn. Study the sample diet designs that follow to gain more of an understanding of crop combinations and garden layout.

# Sample Diets

Sample Diets

The educated person in our society probably has a better understanding of how someone might be sent to the moon and back than how they might produce their own food. Of those with some understanding of space travel, though, most would be lost once the discussion moved from the general principles to the actual laws and equations of physics that are involved in getting someone to the moon. Of those few who have a knowledge of astrophysics, only a handful of people in the world understand the process down to the hardware--the nuts and bolts reality of how to put a person on the moon, and no one person carries all the necessary knowledge in their head. It is simply too complex. Yet it has been done. We have been there and back.

We do not now know how to design a food system capable of feeding the world's population on existing resources in a sustainable way. Certainly no one person has this knowledge. Maintaining an entire planet--spaceship earth--indefinitely, is bound to be infinitely more complex than sustaining a few people, in a small space-craft, for but a few days. Do not be disappointed that there is no easy answer or universal formula for how to sustainably feed yourself.

The broad principles and even a good start on the theories and equations for a science capable of answering the question have been presented. If you want calories from a limited area in an appropriate concentration, consider tubers and roots, balanced with small amounts of nuts, seeds, grains, or beans--which also supply fat and essential fatty acids. For an efficient source of vitamins and minerals, look to leafy green vegetables. Grains will help feed the soil with the carbon in the organic matter from the straw. Legumes help with nitrogen. Deep-rooted plants help cycle minerals. Trees help with water, minerals, carbon dioxide, and other important factors. These are some of the broad principles. The _Efficiency Values_ and _Efficiency Coefficients_ are an initial step in formulating a science from these principles. Similar tools could be developed that would compare the contribution of organic matter and minerals from crop residues or from "compost crops"--crops that are grown especially for the production of organic matter. More of the basic information concerning the factors of sustainability is needed before we can develop the sort of general model that would be needed for a design process--e.g. we know that we need legumes in a parti-cular agricultural system, but we can't tell exactly how many of them we would need in order to bring the nitrogen cycle into balance given climate, cultural practices, and other factors.

You can apply these ideas to your garden and immediately increase the amount of nutrition you can get from a limited area. You can also begin applying the concepts of sustainability and make major steps in that direction as well. For most, huge leaps of improvement are possible without lifting a slide rule or checking a decimal place. *You don't need an exact answer or plan to get most of the way there.* The numbers will help you plan, but it is only the experience of attempting to grow your own food that can teach you what you need to know.

The sample diets that follow are not directions. They are not "the way" to do it. They are useful guides, but as "answers", they will prove disappointing. Look within them for the design principles--the broad concepts--and perhaps select and modify one of the plans as a starting point.

What to plant, where, when, how to care for it--these are the nuts and bolts of intensive food production. You will need to work out the details of these questions for yourself. Use One Circle, How to Grow More Vegetables, The Backyard Homestead, and other resources to help guide you initially, and your own garden will guide you as you progress.

Examine the sample plans, but be sure to first examine them in broad terms. How much area is needed in crops that are *Area Efficient* for calories? Probably somewhere from 300 square feet to 1200 square feet or more, and possibly double that range for a four month growing season, or if less efficient crops are chosen. How much more area do you need in the additional staple crops that are needed for their efficiency in supplying fats and essential fatty acids? This can range from around 50 square feet to get a minimal amount of linoleic acid and very little fat; to 200 or 300 square feet as a minimal area to get 10 percent of your calories from fat; to 1,000 square feet or more for higher levels of fat or when using less efficient crops. After these staple crops, how much additional area will it take to complete one's vitamin and mineral needs? This might be as little as 50 square feet for crops such as turnips, collards, and parsley, but might be several hundred square feet or even more if your tastes run more to broccoli and asparagus.

These figures are an oversimplification, but for many, this summary can serve as an adequate first year planting guide, and if it is followed up with a careful examination of your yields and the amount of nutrients produced by the various crops, this may be a good way to start without having to go through the more cumbersome process of calculating a well-balanced plan. It is important, though, that some people explore the theory and numbers in depth, so that the general understanding and broad principles can continue to be improved upon for all. It is also important that you monitor your nutritional intake if you are significantly changing your weekly diet.

What follows this introduction is the basic information for six sample diets. They do not neatly fit into their plans in every case, and there are other ways to produce the same crops using different rotations and timing. While it may not feel as secure or as attractive, a loose approach to planning for the first few years might prove better than a precise plan that leaves little room for error.

We at Ecology Action often perceive the minimum area diet plan as being best applied in the context of what we call the 21 bed scenario. In the general model, seven 100 square foot beds would be for diet, seven would be for income producing crops, and seven would be for crops grown to help feed the soil. When possible, additional compost crops would be grown in the "off season" in both the income and diet sections--this is the season, whether cool, hot, dry, or wet, that is unfavorable for most food or income crops. Rotations would move the 7 diet beds into each of the other two seven bed sections over time as the income and soil improvement crops were similarly rotated. Another kind of "rotation" can also be done by composting plant wastes together, decreasing chances of disease or depletion of a particular mineral.

When taken in isolation, the designs presented may seem immediately inadequate to the experienced gardener. Crops are planted at times that may not be best for them, a single crop such as potatoes is nearly mono-cropped, there aren't enough legumes, or grains, or trees...It is easy to find the problems, but the potential expressed in these plans should be even more striking. The possibility of producing a complete human diet in 700 square feet, or 1400, or even 2800 square feet is a remarkable breakthrough, and merits the additional effort that may be needed to turn the progress that has already been made in One Circle into a plan that will work for you.

Within the broader context of the 21 bed scenario, and with additional garden research, many apparent "problems" will become much simpler. None of these plans may be the best initial design for you and your location, and if you know enough about gardening to realize this, then rather than rejecting the possibility of producing a complete diet in a minimal area, take the design tools in this book together with your own knowledge of how to garden in your particular locality and design something that will work. Good answers are not found in tools, but in people who possess the wisdom to know how to properly use the tools. The responsibility for a good answer is yours.

The first two plans, averaging about 700 square feet, are called prototype diets because they establish one end of the spectrum of theoretical possibilities. They represent reasonable goals to work toward, but should probably not be used as a first year model. The next two pairs of plans contain the same mix of foods for both men and women, with the man's diet increased by a factor of 1.35 to allow for his additional nutritional needs.  Both pairs require an average of 1400 square feet.  The first design features more cool season crops and the second more hot season crops.

For each design, there is a summary of the areas and number of plantings of each crop, and the projected annual yields and daily intake amounts (this is given in the form of the crop as it is harvested--e.g. dry, uncooked soybeans).  There is also a summary of the daily nutrition from the amounts of the foods as consumed (e.g. cooked soybeans).  A nutrition section comments on the strengths and weaknesses of the diet.  A garden plan section illustrates one possible way that the diet might be worked into a garden plan, and comments on its strengths and weaknesses.  Examine these plans carefully and you can learn much about the design of a diet and a garden plan.  Use this knowledge to develop your own individual plan.  Know that it will not be a complete answer but will be a first step towards one.

The more you know, the more complex the question of how to sustainably produce a complete diet in a minimal area will seem.  If you examine some of the more sustainable traditional systems of agriculture (and there are few of these around today), you will often find extremely complex systems using hundreds of crops and varieties, complex cultural practices, and precise timing.  It is not unusual to find dozens of varieties of the staple crop being planted, with different ones doing better different years depending on the weather.  In F.H. King's Farmers of Forty Centuries, you find a portrait of traditional Asian paddy rice agriculture that includes careful attention to composting, nutrient recycling, and even the production of special crops just for composting (such as milk vetch, a legume that was sown among rice plants near the end of their season, specifically so that it could be harvested and composted).

Traditional food systems represent not goals to aim towards, but models to learn from.  Attempting to immitate a system that developed through forty centuries of adjusting to local conditions will not prove to be a good answer to your own local conditions.  We must begin in a simple and incomplete way.  It is critical that you keep things as simple as you can in the beginning so that the lessons available from your garden will not be obscured by the use of too many crops, too many varieties, and too many experiments in technique.  It is important to develop a base line of under- standing, and this is difficult if too many of the variables are kept constantly changing.  Start simply, observe with all the focus that you can, make changes slowly, and you will proceed step-by-step towards the development of your own minimal area diet plan that will be able to sustain you, the fertility of your soil, and the well- being of the planet.

# A WOMAN'S PROTOTYPE DIET

Nutrition - Nutritionally, this is a nearly adequate, but still marginal diet. A fat intake level of at least ten percent of calories is probably wise, especially when one is shifting from a relatively high fat diet such as is common in the U.S. This diet's fat level falls well below this. Linoleic acid is however at an acceptable level.

The vitamin A comes almost entirely from turnip greens, and even though the body can store this vitamin, the turnips should be grown in several plantings spread throughout the year. The sunflower seeds may be sprouted for extra vitamin A, an extra five square feet of parsley could be grown, or edible weeds, often high in vitamin A, could be eaten. In places with harsh winters, sprouts and a small indoor garden of parsley are both excellent strategies for supplementing vitamin A during the winter.

Pantothenic acid is marginal, but this nutrient lacks an established RDA, and at 96 percent of target may still be fully adequate. Vitamin E is below the RDA, but in the upper range of what was suggested in the RDA text as an acceptable level for vitamin E in a diet low in essential fatty acids, which this diet is. Zinc surpasses both the design target of 10 mg and the RDA of 15 mg. Calcium is above the target, which corresponds to the FAO/WHO figure of 400 to 500 mg, but short of the RDA of 800 mg

## DIET SUMMARY

| Crop | Area sq. ft. | Crops per Year | Area Planted per Year sq. ft. | Yield per 100 sq. ft. pounds | Annual Production pounds | Daily Production pounds | Other Units |
|------|------|------|------|------|------|------|------|
| Potatoes | 400 | 2 | 800 | 200 | 1600 | 4.38 | 4 lbs 6 oz, 14-15 medium potatoes |
| Sunflower | 60 | 2 | 120 | 5 | 6 | .016 | ¼ oz or 1+ Tablespoon |
| Onions | 40 | 2 | 80 | 400 | 320 | .88 | 14 oz or 2¼+ cups diced |
| Turnips | 18 | 2 | 36 | 200 greens 70 roots | 72 gr. 25.2 rts. | .20 .07 | 3+ oz 1+ oz or ¼ cup diced |
| Parsnips | 7 | 2 | 14 | 238 | 33.3 | .09 | 1½ oz or ¼ cup diced |
| Garlic | 25 | 1 | 25 | 120 | 30 | .08 | 1¼+ oz or 2 bulbs |

This amount may prove too low for someone used to a high calcium, high protein diet--the diet of most Americans. The calcium to phosphorous ratio is 2.79:1, higher than the optimal 2:1 ratio, but should be fine if vitamin D is adequate. Iron is sufficient. The diet lacks any direct provision for vitamin $B_{12}$ (see $B_{12}$ section).

This diet is marginal but adequate in quite a number of nutrients, making it a questionable choice as a place to start, especially for those used to a standard, U.S.-type diet. It could, however, be a major improvement in diet for many people in the world, and for those whose diets are currently inadequate, pose no adjustment problems whatsoever. For a woman used to a low fat, vegetarian diet, not excessive in either calcium or protein, the adjustment problems should not be too great, and a switch to this diet for one or two days a week should be no great problem.

Garden Planning - The difficult timing and rotations recommend against this as a place to start. The plan is feas ble, however, and establishes what is possible. Such a plan within the 21 bed scenario outlined earlier could actually probably work out quite well. Part of the problem is that you are forced to double crop potatoes back-to-back. Lacking a larger rotation, such as is possible within a 21 bed scenario, this plan may eventually lead to disease and insect problems. The 21 bed scenario would also help with other weaknesses, such as a lack of legumes for fixing nitrogen, or other crops for supplying large amounts of organic matter for the compost pile.

The following schedule represents one way such a plan might work. The garden is divided into four separate rotation areas. Two are identical two year rotations that have been offset a year, one is a 289 square foot section that repeats itself in the second year, as does the fourth area, a 21 square foot section. All the area requirements for all the crops are supplied each year.

## TWO YEAR PLANTING SCHEDULE*

| Season | Area 1-120 sq. ft. | Area 2--120 sq. ft. | Area 3--289 sq. ft. | Area 4--21 sq. ft. |
|---|---|---|---|---|
| Early spring | 120 potatoes | (garlic, onions + turnips from fall) | 289 potatoes | 14 parsnips + 7 turnips |
| Late spring/ summer | 120 sunflowers | | | 14 turnips + 7 potatoes |
| Fall/winter | 25 garlic + 80 onions + 15 turnips | 120 potatoes | 250 potatoes + 39 in cover crops | 14 potatoes + 7 winter cover |
| Early spring | | 120 potatoes | 289 potatoes | 14 parsnips + 7 turnips |
| Late Spring | | 120 sunflowers | | 14 turnips + 7 potatoes |
| Fall/winter | 120 potatoes | 25 garlic + 80 onions + 15 turnips | 250 potatoes + 39 in cover crops | 14 potatoes + 7 winter cover |

*All figures in square feet. Assumes an eight month growing season.

| Prototype Woman's Diet Nutritional Analysis Area: 550 sq. ft. Weight: 5.45 lbs. | | Potatoes | Sunflower seeds | Onions | Turnips | Parsnips | Garlic | Total | Design Target | Percent of Target Supplied by Diet |
|---|---|---|---|---|---|---|---|---|---|---|
| Weight/day | lbs. | 4.12 | .016 | .876 | .266 | .091 | .082 | 5.45 | 5.5 | 99 |
| Calories | kcal | 1739 | 41 | 152 | 34 | 31 | 51 | 2048 | 2000 | 102 |
| Protein | g | 48.6 | 1.7 | 6.0 | 3.0 | .7 | 2.3 | 62.3 | 46 | 135 |
| Isoleucine | mg | 1421 | 46 | 80 | 102 | -- | -- | 1649 | 1044 | 158 |
| Leucine | mg | 2262 | 69 | 147 | 199 | -- | -- | 2677 | 1392 | 192 |
| Lysine | mg | 1796 | 39 | 251 | 146 | -- | -- | 2232 | 1044 | 214 |
| Cystine+Methionine | mg | 713 | 37 | 64 | 55 | -- | -- | 869 | 870 | 100 |
| Tyrosine+Phynal. | mg | 2526 | 69 | 152 | 214 | -- | -- | 2961 | 1392 | 213 |
| Tryptophan | mg | 618 | 15 | 80 | 43 | -- | -- | 756 | 261 | 289 |
| Threonine | mg | 1479 | 66 | 80 | 120 | -- | -- | 1745 | 696 | 251 |
| Valine | mg | 1739 | 55 | 119 | 128 | -- | -- | 2041 | 1218 | 168 |
| Histidine | mg | 544 | 43 | 56 | 33 | -- | -- | 676 | -- | -- |
| Carbohydrates | g | 395 | 1 | 35 | 7 | 7 | 12 | 457 | 300 | 152 |
| Fat | g | 2.1 | 3.4 | .4 | .3 | .2 | .1 | 6.55 | -- | -- |
| Linoleic Acid | g | 1.07 | 2.16 | -- | .05 | -- | -- | 3.28 | 3.33 | 98 |
| Vitamin A | RE | -- | 1 | 26 | 1133 | 2 | -- | 1162 | 800 | 145 |
| Thiamin | mg | 1.85 | .14 | .12 | .20 | .03 | .09 | 2.43 | 1.0 | 244 |
| Riboflavin | mg | .74 | .02 | .16 | .37 | .04 | .03 | 1.36 | 1.2 | 113 |
| Niacin | mg | 31.7 | .39 | .79 | .90 | .08 | .19 | 34.1 | 13 | 262 |
| Vitamin B6 | mg | 4.37 | .09 | .25 | .11 | .04 | -- | 4.86 | 2.0 | 243 |
| Folic Acid | mg | .29 | -- | .28 | .04 | .01 | .37 | .99 | .4 | 248 |
| Pantothenic Acid | mg | 4.37 | -- | .07 | .13 | .25 | -- | 4.82 | 5 | 96 |
| Vitamin C | mg | 375 | -- | 40 | 136 | 7 | 6 | 564 | 45 | 1250 |
| Vitamin E | IU | .8 | -- | 1.2 | 3.0 | .6 | -- | 5.6 | 6 | 93 |
| Iodine | mcg | 280 | -- | 56 | 69 | 1 | 1 | 407 | 100 | 407 |
| Zinc | mg | 11.2 | -- | 1.4 | 3.1 | -- | .5 | 16.2 | 10 | 162 |
| Calcium | mg | 169 | 9 | 108 | 232 | 21 | 11 | 550 | 500 | 110 |
| Iron | mg | 13.2 | .5 | 2.0 | 1.8 | .3 | .6 | 18.4 | 18 | 102 |
| Phosphorous | mg | 1215 | 6 | 143 | 61 | 32 | 75 | 1532 | 800 | 192 |
| Potassium | mg | 9410 | 67 | 625 | 84 | 223 | 197 | 10606 | 2500 | 424 |
| Magnesium | mg | 634 | 3 | 47 | 58 | 13 | 13 | 768 | 300 | 256 |
| Copper | mg | 3.38 | .13 | -- | .04 | -- | -- | 3.55 | 2 | 177 |

# A MAN'S PROTOTYPE DIET

**Nutrition** - The filbert tree in this diet makes possible the inclusion of a significant amount of fat--filberts are the most area efficient of the crops for fat. The man's prototype diet contains 27.1 grams of fat, or about 9 percent of its calories. This diet fulfills the RDA for zinc and vitamin E. One potential problem is the calcium to phosphorous ratio of 1:3.66, which, while still within the typical range for Americans, is beyond the optimal 1:2 ratio. Using tree collards as the main source of vitamin A makes it easier to ensure a more continuous supply of vitamin A. Alternately, planting annual collards in the spring and then again in the fall should work fairly well.

## DIET SUMMARY

| Crop | Area sq. ft. | Crops per Year | Area Planted per Year sq. ft. | Yield per 100 sq. ft. pounds | Annual Production pounds | Daily Production pounds | Other Units |
|------|------|------|------|------|------|------|------|
| Filberts | 240 | 1 | 240 | 12.4 | 29.8 | .08 | 1¼ oz or 27 nuts |
| Potatoes | 520 | 2 | 1040 | 200 | 2080 | 5.7 | 5 lbs 11 oz 18-19 medium potatoes |
| Collards | 25 | 1 | 25 | 300 | 75 | .21 | 3¼+ oz |
| Parsnips | 10 | 2 | 20 | 238 | 47.6 | .13 | 3 oz or 3/8 cup diced |
| Garlic | 60 | 1 | 60 | 120 | 72 | .20 | 3¼ oz or 5 bulbs |

**The Garden Plan** - Many places will be unsuitable to filberts due either to climatic factors or the problem of the Eastern filbert blight. More than one tree is also needed for good pollination and may work best as a cooperative effort. More research may reveal other crops, quite possibly also trees, which would also be area efficient for fat and which might be better suited for areas where filberts would be inappropriate.

Filberts, collards, and garlic are all full-season crops, and occupy their area for the entire season. Potatoes pose the same problems as in the woman's prototype, and again, the best solution will be to incorporate this diet within the 21 bed scenario. As a theoretical model, though, assume that potatoes follow potatoes. It may be best to grow 510 square feet of potatoes and all 20 square feet of parsnips in the spring, followed in the fall by 530 square feet of just potatoes.

189

| Prototype Man's Diet<br>Nutritional Analysis<br>Area: 855 sq. ft.<br>Daily Weight: 5.98 lbs | | Filberts | Potatoes | Collards | Parsnips | Garlic | Total | Design Target | Percent of Target Supplied by Diet |
|---|---|---|---|---|---|---|---|---|---|
| Weight/day | lbs. | .082 | 5.36 | .206 | .130 | .197 | 5.98 | 6.0 | 100 |
| Calories | kcal | 236 | 2262 | 37.5 | 44.3 | 123 | 2702 | 2700 | 100 |
| Protein | g | 4.69 | 63.2 | 3.36 | 1.00 | 5.54 | 77.8 | 56 | 139 |
| Isoleucine | mg | 545 | 1849 | 105 | -- | -- | 2499 | 1260 | 198 |
| Leucine | mg | 542 | 2943 | 189 | -- | -- | 3674 | 1680 | 219 |
| Lysine | mg | 257 | 2337 | 175 | -- | -- | 2769 | 1260 | 220 |
| Cystine+Methionine | mg | 108 | 927 | 98 | -- | -- | 1133 | 1050 | 108 |
| Tyrosine+phenyl. | mg | 637 | 3286 | 257 | -- | -- | 4180 | 1680 | 249 |
| Tryptophan | mg | 98 | 804 | 47 | -- | -- | 949 | 315 | 301 |
| Threonine | mg | 154 | 1924 | 107 | -- | -- | 2185 | 840 | 260 |
| Valine | mg | 558 | 2262 | 168 | -- | -- | 2988 | 1470 | 203 |
| Histidine | mg | 107 | 708 | 81 | -- | -- | 896 | -- | -- |
| Carbohydrates | g | 6 | 513 | 7 | 10 | 28 | 564 | 405 | 139 |
| Fat | g | 23.2 | 2.7 | .7 | .3 | .2 | 27.1 | -- | -- |
| Linoleic Acid | g | 3.7 | 1.4 | -- | -- | -- | 5.1 | 4.5 | 114 |
| Vitamin A | RE | 7 | -- | 1013 | 3 | -- | 1023 | 1000 | 102 |
| Thiamin | mg | .17 | 2.41 | .19 | .05 | ..23 | 3.06 | 1.4 | 219 |
| Riboflavin | mg | ..20 | ..97 | ..29 | ..05 | ..07 | 1.58 | 1.6 | 99 |
| Niacin | mg | .34 | 41.3 | 1.59 | ..12 | ..45 | 43.8 | 18 | 243 |
| Vitamin B6 | mg | .21 | 5.68 | .18 | .05 | -- | 6.12 | 2.0 | 306 |
| Folic Acid | mg | .03 | .38 | .10 | .02 | .89 | 1.42 | .4 | 351 |
| Pantothenic Acid | mg | .42 | 8.84 | .41 | .35 | -- | 10.0 | 5 | 200 |
| Vitamin C | mg | -- | 488 | 86 | 9 | 13 | 596 | 45 | 1326 |
| Vitamin E | IU | 12.5 | 1.1 | 2.8 | .9 | -- | 17.3 | 6 | 288 |
| Iodine | mcg | 1 | 364 | 16 | 2 | 2 | 385 | 130 | 296 |
| Zinc | mg | 1.14 | 14.6 | -- | -- | 1.19 | 16.9 | 10 | 169 |
| Calcium | mg | 78 | 220 | 190 | 30 | 26 | 544 | 500 | 109 |
| Iron | mg | 1.3 | 17.2 | .9 | .4 | 1.3 | 21.1 | 10 | 211 |
| Phosphorous | mg | 125 | 1581 | 59 | 46 | 181 | 1992 | 800 | 249 |
| Potassium | mg | 262 | 12242 | 375 | 319 | 473 | 13671 | 2500 | 547 |
| Magnesium | mg | 69 | 825 | 53 | 19 | 32 | 998 | 350 | 285 |
| Copper | mg | .5 | 4.4 | -- | -- | -- | 4.9 | 2 | 245 |

## 1400 SQUARE FOOT DIET A
### Woman's = 1190 sq. ft., Man's = 1610 sq. ft.

Nutrition - The two 1400 square foot diets are designed so that both men and women can eat the same mix or ratio of foods and still fulfill their own separate nutritional needs. The woman's diet is presented, and the man's is the same mix with all the quantities increased by a factor of 1.35. This design feature keeps the woman's diet to below $4\frac{1}{2}$ pounds, which should make it a fairly easy diet to consume.

The diet gets a sizable, 15 percent of its calories from fat, still low by U.S. standards, but considerably more than the prototype diets. It has no marginal nutrients, with the possible exception of vitamin $B_{12}$ (see $B_{12}$ section), and even meets the RDA for both vitamin E and zinc. The calcium to phosphorous ratio is an excellent 1:1.77. The vitamin A comes from a diversity of foods that can be harvested throughout the year in most climates, with proper timing.

Garden Planning - In one approach, the 1190 square foot woman's version of this plan may be thought of as being divided into the following sections:

1) 265 square feet for the 240 square foot filbert and the 25 square feet of tree collards (or annual collards planted both spring and fall).

2) 50 square feet in two 25 square foot sections that are planted in a two year rotation of fall-planted garlic followed the next fall by winter wheat, followed the following late spring by potatoes. These two sections are planted "offset" to one another, so that that in one year, wheat and potatoes are being harvested in one while garlic is harvested in the other.

3) A 375 square foot section in which winter wheat is planted each fall, and followed each late spring in the same area by 50 square feet of parsley, 25 square feet of turnips, 25 square feet of parsnips, 50 square feet of onions, and 225 square feet of potatoes.

4) A 400 square foot section that is planted each spring with spring wheat, with 100 square feet of this followed by a summer planting of sunflowers, and the rest followed with fall plantings of 50 square feet of parsley, 25 square feet of turnips, 25 square feet of parsnips, and 200 square feet of potatoes. It may be possible to follow some of this area, particularly the potatoes, with a winter cover crop that would come out before the wheat went in in the spring.

5) A 100 square foot area in which wheat is followed by wheat, a difficult rotation, but one necessitated by this crop selection. Special varieties and techniques may help.

The large area of wheat should help in the production of organic matter for composting, but the plan still lacks in legumes. The use of this plan with the 21 bed scenario could balance this through the use of leguminous cover crops.

## 1400 SQUARE FOOT DIET A SUMMARY

| Crop | Crops per Year | Yield per 100 sq. ft. (pounds) | Women Area per Crop (sq. ft.) | Area per Year (sq. ft.) | Annual Yield (pounds) | Daily Yield (pounds) | Other Units | Men Area per Crop (sq. ft.) | Area per Year (sq. ft.) | Annual Yield (pounds) | Daily Yield (pounds) | Other Units |
|---|---|---|---|---|---|---|---|---|---|---|---|---|
| Wheat | 2 | 10 | 500 | 1000 | 100 | .274 | 4¼+ oz or 3/4 cup berries | 675 | 1350 | 135 | .370 | 6oz or a scant cup berries |
| Garlic | 1 | 120 | 25 | 25 | 30 | .08 | 1¼+ oz or 2 bulbs | 34 | 34 | 41 | .161 | 1 3/4 oz or almost 3 bulbs |
| Sunflower Seeds | 2 | 5 | 50 | 100 | 5 | .014 | ¼ oz or 1 Tbsp | 68 | 135 | 6.75 | .018 | ¼+ oz or 1¼+ Tbsp |
| Potatoes | 2 | 200 | 225 | 450 | 900 | 2.47 | 2# 7½ oz, 8-9 medium potatoes | 304 | 608 | 1215 | 3.33 | 3# 5¼ oz, 11 medium potatoes |
| Onions | 2 | 400 | 25 | 50 | 200 | .548 | 8 3/4+ oz, 1½ cups chopped | 34 | 68 | 270 | .74 | 12 oz or 2 cups chopped |
| Parsley | 2 | 35 | 50 | 100 | 35 | .096 | 1½ oz or scant 3/4 cups chopped | 68 | 135 | 47 | .129 | 2 oz, scant cup chopped |
| Turnips | 2 | 200 grns. 70 rts. | 25 | 50 | 100 / 35 | .274 / .096 | 4¼+ oz / 1½ oz, or 1/3 cup chopped | 34 | 68 | 135 / 47.3 | .370 / .129 | 6 oz / 2 oz or ½ cup chopped |
| Collards | 1 | 300 | 25 | 25 | 75 | .205 | 3¼ oz | 34 | 34 | 101 | .277 | 4½ oz |
| Parsnips | 2 | 238 | 25 | 50 | 119 | .326 | 5¼ oz or 1 1/8 cups diced | 34 | 68 | 161 | .44 | 7 oz or 1½ cups diced |
| Filberts | 1 | 12.4 | 240 | 240 | 29.8 | .082 | 1¼+ oz or 27 nuts | 324 | 324 | 40.2 | .11 | 1 3/4 oz or 37 nuts |

| 1400 sq. ft. Diet A Nutritional Analysis of sample diet for women: 1190 sq. ft. 4.42 pounds men: (multiply all amounts by 1.35) 1607 sq. ft. 5.97 pounds | Wheat | Garlic | Sunflower seeds | Potatoes | Onions | Parsley | Turnips | Collards | Parsnips | Filberts | Total | Woman's Design Targets | % of Woman's Target Supplied by diet |
|---|---|---|---|---|---|---|---|---|---|---|---|---|---|
| Weight/day lbs. | .38 | .082 | .014 | 2.32 | .548 | .096 | .37 | .206 | .325 | .082 | 4.42 | 4.44 | 100 |
| Calories kcal | 415 | 51.0 | 35.6 | 979 | 94.8 | 19.0 | 47.7 | 37.5 | 111 | 236 | 2027 | 2000 | 101 |
| Protein g | 16.6 | 2.30 | 1.53 | 27.4 | 3.73 | 1.56 | 4.18 | 3.36 | 2.50 | 4.69 | 67.9 | 46 | 148 |
| Isoleucine mg | 531 | -- | 40.4 | 800 | 49.9 | -- | 141 | 105 | -- | 545 | 2212 | 1044 | 212 |
| Leucine mg | 1086 | -- | 60.6 | 1274 | 92.1 | -- | 277 | 189 | -- | 542 | 3521 | 1392 | 253 |
| Lysine mg | 466 | -- | 34.1 | 1012 | 157 | 231 | 203 | 175 | -- | 257 | 2535 | 1044 | 243 |
| Cystine+methionine mg | 658 | -- | 32.0 | 401 | 40.0 | 7.87 | 75.9 | 98.3 | -- | 108 | 1421 | 870 | 163 |
| Tyro. + Phen. mg | 1222 | -- | 59.9 | 1422 | 94.8 | -- | 297 | 257 | -- | 637 | 3990 | 1392 | 287 |
| Tryptophan mg | 173 | -- | 12.8 | 348 | 49.9 | 32.3 | 59.6 | 46.8 | -- | 97.9 | 820 | 261 | 314 |
| Threonine mg | 661 | -- | 57.9 | 833 | 49.9 | -- | 167 | 107 | -- | 154 | 2030 | 696 | 292 |
| Valine mg | 719 | -- | 47.9 | 979 | 74.5 | -- | 179 | 168 | -- | 558 | 2725 | 1218 | 224 |
| Histidine mg | 476 | -- | 37.2 | 306 | 34.9 | -- | 45.1 | 81.4 | -- | 107 | 1079 | -- | -- |
| Carbohydrates g | 88.5 | .941 | 1.26 | 222 | 21.6 | 3.71 | 9.10 | 6.74 | 25.8 | 6.22 | 386 | 300 | 129 |
| Fat g | 2.49 | .074 | 3.01 | 1.16 | .274 | .259 | .459 | .659 | .748 | 23.2 | 32.3 | 22 | 147 |
| Linoleic Acid g | .832 | -- | 1.89 | .603 | -- | -- | .063 | -- | -- | 3.72 | 7.11 | 3.33 | 213 |
| Vitamin A RE | -- | -- | .532 | -- | 16.4 | 617 | 1576 | 1013 | 7.48 | 6.64 | 3237 | 800 | 405 |
| Thiamin mg | .711 | .093 | .125 | 1.04 | .077 | .052 | .278 | .187 | .117 | .171 | 2.85 | 1.0 | 285 |
| Riboflavin mg | .148 | .030 | .015 | .418 | .099 | .113 | .514 | .290 | .133 | .198 | 1.96 | 1.2 | 163 |
| Niacin mg | 5.36 | .186 | .343 | 17.9 | .493 | .523 | 1.25 | 1.59 | .293 | .336 | 28.3 | 13 | 217 |
| Vitamin $B_6$ mg | 1.16 | -- | .079 | 2.46 | .159 | .070 | .159 | .183 | .133 | .212 | 4.62 | 2.0 | 231 |
| Folic Acid mg | .072 | .372 | -- | .162 | .175 | .015 | .056 | .095 | .039 | .025 | 1.01 | .4 | 253 |
| Pantothenic Acid mg | 1.35 | -- | -- | 3.83 | .044 | .132 | .174 | .412 | .884 | .422 | 7.25 | 5 | 145 |
| Vitamin C mg | -- | 5.58 | -- | 211 | 24.7 | 75.0 | 189 | 85.9 | 23.7 | -- | 615 | 45 | 1366 |
| Vitamin E IU | 3.12 | .006 | .001 | .464 | .734 | 2.03 | 4.11 | 2.80 | 2.21 | 12.5 | 28.0 | 6 | 466 |
| Iodine mcg | 1.25 | 1.01 | -- | 158 | 35.1 | -- | 95.8 | 15.9 | 5.30 | .738 | 313 | 100 | 313 |
| Zinc mg | 3.01 | .496 | -- | 6.31 | .877 | .394 | 4.37 | -- | -- | 1.14 | 16.6 | 10 | 166 |
| Calcium mg | 51.3 | 10.8 | 7.63 | 95.1 | 67.4 | 88.5 | 323 | 190 | 73.8 | 77.8 | 985 | 500 | 197 |
| Iron mg | 4.10 | .558 | .451 | 7.42 | 1.26 | 2.70 | 2.47 | .927 | 1.04 | 1.26 | 22.2 | 18 | 123 |
| Phosphorous mg | 478 | 75.2 | 5.32 | 684 | 89.3 | 27.5 | 85.1 | 58.9 | 114 | 125 | 1742 | 800 | 218 |
| Potassium mg | 461 | 197 | 58.5 | 5299 | 391 | 317 | 117 | 375 | 798 | 262 | 8276 | 2500 | 331 |
| Magnesium mg | 195 | 13.4 | 2.42 | 357 | 29.6 | 17.9 | 80.7 | 53.4 | 47.1 | 68.5 | 865 | 300 | 288 |
| Copper mg | .749 | -- | .113 | 1.90 | -- | .156 | .052 | -- | -- | .496 | 3.47 | 2 | 173 |

193

One possibility would be to plant legumes under the perennials, such as alfalfa under the filbert and Dutch white clover under the tree collards. These could be harvested periodically and the cuttings added to the compost pile. The two parsnip plantings, in sections 3) and 4) above could both prove difficult to bring to maturity due to timing problems. The plan overall though, could be a useful starting place.

## 1400 SQUARE FOOT DIET B
### Woman's = 1190 sq. ft. Man's = 1610 sq. ft.

<u>Nutrition</u> - This diet looks very good nutritionally. It surpasses the RDA for zinc, is very high in vitamins E and A, has an adequate amount of fat, and a calcium to phosphorous ratio of 1:2.08. If small amounts of sweet potato greens are also included in the diet, even higher amounts of iron and vitamin A will be consumed. Again, vitamin $B_{12}$ could be a concern, but the diet includes plenty of soybeans, sunflower seeds, and peanuts, which are all good crops for the production of tempeh, which can be rich in vitamin $B_{12}$. Sweet potatoes may also soon be considered a good base for the production of tempeh.

<u>Garden Planning</u> - For climates where these crops would be suitable, the planning is fairly simple. Each year there needs to be 750 square feet of warm season crops-- 325 of sweet potatoes, 75 of soybeans, 100 of sunflowers, and 250 of peanuts. Each year there also needs to be 873 square feet of cool season crops--500 square feet of potatoes, 50 of turnips, 30 of onions, 200 of wheat, 30 of parsley, 38 of garlic, and 25 of leeks. The total of cool and warm season crops is 1623 square feet, or 433 square feet over the target of 1190. Thus, 433 square feet of the plan will need to include both a warm season crop and a cool season crop each year. This could include, for the warm season crops: 233 square feet of sweet potatoes, 100 square feet of peanuts, and 100 square feet of sunflowers; and the same area in cool season crops would include: 153 square feet of fall potatoes, 25 of spring turnips, 25 of fall turnips, 15 of spring parsley, 15 of fall parsley, and 200 of winter wheat. These cool season crops could be fit in before or after the warm season crops.

This plan includes both a fair amount of legumes and also some 757 square feet-- the area left of the 1190 that isn't double cropped--that could be planted in winter cover crops. Thus, this plan does well in nutrition, well in planning aspects, and even fair in matters of sustainability. This appears to be an excellent starting place for many. If you wish to plant a scaled down version of this plan in either 550 square feet for women, or 850 square feet for men, simply multiply all the areas of the 1190 plan by .462 for a woman's diet and by .714 for a man's diet.

| Crop | Crops per Year | Yield per 100 sq. ft. pounds | Women | | | | | Men | | | | |
|---|---|---|---|---|---|---|---|---|---|---|---|---|
| | | | Area per Crop sq. ft. | Area per Year sq. ft. | Annual Yield pounds | Daily Yield pounds | Other Units | Area per Crop sq. ft. | Area per Year sq. ft. | Annual Yield pounds | Daily Yield pounds | Other Units |
| Sweet Potatoes | 1 | 82 | 325 | 325 | 267 | .73 | 11½ oz | 439 | 439 | 360 | .99 | |
| Soybeans | 1 | 8 | 75 | 75 | 6 | .016 | 1¼ oz or ½+ Tbsp | 101 | 101 | 8.1 | .022 | ¼+ oz or 3/4+ Tbsp |
| Potatoes | 2 | 200 | 250 | 500 | 1000 | 2.74 | 2# 12 oz or 9 medium potatoes | 338 | 675 | 1350 | 3.70 | 3# 11oz or 12 medium potatoes |
| Sunflowers | 2 | 5 | 50 | 100 | 5 | .014 | ¼ oz or 1 Tbsp | 68 | 135 | 6.75 | .018 | ¼+ oz or 1¼+ Tbsp |
| Peanuts | 1 | 10 | 250 | 250 | 25 | .068 | 1 oz or 2 Tbsp | 338 | 338 | 33.8 | .092 | 1½ oz or 2 3/4 Tbsp |
| Turnips | 2 | 200 grns. 70 rts. | 25 | 50 | 100 35 | .274 .096 | 4¼+ oz 1½ oz or 1/3 cup chopped | 34 | 68 | 135 47.3 | .370 .129 | 6oz 2 oz or ½ cup chopped |
| Onions | 2 | 400 | 15 | 30 | 120 | .33 | 5¼ oz or 3/4+ cup chopped | 20 | 41 | 162 | .444 | 7 oz scant ¼ cup chopped |
| Wheat | 2 | 10 | 100 | 200 | 20 | .055 | 7/8 oz or 2¼ Tbsp berries | 135 | 270 | 27 | .074 | 1¼ oz or 3 Tbsp berries |
| Parsley | 2 | 35 | 15 | 30 | 10.5 | .029 | ½ oz or scant ¼ cup chopped | 20 | 41 | 14.2 | .039 | ½+ oz ¼+ cup chopped |
| Garlic | 1 | 120 | 38 | 38 | 45.6 | .125 | 2 oz or 3 bulbs | 51 | 51 | 61.6 | .169 | 2½+ oz 4 bulbs |
| Leeks | 1 | 240 | 25 | 25 | 60 | .164 | 2½+ oz | 34 | 34 | 81 | .222 | 3½ oz |

| 1400 sq. ft. Sample Diet B for women: 1143 sq. ft. 4.41 lbs./day. For men:(multiply all amounts by 1.35) 1543 sq. ft. 5.95 lbs./day | Sweet Potatoes | Soybeans | Potatoes | Sunflower seeds | Peanuts | Turnips | Onions | Wheat | Parsley | Garlic | Leeks | Total | Woman's Design targets | % of Woman's Target Supplied by diet |
|---|---|---|---|---|---|---|---|---|---|---|---|---|---|---|
| Weight/day lbs. | .608 | .050 | 2.58 | .014 | .068 | .37 | .329 | .076 | .029 | .125 | .165 | 4.41 | 4.44 | 99 |
| Calories kcal | 389 | 27 | 1089 | 36 | 175 | 48 | 57 | 83 | 6 | 78 | 39 | 2027 | 2000 | 101 |
| Protein  g | 5.8 | 2.2 | 30.4 | 1.5 | 8.1 | 4.2 | 2.2 | 3.3 | .5 | 3.5 | 1.7 | 63.4 | 46 | 138 |
| Isoleucine mg | 133 | 143 | 890 | 40 | 303 | 141 | 30 | 106 | -- | -- | 131 | 1917 | 1044 | 184 |
| Leucine mg | 196 | 245 | 1416 | 61 | 579 | 277 | 55 | 217 | -- | -- | 225 | 3271 | 1392 | 235 |
| Lysine mg | 124 | 201 | 1125 | 34 | 320 | 203 | 94 | 93 | 70 | -- | 211 | 2478 | 1044 | 237 |
| Cyst. + meth. mg | 99 | 82 | 446 | 32 | 217 | 176 | 24 | 132 | 2 | -- | 150 | 1360 | 870 | 156 |
| Tyro. + phen. mg | 224 | 254 | 1582 | 60 | 803 | 297 | 57 | 244 | -- | -- | 169 | 3690 | 1392 | 265 |
| Tryptophan mg | 61 | 40 | 387 | 13 | 94 | 60 | 30 | 35 | 10 | -- | -- | 730 | 261 | 280 |
| Threonine mg | 235 | 341 | 926 | 58 | 256 | 167 | 30 | 132 | -- | -- | -- | 2145 | 696 | 308 |
| Valine mg | 163 | 151 | 1089 | 48 | 378 | 179 | 45 | 144 | -- | -- | 253 | 2450 | 1218 | 201 |
| Histidine | 99 | 207 | 341 | 37 | 231 | 45 | 21 | 93 | -- | -- | -- | 1074 | -- | -- |
| Carbohydrates g | 91 | 2 | 247 | 1 | 5 | 9 | 13 | 18 | 1 | 18 | 8 | 414 | 300 | 138 |
| Fat g | 1.4 | 1.2 | 1.3 | 3.0 | 15.0 | .5 | .2 | .5 | .1 | .1 | .2 | 23.5 | 22 | 107 |
| Linoleic acid g | .47 | .68 | .67 | 1.89 | 4.32 | .06 | -- | .17 | -- | -- | -- | 8.26 | 3.33 | 248 |
| Vitamin A    RE | 3726 | 1 | -- | 1 | -- | 1576 | 10 | -- | 187 | -- | 5 | 5506 | 800 | 688 |
| Thiamin mg | .25 | .07 | 1.16 | .12 | .31 | .28 | .05 | .14 | .02 | .02 | .08 | 2.54 | 1.0 | 254 |
| Riboflavin mg | .19 | .02 | .46 | .01 | .04 | .51 | .06 | .03 | .03 | .05 | .05 | 1.45 | 1.2 | 121 |
| Niacin mg | 1.95 | .14 | 19.9 | .34 | 4.88 | 1.25 | .30 | 1.07 | .16 | .28 | .38 | 30.7 | 13 | 236 |
| Vitamin B$_6$ | .60 | .15 | 2.73 | .08 | .09 | .16 | .10 | .23 | .02 | -- | .15 | 4.31 | 2.0 | 216 |
| Folic Acid mg | .04 | .05 | .18 | -- | -- | .06 | .11 | .01 | -- | .57 | -- | 1.02 | .4 | 255 |
| Panto. Acid mg | 2.26 | .38 | 4.26 | -- | .74 | .17 | .03 | .27 | .04 | -- | -- | 8.15 | 5 | 163 |
| Vitamin C  mg | 61 | 4 | 235 | -- | -- | 189 | 15 | -- | 23 | 9 | 13 | 549 | 45 | 1220 |
| Vitamin E IU | 26.8 | 1.7 | .5 | -- | 3.6 | 4.1 | .4 | .6 | .6 | -- | 3.2 | 41.5 | 6 | 692 |
| Iodine  mcg | 30 | -- | 175 | -- | 6 | 96 | 21 | -- | -- | 2 | -- | 330 | 100 | 330 |
| Zinc mg | .2 | .15 | 7.02 | -- | 1.03 | 4.4 | .5 | .6 | .1 | .8 | .23 | 15.0 | 10 | 150 |
| Calcium mg | 111 | 16 | 106 | 8 | 18 | 323 | 40 | 10 | 27 | 17 | 39 | 715 | 500 | 143 |
| Iron mg | 2.5 | .6 | 8.3 | .5 | .6 | 2.5 | .8 | .8 | .8 | .9 | .8 | 19.1 | 18 | 106 |
| Phosphorus  mg | 160 | 43 | 761 | 5 | 126 | 85 | 54 | 96 | 8 | 115 | 37 | 1490 | 800 | 186 |
| Potassium  mg | 828 | -- | 5893 | 58 | 208 | 117 | 235 | 92 | 96 | 300 | 260 | 8087 | 2500 | 323 |
| Magnesium mg | 86 | 30 | 397 | 2 | 64 | 81 | 18 | 39 | 5 | 20 | 17 | 759 | 300 | 253 |
| Copper mg | .41 | .3 | 2.11 | .1 | .3 | .05 | -- | .1 | .05 | -- | .1 | 3.52 | 2 | 176 |

"Everything that man accomplish-
es or does, that he teaches or wants
to learn, must have its right proportion, it must follow its own line and
remain within its circle, to the end
that a balance be preserved, that
there be no crooked thing, that
nothing exceed the circle..."

Paracelcus

# SOME BIOGRAPHICAL NOTES

While growing up in rural Louisiana, I was exposed to home food production in the form of a cow, chickens, and organic vegetable gardening. I left Louisiana to attend Stanford University, where I received a B.A. in political science in 1975. A greater portion of my work, particularly in the last two years, was done at the Stanford Food Research Institute. I focused on political economies within the context of development.

Through the Peace Corps I worked within the Planning Division of the Ministry of Agriculture of Liberia. Working first for a short while as an agricultural economist doing cost benefit analyses of farm loan applications, and later as an agricultural statistician attempting to draw policy implications from a recently completed agricultural survey, I gained insights which changed my career plans, and have led me to the work involved in One Circle.

In 1979, I apprenticed with John Jeavons at the Ecology Action garden in Palo Alto. Since that time I have been gardening as my primary focus. Along the way I have also worked on a 500 acre soybean farm, published a newsletter dealing with food and energy alternatives for the Gulf South, managed a food co-op, and managed a market garden in the San Francisco Bay area.

In 1984, I completed the first volume of a continuing work, A History of Intensive Food Gardening. This first volume deals with Europe from Roman times until the early part of the century. Many of the perspectives in One Circle draw from the work done on this volume.

I returned to work with John Jeavons in 1984, and am currently working at the Willits, CA site as garden manager. My wife, Cindy Gebhard, and I are expecting a child and looking forward to a life that draws most of its income from market gardening and includes research and the process of sharing with others who are pursuing similar work. We hope that by learning how to take care of ourselves in a sustainable way that our research and experiences can help and inspire others.

David L. Duhon

Additional copies of _One Circle_ are available for $9.00, postpaid, worldwide.
Copies of _How to Grow More Vegetables_... are available for $10.00, postpaid,
worldwide, and copies of _The Backyard Homestead_... are available for $11.00,
postpaid, worldwide.  Make checks payable (_in U.S. funds only_) to:

Ecology Action of the Midpeninsula
5798 Ridgewood Road
Willits, California, 95490

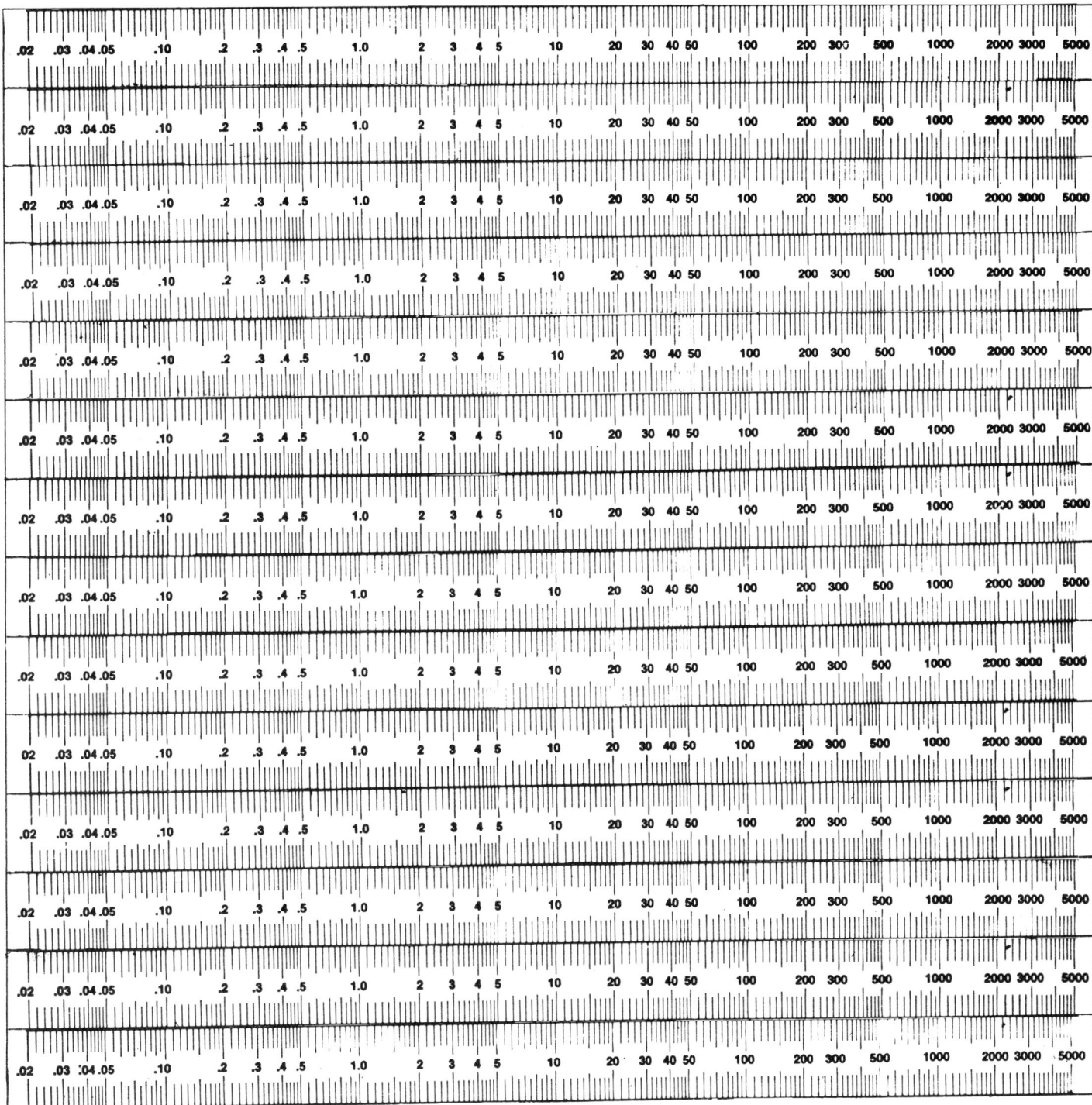